THE SCOTS KITCHEN

The
SCOTS
Kitchen

Its TRADITIONS *and* LORE
with OLD-TIME RECIPES

F. Marian MᶜNeill

MERCAT PRESS
EDINBURGH

First published in 1929 by Blackie & Son Ltd
Reprinted 1993 by Mercat Press
James Thin, 53 South Bridge, Edinburgh
from a copy supplied by Kate Blackadder

ISBN 1873644 23x

Printed in Great Britain by the Cromwell Press, Melksham

To

The " Land o' Cakes and sister *Scots*
Frae Maidenkirk to Johnnie Groat's,"
and over the Firth to
Orkney

PREFACE

The object of this book is not to provide a complete compendium of Scottish Cookery, ancient or modern—for many of the dishes prepared in the Scots kitchen are common to the British Isles; some, indeed, to Europe—but rather to preserve the recipes of our old national dishes, many of which, in this age of standardization, are in danger of falling into an undeserved oblivion. Recipes available in contemporary Scottish cookery books are as a rule omitted, unless hallowed by age or sentiment.

All parts of the country, from the Shetlands to the Borders, have been levied, and all types of kitchen, from Old Holyrood to island sheiling. A few of the simple folk recipes collected in Orkney and the Hebrides have, I believe, never before been published.

In the preliminary sketch, I have tried to show how from the earliest times—through the period of romantic semi-savagery in the Highlands, the period of cosmopolitan elegance (Edinburgh's golden age) in the days of the Auld Alliance, the

Preface

sober kail-and-brose period that succeeded the Reformation, and on to modern times — the pageant of Scottish History is shadowed in the kitchen.

In Scotland to-day, as perhaps the world over, there is of good home cooking less and less. The old women say there is neither the variety there used to be, nor the respect for quality. But we may rest confident that out of the domestic travail through which our women folk are now passing there will emerge a new delight in the home, and, not least, in the kitchen.

" Lean gu dlùth ri cliù do shinnsre," says the Gaelic proverb: Let us follow in the brave path of our ancestors.

F. M. McNEILL.

EDINBURGH, 1929.

ACKNOWLEDGMENTS

I have to express my indebtedness to Mrs. Metzger, New York, for permission to reproduce the photograph of an Orkney ingle-neuk taken by her sister, the late Miss Sinclair, Kirkwall; to Dr. W. Watson, Professor of Celtic in the University of Edinburgh, for the Fire-kindling and Fire-smooring Runes from his father-in-law, the late Alexander Carmichael's collection, *Carmina Gadelica*; to the Rev. Kenneth Macleod, Isle of Gigha, for his translation of an ancient Gaelic Rune of Hospitality; to Messrs. Constable & Sons, London, for three recipes from *The Cookery Book of Lady Clark of Tillypronie*; to Messrs. Andrew Elliot, Edinburgh, for an original recipe from Mrs. Williamson's *Practice of Cookery and Pastry*; and to friends and correspondents all over the country for their valuable help.

F. M. McN.

CONTENTS

AN HISTORICAL SKETCH

RECIPES

SOUPS

ix

DISHES OF FISH

DISHES OF GAME AND POULTRY

Contents

DISHES OF MEAT

DISHES OF VEGETABLES

PUDDINGS AND PIES

SWEETS

SAVOURIES

Contents

BANNOCKS, SCONES, AND TEA-BREAD

CAKES AND SHORTBREADS

MISCELLANEOUS

PREPARATIONS OF OATMEAL, OF BLOOD, OF MILK, OF SEAWEEDS, ETC.

1. *Preparations of Oatmeal*

2. *Preparations of Blood*

3. *Preparations of Milk*

Contents

BEVERAGES

APPENDICES

AN
HISTORICAL SKETCH

I

INTRODUCTORY: INSTITUTION OF THE CLEIKUM CLUB

" Man," said Mr. Peregrine Touchwood, " is a cooking animal."

The occasion was a memorable one—none other than the institution of the celebrated Cleikum Club at the old Border Inn presided over by Meg Dods [1] and immortalized by Sir Walter Scott in *St. Ronan's Well.* This red-letter day in the annals of Scottish gastronomy is commemorated in the introduction to *The Cook and Housewife's Manual*, by Mistress Margaret Dods (Edinburgh, 1826),[2]

---

[1] Lockhart, in his *Life* of Scott, tells us that Scott borrowed the name from Mrs. Margaret Dods, at whose little inn at Howgate, among the Moorfoots, with Will Clark, and John Irving, and George Abercrombie, he often spent a night during a fishing excursion in their student days. When the novel was published, Clark met Scott in the street and observed, " That's an odd name; surely I've met with it somewhere before." Scott smilingly replied, " Don't you remember Howgate?"

The name alone, however, was taken from the Howgate hostess. According to a well-known Peebles tradition, supported by William Chambers, Miss Marian Ritchie was the true original of the termagant landlady of the " Cleikum Inn ", which, as the " Cross Keys ", still exists. Meg appears to have been a caricature of Miss Ritchie, but the characteristics, though exaggerated, are said to agree, in the main. Marian's Bible, punch-bowl, &c., are still preserved in Peebles.

—F. M. McN.

[2] " The individual who has so ingeniously personated Meg Dods is evidently no ordinary writer, and the book is really most excellent miscellaneous reading. Here we have twenty or thirty grave, sober, instructive, business-like pages right on end, without one particle of wit whatever; then come as many more, sprinkled with

a work not unworthy to be placed alongside its French contemporary, Brillat-Savarin's *Physiologie du Goût*.

After the catastrophe which befell the ancient and honourable house of St. Ronan's, our friend Mr. Touchwood, more commonly styled the Cleikum Nabob, was, it appears, in some danger of falling into hypochondria—" vulgarly, *fidgets*, a malady to which bachelor gentlemen in easy circumstances, when turned of fifty, are thought to be peculiarly liable "—but evaded the disaster by the happy thought of founding a club of gastronomes. In addition to the founder, " who understood and loved good cheer ", the club included Mr. Winterblossom, " an old coxcomb, but deep in the mystery "; Dr. Redgill, an English divine who chanced to be taking the waters at

---

facetiae—and then half a dozen of broad mirth and merriment. This alternation of grave and gay is exceedingly agreeable—something in the style of *Blackwood's Magazine*."—Christopher North, in *Blackwood's Magazine*, June, 1826.

" We have no hesitation in saying that if the humorous introduction is not written by Sir Walter Scott, the author of it possesses a singular talent of mimicking his best comic manner, and has presented us with an imitation of the great novelist, as remarkable for its fidelity, facility, and cleverness as anything in the *Rejected Addresses*."
—*The Monthly Review*.

Whether or not Scott had a hand in it, the book was actually compiled by Mrs. Johnston, the wife of an Edinburgh publisher, the author of *The Edinburgh Tales* and other works, and in after years the editor of *Tait's Magazine*.

" Her sense of humour and power of delineating character are shown in her stories and sketches in *Tait*, and a good example of her ready wit has been told by Mr. Alexander Russell, editor of the *Scotsman*. On a visit to Altrive, Mrs. Johnston and her party were kindly received by the Ettrick Shepherd, who did the honours of the district, and among other places took them to a Fairy Well, from which he drew a glass of sparkling water. Handing it to the lady, the bard of Kilmeny said, ' Hae, Mrs. Johnston, ony merit wummin wha drinks a tumbler o' this will hae twuns in a twalmont.' ' In that case, Mr. Hogg,' said the lady, ' I shall only take half a tumbler '."—Sir Walter Scott: *Journal*, Vol. I, Note.

Mrs. Johnston died in 1857.

St. Ronan's,[1] and who, " like a true churchman,
had a strong leaning to dishes as they are "; Mr.
Jekyl, a young life-guardsman who had served in
the Peninsula, had " French theory " in the
affairs of the kitchen, and was " to the full as
flighty and speculative as the Doctor was dog-
matic "; and lastly, on Meg's recommendation,
Mr. Matthew Stechy, " St. Ronan's auld butler,
that kept the first hottle in Glasgow ". Mrs.
Dods herself was elected " high priestess of the
mysteries ".

The Nabob explains his design to Dr. Redgill:

" ' To this ancient hostel now—you will scarce
believe it—have been confined scores of admirable receipts in cookery, ever since the jolly friars
flourished down in the monastery yonder:

> The Monks of Melrose made fat brose
> On Fridays, when they fasted.

You remember the old stave, Doctor?'

" The doctor remembered no such thing. His
attention was given to more substantial doctrine.
' Sir, I should not be surprised if they possessed the original receipt—a local one too, I

[1] St. Ronan's is in fact Innerleithen, in the county of Peebles. Innerleithen had
a Spa, known as the Doos' Well, from the flocks of pigeons who made it their haunt.
" The publication of Scott's novel ushered in the period of its greatest glory, and
visitors were further attracted by an annual festival established by an association
known as the St. Ronan's Border Club. Among those who countenanced, or took
part in the proceedings, were Scott and Adam Ferguson, Christopher North and
the Ettrick Shepherd, Sheriff Glassford Bell and others."
—W. S. Crockett: *The Scott Originals.*

am told—for dressing the red trout,[1] in this hereditary house of entertainment.'

" ' Never doubt it, man—claret, butter, and spiceries. Zounds, I have eat of it till— It makes my mouth water yet. As the French adage goes, " Give your trout a bottle of good wine, a lump of butter, and spice, and tell me how you like him ". Excellent trout in this very house—got in the *Friar's cast*, man—the best reach of the mere. Let them alone for that. These jolly monks knew something of the mystery. Their warm, sunny old orchards still produce the best fruit in the country. You English gentlemen never saw the Grey-gudewife pear. Look out here, sir. The Abbot's Haugh yonder—the richest carse-land and fattest beeves in the country. Their very names are genial and smack of milk and honey! But there comes a brother of the reformed order, whom I have never yet been able to teach the difference between Béchamel and buttermilk, though he understands ten languages. Dr. Redgill—give me leave to present you to my friend, Mr. Josiah Cargill, the minister of this parish.[2] I have been telling my friend that the Reformation has thrown the science of cookery three centuries back in this corner of the island. Popery and made dishes, eh, Mr. Cargill?—Epis-

---

[1] See p. 113.
[2] The original of Josiah Cargill was the Rev. Alexander Duncan, D.D., the minister of Scott's Smailholm boyhood. See *The Scott Originals*, by W. S. Crockett.

copacy, roast beef, and plum-pudding—and what is left to Presbytery but its lang-kail, its brose, and mashlum bannocks?'

" ' So I have heard,' replied Mr. Cargill; ' very wholesome food indeed.'

" ' Wholesome food, sir! Why, your wits are wool-gathering. There is not a bare-foot monk, sir, of the most beggarly abstemious order but can give you some pretty notions of tossing up a fricassee or an omelet, or of mixing an olio. Scotland has absolutely retrograded in gastronomy. Yet she saw a better day, the memory of which is savoury in our nostrils yet, Doctor. In old Jacobite families, and in the neighbourhood of decayed monasteries—in such houses as this, for instance, where long succeeding generations have followed the trade of victuallers—a few relics may still be found. It is for this reason I fix my scene of experiment at the Cleikum,[1] and choose my notable hostess as high priestess of the mysteries.' "

The choice was justified.

" The dinner was served punctual to the second; for Meg and the Nabob, though they did not quite agree in harmony, always agreed in time: a true gourmand dinner; no sumptuous feast of twenty

[1] The name Cleikum derives from the legend of St. Ronan, a seventh-century monk, whose method of dealing with the evil and ignorance of his time was symbolically displayed on the sign hung over the doorway of " Meg Dods' " establishment, where the saint is represented with his crook " cleeking * the De'il by the hind leg ". A ceremony in celebration of the saint is performed annually by the school-boys of Innerleithen.—F. M. McN.

* Catching as by a hook.

dishes in the *dead-thraw*, but a few well-chosen
and well-suited—each relieving each—the boils
done to a *popple*, the roast to a *turn*, the stews to the
nick of time.[1] First came the soup—the hare soup;
Meg called it rabbit-soup, as this was close-time.

" ' Sir, if you please,' replied the doctor, bowing
to the tureen, and sipping his heated Madeira, as
he answered the inquiry of the Nabob, if he would
take soup, ' as our great moralist, Dr. Johnson,
said of your Scotch barley-broth, " Sir, I have
eat of it, and shall be happy to do so again." '

" Stewed red trout, for which the house was
celebrated; a fat, short-legged, thick-rumped
pullet, braised and served with rice and mushroom sauce; a Scotch dish of venison-collops;
and though last, not least in the Doctor's good
love, one of the young pigs, killed since his adventure in the sty: these formed the dinner. And
all were neatly dished—the whole in *keeping* that
would have done honour to the best city-tavern
in London. ' Sir, I say city-tavern,' said Redgill;
' for I humbly conceive that, in all save flimsy show,
business is best understood in the city, however
finely they may talk the matter at the West End.' "

Cranberry-tart and a copious libation of rich
plain cream concluded one of the most satisfactory

[1] " *The Nabob*: The Scots may, and do fail in a grand dinner, Doctor,—no doubt
of it; but as a *nation* they manage better than most of their neighbours."
—Annals of the Cleikum Club (incorporated in the Introduction and
Notes to Meg Dods's *Manual of Cookery*).

dinners Dr. Redgill had ever made in his life, and the racy flavour of Meg's old claret completed the conquest of his affections.

After "much smacking of green seals and red seals", much "cracking of nuts and of jokes", "to conclude the entertainment, the Nabob produced a single bottle of choice Burgundy, Mont Rachet; and a special bumper was dedicated to the new-comer. Coffee, four years kept, but only one hour roasted, was prepared by the Nabob's own hands—coffee which he himself had brought from Mocha, and now made in a coffee-pot of Parisian invention patronized by Napoleon."

" The meal concluded, the Nabob wiped his mouth with his ample Bandana and proceeded:

" ' Gentlemen, Man is a cooking animal; and in whatever situation he is found, it may be assumed as an axiom, that his progress in civilization has kept exact pace with the degree of refinement he may have attained in the science of gastronomy. From the hairy man of the woods, gentlemen, digging his roots with his claws, to the refined banquet of the Greek, or the sumptuous entertainment of the Roman; from the ferocious hunter, gnawing the half-broiled bloody collop, torn from the still-reeking carcass, to the modern *gourmet*, apportioning his ingredients and blending his essences, the chain is complete!

" ' First, we have the brutalized *digger* of roots;

then the sly *entrapper* of the finny tribes; and next the fierce, foul feeder, devouring his ensnared prey, fat, blood, and muscle!'

" ' What a style o' language!' whispered Mistress Dods. ' But I maun look after the scouring o' the kettles.'

" ' The next age of cookery, gentlemen, may be called the pastoral, as the last was that of the hunter. Here we have simple, mild broths, seasoned, perhaps, with the herbs of the field, decoctions of pulse, barley-cake, and the kid seethed in milk. I pass over the ages of Rome and Greece, and confine myself to the Gothic and Celtic tribes, among whom gradually emerged what I shall call the chivalrous or feudal age of cookery—the wild boar roasted whole, the stately crane, the lordly swan, the full-plumaged peacock, borne into the feudal hall by troops of vassals, to the flourish of trumpets, warlike instruments, marrow-bones, and cleavers.' [1]

[1] The spousal rites were ended soon;
'T was now the merry hour of noon,
And in the lofty arched hall
Was spread the gorgeous festival.
Steward and squire, with heedful haste,
Marshalled the rank of every guest;
Pages, with ready blade, were there,
The mighty meal to carve and share;
O'er capon, heron-shew, and crane,
And princely peacock's gilded train,
And o'er the boar-head, garnished brave,
And cygnet from St. Mary's wave; *
O'er ptarmigan and venison
The priest had spoke his benison.
　　　　　—Scott: *The Lay of the Last Minstrel.*

* St. Mary's Loch, at the head of the Yarrow.

" The peacock, it is well known, was considered during the times of chivalry, not merely as an exquisite delicacy, but as a dish of peculiar solemnity. After being

" ' Bravo!' cried Jekyl.

" ' Cookery as a domestic art, contributing to the comfort and luxury of private life, had made considerable progress in England before the Reformation; which event threw it back some centuries. . . . Gastronomy, violently expelled from monasteries and colleges, found no fitting sanctuary either in the riotous household of the jolly Cavalier, or in the gloomy abode of the lank, pinched-visaged Roundhead, the latter, as the poet has it, eager to

> . . . fall out with mince-meat and disparage
> His best and dearest friend, plum-porridge,

the former broaching his hogshead of October beer, and roasting a whole ox, in the exercise of a hospitality far more liberal than elegant.

" ' But, gentlemen, in our seats of learning the genial spark was still secretly cherished. Oxford watched over the culinary flame with zeal proportioned to the importance of the trust! From

roasted, it was again decorated with its plumage, and a sponge, dipped in lighted spirits of wine, was placed in its bill. When it was introduced on days of grand festival, it was the signal for the adventurous knights to take upon them vows to do some deed of chivalry, ' before the peacock and the ladies '.

" The boar's head was also a usual dish of feudal splendour. In Scotland it was sometimes surrounded with little banners, displaying the colours and achievements of the baron at whose board it was served."

—Pinkerton's *History of Scotland*, Vol. I.

" At a Feeste Roiall Pecokkes shall be dight on this manere: Take and flee off the skynne with the fedurs, tayle, and the nekke, and the hed theron; then take the skyn with all the fedurs, and lay hit on a table abrode; and strawe theron grounden comyn; then take the pecokke, and roste hym, and endore hym with rawe zolkes of egges; and when he is rosted, take hym of, and let hym coole awhile, and take and sowe hym in his skyn, and gilde his combe, and so serve hym forthe with the last cours."—From an old coverless Anthology.

this altar were rekindled the culinary fires of Episcopal palaces, which had smouldered for a time; and Gastronomy once more raised her parsley-wreathed front in Britain, and daily gained an increase of devoted, if not yet enlightened worshippers.' "

An extended correspondence, we learn, was arranged by the Club " with well-known amateur gourmands, as well as practical cooks, and also with those clubs, provincial and metropolitan, of which the eating, rather than the erudite preparation of dishes, has hitherto been the leading business ".

Not only Scotland, but Ireland, England, and Wales were levied, and several continental countries as well. The later editions of the *Manual* contain over twelve hundred recipes. The unique feature of the work, however, is the section on Scottish National Dishes, and the sixty (or thereabouts) recipes it contains form the nucleus of the present collection.

II

THE NATIONAL LARDER

' The fate of nations depends on how they are fed."—Brillat-Savarin.

The art of a country always has its roots in the soil, and the study of comparative cookery shows that however plentiful and varied the imported foodstuffs, it is the natural conditions and products that determine the general character of the national cuisine.

Despite certain natural disadvantages, Scotland has always been in a special sense a food-producing country. It is true that little more than a fourth of her total area is under cultivation; the soil, too, though of very diverse quality, is on an average poorer than that of England, and the climate wetter and colder, so that neither crops nor fruits reach the same perfection, nor is the harvest so certain.[1] On the other hand, certain districts, such as the Lothians, Clydesdale, Angus, Moray, and the Carse of Gowrie are as fertile as any in the British Isles, and in certain sheltered districts in Moray, Ross, and the Isles, exotic fruits and flowers grow freely in the open air. And nowhere in the world are farming and gardening prosecuted with greater skill and enterprise.

In olden times, when the population was small and sparse—by the beginning of the sixteenth century it did not exceed half a million—the means of sustenance were on the whole plentiful. The moors and forests abounded with game, whilst in Argyll and elsewhere " herds of kye nocht tame " with flesh " of a marvellous sweet-

[1] " No nation has so large a stock of benevolence of heart as the Scotch. Their temper stands anything but an attack on their climate. They would have you even believe they can ripen fruit; and, to be candid, I must own in remarkably warm summers I have tasted peaches that made excellent pickles. . . . Even the enlightened mind of Jeffrey cannot shake off the illusion that myrtles flourish at Craig Crook."—Sydney Smith.

ness, of a wonderful tenderness, and excellent delicateness of taste " ranged the hills. Rivers, lochs, and seas teemed with fish. Sheep were valued mainly for their wool, cows for their milk. Butter and cheese were in use in the earliest times, and the oat and barley crops have always provided the staple bread.[1]

Oatmeal has gradually ousted barley from its supremacy, and is in turn threatened by wheaten flour, the victory of which would be regarded by many as a national disaster.[2]

Since the Reformation, which effected a radical change in the national character, the proverbial Scot has been reared on porridge and the Shorter Catechism, a rigorous diet, but highly beneficial to those possessed of sound digestive organs.[3] Many a "lad o' pairts" who ultimately rose to fame studied his Bain and Aristotle by guttering

[1] " It was not for his benefactions to broth-pot and bake-board that John Barley-corn got title to rank as King of Grain. It was for the gift of his strong heart's blood . . . From the Lothians in the south, to the scarcely inferior barley-soils of Moray in the north, the great mass of the bear harvest is destined for distillation and brewing, and only an insignificant proportion will find its way to the mill. The flower of it goes to the brewer; the distiller gets the inferior quality; but even when barley bread was a staple food in the farm-house and burgh towns of Scotland, it was still the lighter qualities of both bigg and barley that were dressed or ground at the mill for pot or girdle."—Hugh Haliburton: *Furth in Field*.

[2] " *Macdonald*: If beer and beef-steaks have made Englishmen, oatmeal cakes and oatmeal porridge have made Scotchmen.

" *Hilarius*: Specially Scotch brains. There is a notable seasoning of phosphorus in oats which produces the *praefervidum ingenium Scotorum*."
　　　　　　　　　　　　　　　　　　　—John Stuart Blackie: *Altavona*.

When the *Edinburgh Review* was founded in 1800, the motto proposed by Sydney Smith was, "Tenui musam meditamur avena". ("We cultivate literature on a little oatmeal.") This was later modified.—F. M. McN.

[3] " An honest, good sort of fellow, made out of oatmeal," said Carlyle of Macaulay The compliment might have been reciprocated.—F. M. McN.

candle-light in a garret in which one of the most conspicuous articles of furniture was a sack of oatmeal,[1] and regular holidays were formerly granted by the authorities to enable the poor student to tramp back to his native glen and replenish his sack.[2]

"The ancient way of dressing corn," writes Martin, who visited the Western Isles in 1703, "which is yet used in several Isles is called Graddan, from the Irish word *Grad*, which signifies quick. . . . A Woman sitting down, takes a handful of corn, holding it by the Stalks in her left hand, and then sets fire to the Ears, which are presently in a flame; she has a Stick in her right hand, which she manages very dexterously, beating off the grain at the very Instant, when the Husk is quite burnt, for if she miss of that, she must use the Kiln, but experience has taught them this Art to perfection. The Corn may be so dressed, winnowed, ground, and baked within an Hour after reaping from the Ground. The

---

[1] Many a promising lad nevertheless died of over-study and malnutrition, and some who did achieve success were cut off in their prime as the result of a too meagre régime.

[2] An annual holiday known as Mealy Monday is still celebrated in the Scottish Universities.

Oatmeal has other uses than as an article of food. "Meat in Scotland is frequently kept a fortnight smothered in oatmeal and carefully wiped every day," says Mrs. Dalgairns in her *Practice of Cookery* (Edinburgh, 1829), "and if it should be a little tainted, it is soaked for some hours before it is used in oatmeal and water."

Oat-cakes, mealie puddings, and cheeses are still commonly kept buried in oatmeal in the girnel or meal-chest. Oatmeal was formerly used as soap, and many country lasses still place a small muslin bagful in their ewer overnight for the benefit of their complexions.—F. M. McN.

Oat-bread dressed as above is Loosening, and that dressed in the Kiln Astringent, and of greater strength for Labourers: but they love the Graddan, as being more agreeable to their taste."

Another mode was the primitive mortar-mill, which was succeeded by the quern,[1] a hand-mill composed of two circular stones with a hole in the centre of the upper one (through which it is fed with corn) and a wooden handle. The meal falls from all sides on to a wide tray, and by means of a wooden spindle can be ground coarse or fine at will.

> The cronach [2] stills the dowie [3] heart,
>   The jurram [4] stills the bairnie,
> The music for a hungry wame [5]
>   Is grinding o' the quernie,

says the old song.

The quern was in common use throughout the Highlands and Islands in the latter part of the nineteenth century, and is still used in the outlying districts, though isolately and sparingly.

As oatmeal was the staple grain, kail [6] was long

---

[1] A.S cweorn .   [2] Gael. coronach, lament.   [3] Sorrowful.
[4] Gael. iorram, song, lullaby.   [5] Belly.   [6] Colewort, cabbage.

" Kail is still the common name in Scotland for broth, and is even used metonymically for the whole dinner, as constituting, among our temperate ancestors, the principal part. Hence, in giving a friendly invitation to dinner, it is common to say, ' Will you come and tak' your kail wi' me?' Black Dwarf."—Jamieson, Dictionary of the Scottish Language.

In Edinburgh the bell rung at two o'clock was popularly known as the kail-bell, and that which was rung at eight as tinkle-sweetie, because the sound of it was so sweet to the ears of apprentices and shop-men, who were then at liberty.

the staple vegetable of Scotland. His kail-yard [1] was in fact to the old Scots crofter what his potato-plot was to the Irish peasant.

> Although my father was nae laird, [2]
> 'T is daffin' [3] to be vaunty,[4]
> He keepit aye a gude kail-yaird,
> A ha' hoose [5] and a pantry.[6]

Meg Dods speaks of *The Land o' Kail* as Burns does of *The Land o' Cakes*.[7] The vogue of kail, however, was originally confined to the Lowlands. The Highlander preferred the common nettle [8] in his broth, and appears to have regarded the use of kail as a symptom of effeminacy.[9]

---

[1] Kitchen-garden. " The most beautiful kitchen-garden, I believe, in the world, was at Blair Castle."—Bishop Pococke (1760).

The term kail-yaird has been applied to a school of fiction including Barrie, Crockett, and Ian Maclaren, who depict Scottish village life. Ian Maclaren took one of his titles, *Beside the Bonnie Brier Bush*, from the song:

> There grows a bonnie brier bush in our kail-yard.

George Douglas's *House with the Green Shutters*, a study of the same theme in colours as sombre as those of the others were roseate, was a protest against the sentimentalism of the " kail-yairders ".—F. M. McN.

[2] Land-owner. [3] Nonsense. [4] Boastful. [5] A superior type of house with a hall or living-room. [6] *Scornfu' Nansy*, from Ramsay's *Tea-Table Miscellany*, where it is marked as old.

[7] Originally oat-cakes.

[8] " Ivar's daughter " is the name given to the nettle plant, which, about St. Patrick's Day, puts her head out of holes in walls loosely built without lime. She is said to have been blessed by the Saint as useful to man and beast.—F. M. McN.

[9] " The Grants, who, living near the Lowland line, had grown fond of it, were condemned as the soft, kail-eating Grants, and a Gaelic poem on the battle of Killiecrankie mocks at Mackay's defeated soldiers as ' men of kail and brose '."
—T. F. Henderson: *Old-World Scotland*.

In the earlier part of the nineteenth century, cabbage and green kail were freely grown in the Hebrides, but after the evictions in South Uist and elsewhere, when the people were deprived of their plots of land, they fell back on certain wild vegetables formerly used only in emergency—wild spinach, wild mustard, the goose-foot, and the root of the little silver-weed, trunkfuls of which were stored for winter use. Pennant tells us that the dried roots of the *cor-meille*, or wood pease (*Orobus*

The potato, like the Gael, travelled to Scotland viâ Ireland, and crossed by the self-same route. " That man has not been dead many years who first introduced from Ireland the culture of the potato into the peninsula of Cantyre; he lived near Campbeltown. From him the city of Glasgow obtained a regular supply for many years; and from him also the natives of the West Highlands and Isles obtained the first plants, from which have been derived those abundant supplies on which the people there now primarily subsist."[1] Its first recorded appearance in Scotland is in 1701, when the Duchess of Buccleugh's Household Book mentions a peck of potatoes as brought from Edinburgh, and costing half a crown.

" About (1733)," Chambers tells us, " it was beginning to be cultivated in gardens, but still with a hesitation about its moral character, for no reader of Shakespere requires to be told that some of the more uncontrollable passions of human nature were supposed to be favoured by its use. . . . (In 1739) a gentleman styled Robert Graham of Tamrawer, factor on the forfeited estate of

tuberosus), were the support of the Highlanders in long journeys where the customary food could not be obtained. A plant called *shemis* (*Ligusticum scoticum*), possessing aromatic and carminative qualities, grows on the rocky shores of the Hebrides and the western seaboard, and is used as a green vegetable, boiled or raw. The wild carrot has always been the favourite " fruit " of the children of the Hebrides. As they seek it, they recite an old Gaelic rhyme:

> Honey underground
> Is the winter carrot
> Between St. Andrew's Day and Christmas.—F. M. McN.

[1] Anderson's *Recreations*, Vol. II (1800).

Kilsyth, ventured to the heretofore unknown step of planting *a field of potatoes*. His experiment was conducted on a half-acre of ground on the croft of Neilstone, to the north of the town of Kilsyth. It appears that the root was now, and for a good while after, cultivated on *lazy-beds*. Many persons —amongst whom was the Earl of Perth, who joined in the insurrection of 1745—came from great distances to witness so extraordinary a novelty and inquire into the mode of culture."[1]

Turnips were introduced from Holland about the same period. " Cockburn of Ormiston . . . sewed turnips in 1725, being the first to raise turnips in drill." [2]

" Piscinata Scotia," says the proverb. During the early Celtic period, when adoration was paid to the waters, fish as food was taboo, and even after the introduction of Christianity it continued for a time to be considered dangerous to the purity of the soul.[3] When, in the eleventh century, the Roman Church superseded the Celtic one, her fast-days and fastings encouraged the development of the fisheries, which at an early period became a source of national wealth.[4] By the

---

[1] *Domestic Annals of Scotland.*   [2] *Farmer's Magazine*, 1804.

[3] Aphrodite was born of the sea, and was commonly held to exercise her influence through certain products of the sea, notably (in the Scottish tradition) trout, skate, shell-fish, and salt. Skate-bree (the liquor in which skate has been boiled) is a famous old Scottish love-potion.—F. M. McN. See *Caledonian Medical Journal*, Ap., 1928. article on Scottish Folk Medicine, by Col. D. Rorie, M.D.

[4] " David I gave the monks of the Isle of May exclusive rights around their own shores, conferred on the community of Holyrood the tithe of his own share of the

thirteenth century Aberdeen was famous for her speldings[1] and other cured fish, and Don Pedro de Ayala, who visited Scotland in 1498, comments on the great quantities of salmon, herring, and " a kind of dried fish which they call stock fish ", which were then exported. Loch Fyne herrings were early celebrated for their delicious flavour, and were sent in barrels to Edinburgh and other towns.[2]

The salmon fisheries were of even greater importance. So plentiful, indeed, was this fish, that it was despised by the upper classes, and farm-hands used to stipulate that it should not be served to them more than so many times a week.[3]

In the seventeenth century the Dutch fishermen

larger fish caught along the southern shore of the Forth, from the Avon to Cockburnspath, and made over to the monastery of Dunfermline every seventh one of the seals caught at Kinghorn, after his own tithe had been set aside; Malcolm IV granted the half of the fat of the royal fishes which might come into the Forth on either shore; and Alexander I gave to the monks of Scone the right to fish in the Tay, near which their house was situated."
—Louis A. Barbé: *Sidelights on Scottish History.*

Seals were extensively used as food in the Hebrides down to the last century Adamnan (624–c. 704) speaks in his *Life of St. Columba* of "the little island (off Iona) where our sea-calves breed", and Martin writes: " The natives salt the seals with the ashes of burnt sea-ware, and say they are good food "(*Description of the Western Islands*, 1703).—F. M. McN.

[1] Called also *speldrins:* small haddocks or whitings split, salted, and rock-dried; to be distinguished from *finnans*, or smoked haddocks. They are mentioned by Boswell.

[2] " Wastlin' Herrin!" (west-coast herring) is an old Edinburgh street cry. A keg of these used to be a popular gift in Edinburgh and the east country. The plump Loch Fyne herring are still jocularly alluded to as *Glasgow Magistrates.*

[3] " I have been told it here as a very good Jest, that a Highland Gentleman who went to London by Sea, soon after his Landing passed by a Tavern where . . . there were among other Things a Rump of Beef and some Salmon: of the Beef he ordered a Steak for himself, ' but ', he says, ' let Duncan have some Salmon '. To be short, the Cook who attended him humoured the Jest, and the Master's eating was Eight Pence, and Duncan's came to almost as many Shillings."
—Burt: *Letters from the North of Scotland* (1730).

were thoroughly at home in Scottish waters.[1]
Every season, year in, year out, and almost the
whole year round, those patient, plodding, but
astute folk came over and fished round our coasts
until they had practically established a monopoly,
out of which their country made enormous gains.
The Firth of Forth was a favourite resort.

> In her the skate and codlin sail,
> The eil, fu' souple, wags her tail,
> Wi' herrin, fleuk,[2] an' mackarel,
>   An' whitens dainty;
> Their spindle-shanks the labsters trail
>   Wi' partans [3] plenty.[4]

It was not till the beginning of the eighteenth
century that the Scots woke up to the fact that
their pockets were being unostentatiously but
systematically picked.   In 1720, the same year
that the South Sea scheme was launched in England, a North Sea scheme was launched in Scotland, its express purpose being to " ding the
Dutch ", and to revive and develop the Scottish
fisheries, as well as stimulate the boat-building
industry.   About two million pounds appear to
have been subscribed, but soon, " by a frost the
origin and nature of which belongs to the social
and political history of those times ", the North
Sea scheme, like its more celebrated contemporary,
was completely blighted.

[1] It is an old saying that Amsterdam was built on Scottish herring-bones.
[2] Flounder.   [3] The large edible crab.   [4] Fergusson: *Caller Oysters.*

Shell-fish, of course, were always a staple article of diet.[1] So, too, were seaweeds, not only in the isles, where the food problem was often acute, but in all the seaboard towns.

Relatively speaking, the Scots were always a piscivorous, the English a carnivorous race. Despite the excellence of their beef [2] and mutton, the Scots have never been great meat-eaters. Burt writes: " The little Highland Mutton, when fat, is delicious, and certainly the greatest of Luxuries. And the small Beef, when fresh, is very sweet and succulent, though it lacks that Substance which should preserve it long when salted. Amongst the poorer classes in Scotland, beef is eaten only at Martinmas,[3] when a Mart or Ox is killed; and

[1] Oysters figure with partans, crabs, and other shell-fish at the royal banquet at Stirling in 1594, on the occasion of the baptism of Prince Henry. They were always immensely popular in the capital.

" What desperate breedy beasts eisters must be," says the Shepherd in *Noctes Ambrosianae*, " for they tell me that Embro devours a hunder thoosand every day." " Why, James," says North, " that is only about two oysters to every three mouths."

" There is perhaps no spot on earth," we read in the annals of the Cleikum Club " where oysters were enjoyed in greater perfection than at the head of the old Fish Market Close in Edinburgh—alas the change!—once the cynosure of all the taverns, fish creels, and book-sellers' shops of that learned city; the place where eating, learning, and law sat enthroned side by side. Here, on any evening from October till March, the oyster-gourmand took his solitary stand and enjoyed his delicious regale in its utmost earthly perfection, swallowed alive with its own gravy the moment it was opened by the fish-wife, who operated on the shell with a dexterity of manipulation, a rapidity of fingering which no piano-player we ever saw could compare with. . . . A precious remnant of genuine oyster-eaters still haunt this favourite spot. Dr. Redgill resolved to visit it on the first night of his sojourn in Edinburgh."

Since the disappearance of the oyster-beds from the Firth of Forth the once familiar cry " Caller Oo!" (fresh oysters) has practically died out in the streets of Edinburgh.

[2] The " roast beef of old England ", at its best, is Scots beef, which always fetches a higher price in the London market.

[3] At this season fodder is scarce. The killing of the mart appears to have been originally sacrificial in character, in honour of St. Martin. The name may be derived, as Jamieson suggests, from *Martin*, but more probably it is simply the Gaelic word *mart*, a cow

the only other butcher meat they eat throughout
the year is an occasional Braxy [1]." [2]

As regards pork, Scott, in a note to *The Fortunes
of Nigel*, reminds us that " the Scots, till within
the last generation, disliked swine's flesh as an
article of food as much as the Highlanders do
at present.   It was remarked as extraordinary
rapacity, when the Border depredators con-
descended to make prey of the accursed race,
whom the fiend made his habitation;" [3] and adds,
in a note to *Waverley*, " King Jamie carried this
prejudice to England, and is known to have
abhorred pork almost as much as he did tobacco ".[4]
Nevertheless Burt tells us that Aberdeen, in 1730,
was furnishing families with pickled pork, " for
winter provision, as well as for their shipping ";
and in the Kingdom of Fife they have an excellent

[1] Braxy mutton, the salted flesh of sheep which have died of braxy, is commonly
eaten by poor herdsmen and shepherds, who may have found its strong flavour
palatable. " In pastoral countries it is used as a food with little scruple," says Scott
in a note to *Redgauntlet*; according to Burns, " moorland herds like good fat braxies ";
and Norman Macleod speaks of " the occasional, dinner luxury of braxy, a species
of mutton which need not be too minutely inquired into."

[2] *Letters from the North of Scotland* (1730).

[3] An old Galloway grace before meat runs:
> Bless the sheep for David's sake, he herdit sheep himsel';
> Bless the fish for Peter's sake, he gruppit fish himsel';
> Bless the soo for Satan's sake, he was yince a soo himsel'.
> —From Dr. Trotter's *Galloway Gossip*.

[4] Ben Jonson has recorded this peculiarity where the gipsy in a masque, ex-
amining the King's hand, says:
> . . . you should by this line
> Love a horse and a hound, but no part of a swine.
> —*The Gipsies Metamorphosed*.

" James's own proposed banquet for the Devil was a loin of pork, a poll of ling,
with a pipe of tobacco for digestion."—Scott: *Waverley*, Note.

" In Scotland we do not manage pork well. In England they kill it at the proper
age and size. . . . Servants [in Scotland] will seldom touch it; in London it is the
greatest treat they can get."—Mrs. McEwen: *Elements of Cookery* (1835).

pie, of ancient pedigree, with rabbit and pickled pork as the main ingredients.

Rabbits were always a popular article of diet in the Lowlands, and in the thirteenth century a rabbit warren and its warrener were attached to every burgh.[1]

Like the fisheries, poultry-rearing, and indeed husbandry generally, owed much to the fostering care of the monks.

The popular belief that before the Union of the Crowns Scotland was a poor and barbarous country is contrary to fact. Like other countries, she had periods of acute poverty, even of destitution; but at the worst of times she was never much worse off than England, and often she fared much better. Her internal resources were frequently drained by costly wars and by internal feuds which occasionally resulted in social anarchy, and she was further handicapped by a vicious economic system—a survival of the Middle Ages —that set town against town, burgh against burgh. Nevertheless at a very early period she had a considerable foreign trade.[2] Rich dresses were

---

[1] Mak kinnen * and capon ready, then,
    And venison in great plentie;
    We 'll welcome here our royal King.
                        —*Ballad of Johnie Armstrang.*

    * Rabbits. Cf. Gael. *coinnin* and E. *coney.*

[2] In the ledger of Andrew Halyburton, an enterprising Scottish commission merchant, we have an authoritative document as to Scottish trade at the end of the fifteenth century. Her foreign trade was based not on any organized industry, but on the primeval callings of fishermen, shepherds, and huntsmen. Her ships took

The National Larder

imported by Malcolm III (Canmore) in the eleventh century, oriental luxuries by Alexander I in the twelfth, whilst David I was praised by Fordun for enriching the ports of his kingdom with foreign merchandise. In the thirteenth century, under Alexander III, Scotland had a large and lucrative trade with Flanders, Germany, and the Low Countries, and during the next hundred years, under the wise rule of three successive kings, she attained a remarkable degree of well-being. In the fourteenth century, however, when a truce with England was on the point of conclusion, and Scotland imagined herself safe from attack, she was raided with more than usual ferocity [1] and her richest provinces utterly laid waste.[2]

wool, hides, and fish to Flanders, and returned with wine, furniture, and plate. (The Netherlands were long the clearing-house for European and extra-European trade.) Under James IV, Berwick, the chief Scottish port, was likened to Alexandria, and her customs were reckoned to equal a third of all England.—F. M. McN.

Aberdeen was an early Flemish settlement. " She served an extensive district— a district which was rich in the staple products of the period. . . . As the bulk of her trade was with the Low Countries, she frequently received accessions to her population from her kinsmen across the water. Down the centuries the true son of Aberdeen has maintained certain characteristics of his own, so much so that even to-day the typical Aberdonian is different from his fellow-Scots elsewhere."
—Evan Barron: *The Scottish War of Independence.*

[1] " The barons of Scotland were not apprised of this invasion, and took the affair much to heart, saying they would revenge it to the utmost of their power."
—Froissart: *Chronicles.*

[2] " Between the fertile and civilized part of England and the march of Scotland, lay a hundred miles of barren and thinly peopled country. . . . The Scotch themselves were less fortunate. . . . From the top of the Cheviot ridge the moss-troopers could descry three of the richest shires of Scotland stretched below them, a helpless prey, whilst southward they could see nothing but desolate moors. The fertile Lothians and the Tweed valley could be raided by Percy, but the English midlands could not be touched by Douglas."
—G. M. Trevelyan: *England in the Age of Wyclif.*

Quhen [1] Alysander oure king was dede,
    That Scotland lede in luve and lé,[2]
Away was sons [3] of ale and brede,
    Of wyne and wax, of gamyn [4] and glé;
Oure gold was changed into lede.
    Cryst borne into Virginité,
Succour Scotland and remede [5]
    That stad [6] is in perplexité. [7]

No wonder that, as Froissart tells us, the French troops were astonished and appalled at the intense poverty of the country which had produced so much of the flower of European scholarship and chivalry.

But with normal conditions she invariably recovered.   Taylor, the Water Poet, primed with travellers' tales of a bleak, barren, and famine-stricken land, was astonished to find, on crossing the border in 1618, that.

There I saw the sky above and earth below,
And, as in England, there the sun did shine;
The hills with sheep replete, with corn the dale,
And many a cottage yielded good Scots ale.

Neither was there any shortage in the Highlands.   Of Lord Lovat (*b.* 1572) we read: " The weekly expenditure of provisions in his house included 7 bolls of malt, 7 bolls of meal, and 1 of flour.   Each year 70 beeves were consumed, besides venison, fish, poultry, lamb, veal, and all

[1] When. [2] Law. [3] Abundance. [4] Sport. [5] Remedy. [6] Fixed.
[7] Ancient Cantus preserved in Wyntoun's *Orygynale Cronykill of Scotland.*

sorts of feathered game in profusion. His lordship imported wines, sugars, and spices from
France, in return for the salmon produced by his
rivers. He was celebrated for a liberal hospitality,
and when he died in 1633, 5000 armed followers
and friends attended his funeral, for all of whom
there would be entertainment provided." [1] And
Captain Burt, who accompanied General Wade
to Scotland in 1724, writes in his *Letters from the
North of Scotland* that while in some parts he
found no decent food, in others he was surfeited
with delicacies—grouse, partridge, salmon, trout,
and excellent honey. There was wine and brandy
of fine quality, but " the glory of the country
was Usky ".[2]

On the whole, the remark of the French traveller, Estienne Perlin, in 1552, " Nothing is
scarce here but money ", is substantially true of
Scotland throughout her history.

III

THE RENASCENCE OF COOKERY
IN SCOTLAND

" Mere hunger, which is the best sauce, will not produce cookery, which is the
art of sauces."

Cookery aims, of course, at much more than
merely supplying the necessities of nutrition. Its
development is dependent on an increasing refine-

[1] Anderson: *History of the Frasers.*   [2] Whisky (Gael. *usque baugh*, living water).

ment of taste, which, in turn, is dependent on a certain degree of wealth and general culture. And if, as we have said, the art of a nation has its roots in the soil, it is equally axiomatic that external influences are necessary to foster its growth.

In cookery, as in all the arts, there is a continuous give-and-take among the nations. The Greeks, through their contact with Asia, added a touch of oriental splendour to their banquets;[1] the Romans, forsaking their old simple ways, borrowed in turn from the Greeks. Then come the Dark Ages of Cookery, as of all culture, and not till the Renascence—then, too, with Italy as the starting-point—does the history of modern cookery begin.

The development of the art in France appears (judging by references in Montaigne) to owe much to Catherine de Medici (1519–89), wife of Henri II of France, who brought Italian cooks to Paris and introduced there a cultured simplicity hitherto unknown. (Ices, incidentally, were an Italian innovation.) The seed was sown on fertile soil. The French rapidly became masters of the art, and have retained their supremacy to this day. The spread of cosmopolitan hotels and restaurants has acquainted the whole civilized

[1] " In Greece the arts of cookery and medicine were associated, and were studied by physicians of the greatest eminence."

—W. C. Hazlitt: *Old Cookery Books.*

world with the type. The French Revolution dealt a severe blow to the art, as to so much else in the *ancien régime*; but it recovered, and in 1804, in the lifetime of Brillat-Savarin, the *Almanach des Gourmands* was started—" the first sustained effort at investing gastronomy with the dignity of an art ".[1]

In the days of the Auld Alliance,[2] the fashions of living of the Scottish nobility were much

[1] The names of its principal exponents are known the wide world over: Béchamel, for example, maître d'hôtel to Louis XIV, celebrated for his sauce; Vatel, the great Condé's cook, the story of whose suicide in despair at the tardy arrival of the fish is so touchingly told by Madame de Sévigné; the chef of the Prince of Soubise, whose name is borne by an onion sauce; and Richelieu, to whom is ascribed the mayonnaise. See *Enc. Brit.*, art. *Cookery*.

[2] Legend attributes to Charlemagne the

Weill keipit ancient alliance
Maid betuix Scotland and the realme of france.*

Its authentic beginnings, however, go no farther back than the twelfth century. Later, when England, led by her Norman conquerors into a series of wars of aggression, had subdued Wales and partially subdued Ireland, she turned to Scotland and France, who were thus drawn to make common cause against a powerful enemy, and it was by this means that Scotland was able to maintain the national independence asserted at Bannockburn in the fourteenth century. The Scottish archers fought with distinction during the Hundred Years' War, one of their leaders, the Earl of Buchan, being created Constable of France. In recognition of their services, Charles VII appointed as Royal bodyguard the famous Scots Guard of France, which consisted of a hundred gendarmes and two hundred archers.† Twenty-four of their number were told off as the special protectors of the Royal person. Louis XIV was reported to trust no other creatures of human make, and history shows that their motto, In omni modo fidelis (*Ever Faithful*), was well merited.

According to the old courtly creed of France, the privileges of the Scots Guard had " an eminence that partook of sacredness ". Its captain was a high officer of state, the first we know of being John Stewart, Lord of Aubigny, founder of a great Scots house in France; many of its members—scions of distinguished houses such as Douglas, Stewart, and Hamilton—received titles and lands from successive French monarchs; and Scottish nobles were as much at home at the French court as at their own.

Conversely, during the regency of Albany in the sixteenth century, French troops

* Sir David Lyndsay: *Deploration of the Death of Queen Magdalene.*

† " The institution of the Scots Guard was an acknowledgement of the service the Scots rendered to Charles VII in reducing France to his obedience, and of the great loyalty and virtue he found in them."—Louis XII: " Letters of General Naturalization for the Whole Scottish Nation in France." (See Daniel's *Histoire de la Milice Française*, Vol. II.)

influenced by the French Court, and the early Stuart kings vied with their continental contemporaries in the magnificence of their banquets.

Hector Boece [1] laments the " extreme diligence " with which his contemporaries searched " so mony deligat courses that they provoke the stomach to ressave more than it may sufficiently digest ", and attributes this deviation from the simpler ways of an earlier generation to the nobility, who introduced them " efter the fassione quhilke they have seen in France ".

In those days, poverty and love of adventure drove many young men of family or " parts " abroad as soldiers of fortune or as scholars, as

were garrisoned in Scotland, and when the Regent was absent in France, he left the Sieur de la Bastie as guardian within the boundaries of Lothian and Merse.

After the Union of the Crowns of England and Scotland in 1603, the native element in the Scots Guard was gradually thinned, but the Guard persisted as part of the pageantry of the French court until the latter went down, with all its pomps and vanities, in the maelstrom of the French Revolution.

Scott's *Quentin Durward* gives a picture of the life of a member of the famous Guard.

The prolonged intercourse between the two countries naturally led to numerous alliances between their royal and noble houses. William the Lion and Alexanders II and III had French wives, and James V had two in succession—the fragile Magdalene, whom he married in Notre Dame and buried two months later in Holyrood Abbey, and Mary of Lorraine, the mother of Mary Stuart. Almost beneath the walls of Craigmillar Castle, on the outskirts of Edinburgh, there nestled the hamlet of Little France, the residence of such of Mary's attendants as could not find accommodation in the Castle, and it is said that French sorrel grows freely in the neighbourhood. In the little historic garden at Croft-an-Righ, there grows another plant introduced from France—*archangelica officinalis*, which is used for purposes of confectionery. It has been in cultivation since 1568, a year or two after Queen Mary's return from France, and is believed to grow nowhere else in the United Kingdom.

The Auld Alliance has left traces in almost every department of Scottish national life, notably in her legal and ecclesiastical systems, and in the common speech. (See Appendix I: *Franco-Scottish Domestic Terms*.) The strong sentimental bond which still persists is crystallized in the flourishing Franco-Scottish Society.—F. M. McN

[1] A fifteenth-century Scottish historian and friend of Erasmus.

now they go to London, India, and the Dominions,
so that we had a cosmopolitan instead of, as to-
day, an anglicized aristocracy.[1] It is not, therefore,
surprising that in the earliest Scottish cookery-
books we learn to dress cod in the Dutch way,
lobsters in the Italian way, a nowt's tongue in the
Polish way, and so forth, as well as numerous
dishes *à la française*.[2]

We learn from the Exchequer Rolls that James I
kept a French cook, and it is not unlikely that his
successors did likewise. During the reign of
James IV, the Scottish court was regarded as the
most romantic and brilliant in Europe.[3] Its
praises were sung by the Italian poet Ariosto,
and it is the subject of a finely-painted frieze
in Siena. It was ornamented by a galaxy of

[1] " Then it was that the name of Scot was honourable over all the world, and that
the glory of their ancestors was a pass-port and safe-conduct for any traveller of
that country. . . . I have heard it related [of James (the Admirable) Crichton] . . .
that after his peragration of France, Spaine, and Italy, and that for speaking some of
these languages with the liveliness of the country accent they would have had him
pass for a native, he plainly told them, without making bones thereof, that truly he
thought he had as much honour by his own country, which did contrevalue the riches
of those nations by the valour, learning, and honesty wherein it did parallel, if not
surpass them."—Sir Thomas Urquhart of Cromarty (*c.* 1605-6*,*: *Ekskybalauron*.

[2] " We of Scotland," said Winterblossom [apropos of soup], probably owe our
superiority in this department to our long and close alliance with that nation which
has ever been most profoundly skilled in the mysteries of the soup-pot. That
Scotland is indebted to France for even the slender proficiency she has attained in
cookery, is abundantly evident from the culinary phraseology of the nation. Kitchen
—cuisine—the word with us comprehends every kind of viand or preparation which
may add to the relish of the coarse cake, and decoction of oatmeal and coleworts,
which formed the staple of the daily meal. A peasant's butter, cheese, fish, meat
and so forth, all are ' kitchen '. Then we have the hachi—the soup Lorraine and
à la Reine, the veal Flory, or Florentine pie—our broche and our turn-broche, and
our culinary adage, ' hunger is good kitchen '."—*Annals of the Cleikum Club*.

[3] " During the sixteenth century, all the leading powers of Europe found it their
interest to court the goodwill of Scotland."—P. Hume Brown: *Life of John Knox*.

poets [1] who virtually alone illumine the barren period
in English literature that separates Chaucer from
Spenser; knights from all over Europe took part
in its jousts, and even negroes from Morocco
arrived at Leith [2] in Scottish ships. James was
as mindful, too, of the elegance of the table as
of the splendours of the tournament.[3] Alas that
so much chivalry and talent should have been
blotted out on Flodden Field!

In the sixteenth century Mary of Lorraine, the
wife of James V, introduced to Edinburgh the
perfected civilization of France.[4] James himself,
according to Buchanan, was temperate in diet and
seldom drank wine, but this apparently had no
effect on the customs of the day, for at the Earl
of Atholl's Buchanan was entertained " with all
sich delicious and sumptuous meattis as was to
be had in Scotland, for fleschis, fischis, and all

[1] Henryson, Dunbar, Gavin Douglas, Sir David Lyndsay, and among lesser
lights, Sir Gilbert Hay, chamberlain to Charles VI of France, who made several
translations of the works of French authors.

[2] Here, in 1511, James IV " buildit the *Michael*, ane verrie monstruous great
ship, whilk tuik sae meikle timber that schee waisted all the woodis in Fyfe, except
Falkland wood, besides the timber that cam out of Norroway ".—Pitscottie.

[3] In his *Dirige to the King at Stirling*, Dunbar invites James to return to the festive halls of Holyrood:

> To eit swan, cran, pertrik * and plever,†
> And every fische that swymis in rever;
> To drynk with ws the new fresche wyne,
> That grew upon the rever of Ryne,
> ffresche, fragrant clairettis ‡ out of France,
> Of Angerss and of Orliance,
> With mony ane courss of grit dyntie:
>   Say ye amen, for cheritie.
>   * Partridge.   † Plover.   ‡ Claret.

In the sixteenth century much French and Flemish furniture and plate was
imported.

kinds of fyne wyne, and spycis, requisit for ane
prince ". Under Mary Stuart the supremacy of
French fashions was maintained.[1] Knox, indeed,
makes special reference to the extravagant banqueting of the queen and nobles: " The affairis of the
kytcheing were so gryping that the mynesteris
stipendis could nocht be payit."

This prolonged period of high living resulted at
last in an actual shortage of food, and in 1581
a law was passed against " superfluous banqueting ".

Dishes and courses were regulated according to
rank, and transgressors not only were fined, but
also suffered moral punishment, being stigmatized
as men " given to voluptuosity, and not for the
weal of their person and the common weal of this
realm ". Exemption was granted, however, in
favour of certain high-days and holidays, including
Yule and Pasch;[2] special occasions such as weddings; and banquets given officially to strangers
from other countries; but no Scotsman was to

[1] They say wyfis are sa delicat
In feiding, feisting, and bankat,*
 Some not content are with such cheir
As weill may suffice thair estate;
 For newfangilness † of cheir and geir.‡

And some will spend mair, I heir say,
In spyce and droggis on ane day
 Than wad thair mothers in ane yeir;
Whilk ‖ will gar § mony pak ¶ decay,
 When they sa vainlie waste thair geir.
  —Sir Richard Maitland (1496–1586): *Satire on the Toun Ladyes.*
* Banquet. † Novelty. ‡ Possessions. ‖ Which. § Make. ¶ Fortune.
[2] Christmas and Easter.

make banquets to any other Scotsman " but in the manner aforesaid ".

Other and severer acts followed, professedly occasioned by the prevailing dearth.[1]

The French dessert was introduced to Scotland in the sixteenth century,[2] the table being disserved or cleared, and the fruits and sweets which followed being served in another room.[3] A Scottish house had " fyne lame pottis for desertis " and " lyttil new plaitis for disertis " as early as 1594. And James VI, when visiting New College, St. Andrews, to hear a disputation between the " Bischope " and Andrew Melville, passed to the College Hall, " where was prepared a banquet of wat and dry confectiones, with all sortes of wyne,[4] wharat His Majestie camped verie merrilie a guid whyll ".

It does not appear, however, that French influences ever extended far beyond Edinburgh and Court circles. Fynes Morison, for example, who visited Scotland in 1598, writes:

[1] To some extent their influence was felt down to the eighteenth century. In 1744, at a meeting held in Portree to discourage the use of foreign luxuries, the Skye chiefs—Sir Alexander Macdonald of Macdonald, John Mackinnon of Mackinnon, Norman Macleod of Macleod, and Malcolm Macleod of Raasay—agreed to discontinue and discountenance the use of brandy, tobacco, and tea, whilst at the University of St. Andrews the bursars, so long as they continued to dine in the common hall, were restricted on three days of the week to fish and eggs, and to broth and beef on the other four.—F. M. McN.

[2] In England, the word dessert does not come into use until the middle of the following century.

[3] " During the old régime, the French moved from table to the ante-room to refresh their lips and fingers immediately after the substantial part of their repast. Madame the Comtesse de Genlis appears to consider the abandonment of this practice and the introduction of finger-glasses as one of the most flagrant innovations of parvenu manners."—Meg Dods: Manual, Note.

[4] One still reads in newspaper reports of municipal or other social gatherings in Scotland of a " banquet " of cake and wine.

" Myselfe was at a Knight's House who had many servants to attend him, that brought in his meate with their heads covered with blew caps, the Table being more than half furnished with great platters of porredge [1] each having a little bit of sodden [2] meat; and when the Table was served, the servants did sit down with us,[3] but the upper messe, insteede of Porredge, had a Pullet with some prunes in the broth.[4] And I observed no Art of Cookery, or furniture of Household stuff, but rather rude neglect of both, though . . . we were entertained after their best manner. . . . They drink pure Wines, not with sugar as the English, yet at Feasts they put comfits in the Wine, after the French manner, but they had not our Vinteners' fraud to mixe their Wines. . . . [They] vulgarly eat hearth-cakes of oats, but in cities have also wheaten bread, which, for the most part, is bought by courtiers, gentlemen, and the best sort of citizens."

The Reformation in Scotland was in fact a

---

[1] Pottage, broth.   [2] Boiled.

[3] " Till within this last (nineteenth) century, the farmers, even of a respectable condition, dined with their work-people. The difference betwixt those of high degree was ascertained by the place of the party above or below the salt, or sometimes by a line drawn with chalk on the dining-table. Lord Lovat, who knew well how to feed the vanity and restrain the appetites of his clansmen, allowed each sturdy Fraser who had the slightest pretensions to be a duinhé-wassel [*] the full honour of the sitting, but at the same time took care that his young kinsmen did not acquire at his table any taste for outlandish luxuries. His Lordship was always ready with some honourable apology why foreign wines and French brandy—delicacies which he conceived might sap the hardy habits of his cousins—should not circulate past an assigned point on the table."—Scott: *Waverley*, Note.

[4] Cock-a-leekie.   [*] (Approximately) gentleman.

revolution, in many ways analogous in its effects to the French Revolution that succeeded it.[1] Drastic ills require drastic remedies, and drastic remedies, that benefit the system in one direction, have inevitably a baneful effect in another. In Scotland there began a praiseworthy cult of mind and character, but the arts declined. Beauty became suspect—she ministered, it was alleged, to the senses, not to the soul—and from the ancient trinity of Beauty, Goodness, and Truth, whose essential oneness it is the aim of civilization to demonstrate, she was ruthlessly expelled. Her natural beauties, her love of literature, and her wealth of folk-music saved the country from æsthetic starvation. Presbyterian Scotland produced, indeed, a Raeburn, a Rennie, and the Adam brothers; but her Knox, her Carlyle, and her Livingstone were more truly representative of the rule of the Kirk.[2] Every department of the

[1] Democratic principles were understood and applied in Scotland long before England or continental countries, though it was not in Parliament, but in the General Assembly of the Kirk, that the voice of the people made itself felt. It has been said with truth that Burns's *A Man's a Man for a' that* has done more for the growth of democracy than a thousand lectures and pamphlets.—F. M. McN.

[2] " Banks . . . are in their modern form a Scottish invention. Besides those that sprang up in Scotland itself, the national banks of England and France owed their origin to two Scotsmen. A system of life insurance represented the provident habits and business talents of the nation. Adam Smith shares with the French economists the honour of founding political economy as the science of the wealth of nations. Mental philosophy became a favourite study, and a distinctively Scottish school produced thinkers who deeply influenced the later systems of the Continent. The history not of Scotland only, but of England and of some portions of Europe was written by Scotsmen. . . . The dawn of the scientific era of the nineteenth century was foreshadowed by Scotsmen of science, the founders of modern geology, chemistry, anatomy, physiology, and the practice of medicine. In Scotland was made the first of

national life was affected, not excepting the kitchen. This radical change was, as T. R. Henderson expresses it, the result " partly of the severance of intercourse with France, partly of the Puritanism of the Reformers,[1] and partly of the increasing insufficiency of the supplies of meat. . . . In the austerer years of the seventeenth and eighteenth centuries, French influence was chiefly discernible in the ingenuity displayed in making the most of nothing."

But even during the troublous Stuart and Jacobite periods, the connexion with France was to

the great line of discoveries in the practical application of science by the use of steam as a motive power."—H. S. Williams, LL.D.: *The Historian's History of the World*, Vol. XXI (New York and London).

In the domain of art—music (in its higher forms), the drama (practically non-existent before Barrie), and painting, literature alone being excepted—the achievement of Scotland is far less distinguished. The assertion, so freely made, that Presbytery is inimicable to æsthetic development contains probably as much truth, but certainly no more, as the assertion, equally freely made, that the rule of Rome is inimicable to intellectual development. A virile nation, Protestant or Catholic, will burst through any ecclesiastical straight-jacket. (To-day it would appear that whilst Protestant Scotland grows steadily less Puritan, Catholic Ireland grows steadily more so.) That the Scottish churches are no longer indifferent, much less hostile to the fullest development of the arts (not excepting the drama), their official organ, *The Scots Observer*, bears witness, and a comparison of this paper with the popular organs of other Churches will show that modern Presbytery is quite as catholic in outlook as Episcopacy, Roman or Anglican.—F. M. McN.

[1] In many devout Presbyterian households, cookery was looked on askance as pandering to the grosser appetites.

" Whilst on Sunday the Presbyterian gentleman took a sparing refection of bread and an egg or cold beef, between sermons, merely to allay the acute pangs of hunger, reserving his energies and carnal appetite for the supper, the (Episcopalian), after going to his meeting-house, had a substantial meal at midday, having no scruples. Hence it was a common saying that ' if you would live well on Sunday, you must take an Episcopalian dinner and a Presbyterian supper '."
—H. Grey Graham: *Social Life in Scotland in the Eighteenth Century.*

In 1778, the cooks and cook-maids of Edinburgh went on strike because they had long been subjected to " the profane practice of dressing meat on the Lord's Day ".

some extent maintained, notably by the old Highland families who were proscribed after the
Fifteen and the Forty-five.[1] There is, indeed, a
certain affinity between the Gaelic and Gallic
races, which cannot be entirely explained by the
long association of their aristocracies, and which
can be traced even in the kitchen.[2] French
influences appear to have persisted in Edinburgh

[1] Capt. Burt, an English officer of Engineers, who was sent to the Highlands as
a contractor about 1730, writes in his *Letters from the North of Scotland*:

" From the state of the country, the political bias of the Highlanders, and the
éclat which they acquired under Montrose and Dundee, the eyes of all Europe
were turned towards them as the only hope of the house of Stewart. Their chiefs
were courted by, and had frequent personal intercourse with the friends of that
family who were of most note, both in Scotland, England, and Ireland, and on the
continent. Studying to accomplish themselves for the part they had to act, and
always received with the greatest distinction in the best society, they became states-
men, warriors, and fine gentlemen. Their sons, after passing through the usual
routine of the schools and Universities of Scotland, were sent to France to finish
their education. As the policy of the whigs was to crush and destroy, not to con-
ciliate, and they found neither countenance nor employment at home, they entered
into the French or Spanish service, and in these countries were, from political views,
treated with a distinction suitable, not to their pecuniary circumstances, but to
their importance in their own country. Great numbers of the more promising youth
of their clans joined them, and in order that the luxurious indulgences of a more
favoured climate might not render them unfit or unwilling to settle in their own
country, at the end of two or three years they returned for a time to their relations,
with all their accomplishments in knowledge and manners, and, with their relish
for early habits still unimpaired, resumed the quilted plaid and bonnet, and were
replaced in their regiments abroad by another set of young adventurers of the same
description. Thus, among the gentry, the urbanity and knowledge of the most
polished countries of Europe were added to a certain mental and moral civilization,
good in its kind, and peculiar to themselves. At home, they conversed with the
lower classes in the most kindly and cordial manner, on all occasions, and gratified
their laudable and active curiosity in communicating all they knew. This advantage
of conversing freely with their superiors, the peasantry of no other country in
Europe enjoyed, and the consequence was that in 1745 the Scottish Highlanders,
of all descriptions, had more of that polish of mind and sentiment which constitutes
real civilization, than in general the inhabitants of any other country we know of,
not even excepting Iceland."

[2] " Scottish and French cooking have a great deal in common," writes one of
the contributors to this collection, a Colonsay woman who became familiar with
French methods in the service of a great Highland chief, " the way we cook up meat
and vegetables together, and go in so much for braising and stewing. I often think
their charcoal stoves are very like our peat embers that keep the broth boiling a
gently and bake the potatoes on the top."

throughout the eighteenth century. " At the best houses," says an English visitor, " they dress their victuals after the French manner." Burns, too, appears to have become acquainted there with French and other foreign survivals, for in his *Ode to a Haggis* he asks:

> Is there that owre his French *ragout*,
> Or *olio* that wad staw a stew,
> Or *fricassee* wad make her spew
>   Wi' perfect scunner,
> Looks down wi' sneerin', scornfu' view
>   On sic a denner?

The merging of the Scottish and English crowns and the removal of James VI and his court from Edinburgh to London, mark the end of the Auld Alliance, and with it the waning of French and the waxing of English influences, social as well as political, in Scotland.[1] These influences, how-ever, were reciprocal, and, relatively to her size, Scotland gave more than she got. As regards

---

[1] From a purely cultural point of view, Scotland lost more than she gained by the Union of the Crowns. She lost the old close contact with the most highly civilized nation in the world, and established a new close contact with a nation for whom efficiency, not culture; comfort, not elegance; manufacture, not art, were paramount things. She lost her reigning family—and the Stuarts, whatever their shortcomings as rulers, were genuinely aristocratic in temperament (in contradistinction to the Houses of Tudor and Hanover) and devoted to the arts; she lost her nobility, who forsook the Canongate for Mayfair; she lost her Parliament; and finally she lost her intelligentsia. Consequently the brilliant capital of the early Stuarts has sunk steadily into semi-provincialism. To-day she is a proud but saddened beauty, living on her memories, yet not entirely without hope of better things—a hope quickened by the life and colour that permeate her grey streets when the Court sits at Holyrood.
—F. M. McN.

cookery, Scottish dishes were very soon popularized in Court circles. King Jamie always enjoyed his native fare.

" Nobody among these brave English cooks," says Laurie Linklater in *The Fortunes of Nigel*, " can kittle up his Majesty's most sacred palate with our own gusty Scottish dishes. So I e'en betook myself to my craft, and concocted a mess of Friar's Chicken for the soup, and a savoury hachis, that made the whole cabal coup the crans."

In the same volume George Heriot, goldsmith to James VI and I, who followed his royal patron to London, and later bequeathed his fortune to charities still flourishing in Edinburgh, thus invites his young compatriot, Lord Glenvarloch, to dine with him:

" ' For the cheer, my Lord, a mess of white broth, a fat capon, well larded, a dish of beef collops for auld Scotland's sake, and it may be a cup of right old wine. . . .' Besides the Scottish fare promised, the board displayed beef and pudding, the statutory dainties of old England."

Even Oliver Cromwell regaled himself occasionally on a dish of Scots veal collops.[1]

There was, however, no general amalgamation of

---

[1] See " The Court and Kitchen of Elizabeth, commonly called Joan Cromwell, the wife of the late Usurper, truly described and represented."—London, 1664.

Scottish and English cookery, and even in London
Scottish influences were limited to narrow, if high
circles. It was not, indeed, until the nineteenth
century, when the magic wand of Sir Walter Scott
had dispelled the hostility and mutual suspicion
bred by centuries of feud, that the middle classes
of the two countries borrowed freely from each
other in this domain. To-day our Scots porridge
and barley broth and scones and orange marmalade are as popular south of the Tweed as are
ham and eggs, Bath buns, and Yorkshire pudding
in the north. But native dishes have a habit of
deteriorating on alien soil, and, despite their
similarity to a casual observer, the cuisines of
the two countries remain, in many respects,
curiously distinctive.

IV

THE PLENISHING OF THE KITCHEN

" The ingle-neuk,* wi' routh † o' bannocks and bairns!"
—*Old Scottish toast or sentiment.*

In most countries, even to-day, one finds the
rudest forms of art co-existing with the highest,
the earliest stage of civilization with the most
advanced. It is not, therefore, surprising that
while the banqueting halls of Linlithgow and
Holyrood vied in elegance with any in Europe,

* Fireside.   † Plenty.

elsewhere in the kingdom the most primitive methods of cookery prevailed.

" I have been assured," writes Burt, in the early eighteenth century, " that in some of the Islands the meaner sort of People still retain the Custom of boiling their Beef in the Hide, or otherwise, being destitute of Vessels of Metal or Earth, they put Water into a Block of Wood, made hollow by the help of the Dirk and burning, and then with pretty large Stones heated red-hot, and successively quenched in that Vessel, they keep the Water boiling till they have dressed their Food."

This was a survival of conditions once universal in the Highlands.

In *The Fair Maid of Perth* Scott describes an *al fresco* kitchen on the shores of Loch Tay. The period is the fourteenth century, the occasion the funeral feast of a Highland Chief.

" The Highlanders, well known for ready hatchet men, had constructed a long arbour or sylvan banqueting-room [in which] the most important personages present were invited to hold high festival. Others of less note were to feast in various long sheds, constructed with less care; and tables of sod, or rough planks, placed in the open air, were allotted to the numberless multitude. At a distance were to be seen piles of glowing char-coal or blazing wood, around which countless

cooks toiled, bustled, and fretted, like so many
demons working in their native element. Pits,
wrought in the hillside and lined with heated
stones, served for stewing immense quantities of
beef, mutton, and venison;[1] wooden spits supported sheep and goats, which were roasted entire;
others were cut into joints and seethed in cauldrons
made of the animals' own skins, sewed hastily
together and filled with water; while huge quantities of pike, trout, salmon, and char were broiled
with more ceremony on glowing embers."

A similar scene from real life is described by
Taylor, the Thames water-poet, who, in 1618,
accompanied the Earl of Mar and a distinguished
company on a shooting expedition into the Highlands, where they put up in temporary lodges
called *lonchards*. " The kitchin was alwayse on the
side of a banke, many kettles and pots boyling, and
many spits turning and winding, with great variety
of cheere, as venison, bak't, sodden, rost and
steu'de beefe, mutton, goates, kids, hares, fresh
salmon, pidgeons, hens, capons, chickens, par-

---

[1] "The Scottish Highlanders in former times had a concise mode of cooking their
venison, or rather of dispensing with cooking it, which appears greatly to have surprised the French whom chance made acquainted with it. The Vidame of Charters,
when a hostage in England, during the reign of Edward VI, was permitted to travel
into Scotland, and penetrated as far as the remote Highlands (*au fin fond des
Sauvages*). After a great hunting party, at which a most wonderful quantity of game
was destroyed, he saw these *Scottish Savages* devour a part of their venison raw,
without any further preparation than compressing it between two batons of wood,
so as to force out the blood, and render it extremely hard. This they reckoned a
great delicacy; and when the Vidame partook of it, his compliance with their taste
rendered him extremely popular."—Scott: *The Lady of the Lake*, Note.

tridges, moor-cootes, heath-cocks, capperkellies,[1] and termagents;[2] good ale, sacke, white, and cleret, tent (or allegant)[3] with most potent *aquavitae*. Thus a company of about fourteen hundred was most amply fed."[4]

The Scottish baronial kitchen, with its great fireplace designed to roast an ox whole, differed little from the corresponding types in other countries. The nation, after all, dwells in the cottage, and it is in the cottage that one finds all that is most truly characteristic of the nation.

The plenishing of a sixteenth-century kitchen of the humbler sort is minutely described in *The Wowing of Jok and Jynny*, one of the oldest surviving Scottish songs.[5] Jynny's mother recites her daughter's " tocher-gud ":[6]

[1] Capercailzie or mountain cock (Gael. *capull coille*).

[2] Ptarmigan (Gael. *tarmachan*).   [3] Alicant.

[4] In the following century, Prince Charlie, according to the Jacobite song, was regaled with much the same fare:

> Come o'er the stream, Charlie, dear Charlie, brave Charlie,
>   Come o'er the stream, Charlie, and dine wi' Maclean;
> And though you be weary, we 'll make your heart cheery,
>   And welcome our Charlie and his loyal train.
>   We 'll bring down the track deer,
>   We 'll bring down the black steer,
>   The lamb from the bracken and doe from the glen;
>   The salt sea we 'll harry,
>   And bring to our Charlie
>   The cream from the bothy and curd from the pen.
>   —James Hogg: *Come O'er the Stream, Charlie.*
>   Air: *The Maclean's Welcome.*

[5] In the Bannatyne MS. (8568), this poem was assigned to Clark, whom Dunbar commemorates for his " balat-making and trigide ", but the name was deleted by the transcriber.

[6] Gael. *tochar*, a dowry.

" My berne," scho sayis, " hes of hir awin,
    Ane guss, ane gryce,[1] ane cok, ane hen,
Ane calf, ane hog,[2] ane fute-braid sawin; [3]
    Ane kirn,[4] ane pin,[5] that ye weill ken,
    Ane pig,[6] ane pot, ane raip [7] thair ben,[8]
Ane fork, ane flaik,[9] ane reill,[10] ane rok;[11]
    Dischis and dublaris [12] nyne or ten:
Come ye to wow our Jynny, Jok?

" Ane blanket, and ane wecht [13] also,
    Ane schule,[14] ane scheit, and ane lang flail,
Ane ark,[15] ane almry,[16] and laidills two,
    Ane milk-syth [17] with ane swine taill,[18]
    Ane rowsty whittil [19] to scheir [20] the kaill,[21]
Ane wheill, ane mell [22] the beir [23] to knok,
    Ane coig,[24] ane caird wantand ane naill: [25]
Come ye to wow our Jynny, Jok?

" Ane furme,[26] ane furlet,[27] ane pott, ane pek,[28]
    Ane tub, ane barrow, with ane wheil-band,
Ane turs,[29] ane troch,[30] and ane meil-sek,
    Ane spurtill [31] braid [32] and ane elwand [33]."

Jok contributes, in addition to a lengthy list
of outdoor implements, " ane trene truncheour,[34]

---

[1] A young pig. [2] Two-year-old sheep. [3] Corn to sow a foot-breadth. [4] Churn.
[5] Skewer. [6] Earthen vessel. [7] Rope. [8] In there. [9] Hurdle. [10] Reel.
[11] Distaff. [12] Large dishes, as tureens. [13] Instrument for winnowing corn.
[14] Shovel. [15] Meal chest. [16] Cupboard. [17] Milk-strainer. [18] Corruption of
seying-tale, sifting-measure (for milk). [19] Rusty gullie. [20] Cut. [21] Colewort.
[22] Mallet. [23] Barley. [24] Large wooden vessel. [25] A carding-comb with a nail
missing. [26] Bench. [27] Fourth of a boll. [28] Sixteenth of a boll. [29] Truss.
[30] Trough. [31] Porridge-stick. [32] Broad. [33] Instrument for measuring an ell.
[34] Wooden platter.

ane ramehorn spoon,[1] . . . ane maskene-fatt ",[2] together with

> Ane pepper-polk [3] made of a padill,[4]
> Ane sponge, ane spindall wantand ane nok,[5]
> Twa lusty lippis to lik ane laiddill,
> To gang togidder, Jynny and Jok.[6]

Here is a description (drawn from an existing inventory) of another sixteenth-century kitchen, that of the Manse of Stobo, which stood at the head of the Drygate of Glasgow.

" There are but two pieces of furniture, one a ' weschell almerie ', which was probably a plainly made kitchen dish-press, and the other a 'dressing-burd ', in other words a table on which meat and other articles of food were dressed. No form or stool or other kind of seat is provided, nor is there any other concession to comfort. There are cauldrons, kettles, ' mekle '[7] pots and ' litel ' pots, frying-pans, goose-pans, roasting-irons, fish ' skimmers ', ' mekle ' speits and ' litel ' speits, stoups,[8] pitchers, and ' piggis ',[9] besides the special

---

[1] In olden times, each man had his horn spoon, which he carried at his side, or fastened to his bonnet, to sup the kail, porridge, or sowens. The old horn spoons had a whistle at the end of the handle. " Better the suppin' end nor the whistle end," says the proverb.

Before the introduction of glass, drinking vessels were commonly made of horn, the better articles being silver-rimmed. Hornware is an old Scottish craft, still extant.—F. M. McN.

[2] Brewing vessel.   [3] Bag.   [4] Pedlar's wallet.   [5] Notch.   [6] For Jenny and Jock to marry on.   [7] Big.

[8] Deep and narrow vessels for holding liquids.

[9] Earthen vessels (Gael. pigadh, pigin).—See Jamieson. "Pigs in the chimnies" are chimney-pots.

paraphernalia of the bakehouse and brew-house.[1]
A capon cave shows that poultry were kept, and
the supply of provisions is on a scale that suggests
that the household was given to what a contemporary calls ' large tabling and belly cheer '.
There are, for example, eight marts, or salted
carcases of beef; a pipe of salmon, containing
eight dozen; a pipe of Loch Fyne herring; an
ark containing eighty bolls of meal; six stone of
butter and a ' kebboc ' or cheese weighing twenty-
two pounds, . . . and his barn is well stored with
wheat, oats, ' beir ', peas, and hay."

In *Marmion*, Scott describes the kitchen of an
inn in the Lammermoors in the early sixteenth
century.[2]

> Soon, by the chimney's merry blaze,
> Through the rude hostel might you gaze;
> Might see, where, in dark nook aloof,
> The rafters of the sooty roof
>   Bore wealth of winter cheer;
> Of sea-fowl dried, and solands store,
> And gammons of the tusky boar
>   And savoury haunch of deer.

[1] " Dishes were commonly pewter, and drinking-cups were of tree with pewter or
silver bases or pedestals. The Protector, Somerset, on landing at Leith, was
astonished at the elegance of the table appurtenances, which included some of the
best continental craftsmanship."—C. Rogers: *Social and Domestic Scotland.*

[2] " The accommodations of a Scottish hostelrie, or inn, in the sixteenth century,
may be collected from Dunbar's admirable tale of *The Friars of Berwick*. Simon
Lawder, ' the gay hostler ', seems to have lived very comfortably; and his wife
decorated her person with a scarlet kirtle, and a belt of silk and silver, and rings
upon her fingers; and feasted her paramour with rabbits, capons, partridges, and
Bordeaux wine."—Note to *Marmion.*

The chimney arch projected wide;
Above, around it, and beside,
   Were tools for housewives' hand;
Nor wanted, in that martial day,
The implements of Scottish fray,
   The buckler, lance, and brand.
Beneath its shade, the place of state,
On oaken settle, Marmion sate,
And viewed around the blazing hearth
His followers mix in noisy mirth;
Whom, with brown ale, in jolly tide,
From ancient vessels ranged aside,
Full actively their host supplied.

The typical Scottish home of later times is the but-and-ben, or two-roomed cottage. The furniture of the but, or kitchen-end, consisted of an aumry [1] (cupboard) generally placed opposite the window, where milk and provisions were kept, and above it the skelf [2] (a wooden frame containing shelves) on which the crockery and utensils were arranged; a kist (chest) containing the family wardrobe; a box-bed, built into the interior wall, with shelves at the head and at the foot, on which part of the apparel was deposited; a muckle chair (a wooden chair with arms) for the man, and stools or creepies for the woman and children. There were also a plunge-churn, a spinning-wheel, a barrel of oatmeal and another of salt fish, and (before the introduction of the modern lamp) a

[1] Fr. *armoire*.　　[2] Gael. *sgealp*.

crusie, with a supply of oil and dried pith of rushes. In addition there was the cottage library, consisting of not less than three volumes—the Bible, the *Pilgrim's Progress*, and (ever since his day) Burns.

All the cooking was done on the wide, open hearth. Over the fire, by means of a jointed iron arch with three legs, called the clips, was suspended whatever utensil was in use, the end of the clips being hooked to hold it fast. The clips was again hooked upon the end of a chain, called the crook, which was attached to an iron rod or beam commonly called the roof- or rantle-tree,[1] and this, in turn, was fixed across the chimney-stalk, at some distance from the fire.

The ordinary cottage bread, consisting mainly of barley and mashlum [2] bannocks and oat-cakes, was baked on the girdle, a round thin plate of malleable or cast iron, with a semicircular handle.[3] An equally indispensable utensil was the kail-pot, a round iron pot with three legs (evolved from the primeval tripod), and a close-fitting convex

---

[1] In Orkney, amer- or emmer-tree.   [2] Mixed grain.

[3] In Roman times, hearth-cakes of oats were the bread of the savage natives, who baked them on stones round the fire. These stones the native Gaels named *greadeal*. They formed a ring round the fire, and hence the peculiar significance of the word girdle in the Scots vocabulary. "

—T. F. Henderson: *Old-World Scotland.*

In the fourteenth century, Froissart tells us, the equipment of the Scottish soldier included a *flat plate of metal* and a wallet of oatmeal, for the purpose of making oat-cakes. In the cottages, the plate was probably placed on a tripod over the peat embers.

The modern girdle was invented and first made in the little burgh of Culross, in Fife. In 1599, James VI granted to the Culrossians the exclusive privilege of its manufacture, and this was confirmed by Charles II in 1666.

lid, in which broth or porridge was cooked. It served too as a rude oven, being on such occasions buried in burning peat.

Oatcakes were " finished " on a toasting-stone[1] on their removal from the girdle. The quern sometimes served this purpose.

In simple homes the kitchen was always the living-room, the focus and core of family life, and its praises have been sung by many of our vernacular poets. Here are glimpses of some typical kitchens:

THE MILLER'S KITCHEN

Merry may the maid be
  That marries the miller:
For foul day and fair day
  He 's aye bringin' till her;
He 's aye a penny in his purse
  For dinner and for supper;
And gin she please, a good fat cheese
  And lumps o' yellow butter.

Behind the door a bag o' meal,
  And in the kist was plenty
Of good hard cakes his mither bakes,
  And bannocks were na scanty.
A good fat sow, a sleeky cow
  Was standin' in the byre;
Whilst lazy puss with mealy mouse
  Was playing at the fire.

---

[1] One of the primitive toasting stones is preserved, with other old Scottish domestic utensils, in the National Museum of Antiquities, Edinburgh.

In winter, when the wind and rain
  Blows o'er the house and byre,
He sits beside a clean hearth-stane
  Before a rousing fire;
With nut-brown ale he tells his tale,
  Which rows him o'er fu' nappy.
Who 'd be a king—a petty thing,
  When a miller lives sae happy.

        SIR JOHN CLERK OF PENNICUIK (1684–1755).

THE FISHERMAN'S KITCHEN

And are ye sure the news is true?
  And are ye sure he 's weel?
Is this the time to think o' wark?
  Ye jauds, fling bye your wheel!
Is this a time to think o' wark,
  When Colin 's at the door?
Rax [1] me my coat, I 'll to the quay,
  And see him come ashore.

Rise up and mak' a clean fireside,
  Put on the muckle [2] pot;
Gie little Kate her cotton gown,
  And Jock his Sunday coat;
And mak' their shoon as black as slaes,
  Their hose as white as snaw;
It 's a' to please my ain gudeman:
  He likes to see them braw. [3]

There 's twa fat hens upon the bauk, [4]
  Been fed this month and mair;

[1] Reach.   [2] Big   [3] Well dressed.   [4] Roosting beam.

Mak' haste and thraw [1] their necks about,
 That Colin weel may fare.
And spread the table neat and clean,
 Gar [2] ilka [3] thing look braw,[4]
For wha can tell how Colin fared
 When he was far awa'?

     —*There's Nae Luck About the House.*[5]

THE FARMER'S KITCHEN

The gudeman, new come hame, is blyth to find,
 When he out o'er the halland [6] flings his een,
That ilka [7] turn is handled to his mind,
 That a' his housie looks sae cosh [8] and clean:
For cleanly house looes he, tho' e'er sae mean.

Weel kens the gudewife that the pleughs [9] require
 A heartsome meltith [10] and refreshing synd [11]
O nappy [12] liquor o'er a bleezin' fire:
 Sair wark and poortith [13] dinna weel be join'd.
Wi' buttered bannocks now the girdle reeks;
 I' the far nook the bowie [14] briskly reams; [15]
The ready kail [16] stand by the chimley cheeks,[17]
 And had the riggin' [18] het wi' welcome steams
Whilk [19] than the daintiest kitchen [20] nicer seems.

   ROBERT FERGUSSON (1750–74): *The Farmer's Ingle.*

[1] Twist.   [2] Make.   [3] Every.   [4] Fine.

[5] This song has been claimed for Jean Adams (1710–65) and for William Julius Mickle (1734–88). According to Burns, with whom it was a favourite, it came first on to the streets as a ballad about 1771 or 1772. It is included in Herd's collection (1776).

[6] An inner wall built between the fire-place and the door, to screen the interior from draughts.   [7] Every.   [8] Snug.   [9] Ploughs.   [10] Meal.   [11] Drink.   [12] Strong. [13] Poverty.   [14] A small barrel.   [15] Froths.   [16] Broth.   [17] The stone pillars at the side of the fire.   [18] Ridge.   [19] Which.   [20] Relish.

THE COTTER'S KITCHEN

At length his lonely cot appears in view,
  Beneath the shelter of an aged tree;
Th' expectant wee things, toddlin', stacher [1] through
  To meet their dad, wi' flichterin' [2] noise and glee.
  His wee bit ingle,[3] blinkin' bonnily,
His clean hearthstane, his thriftie wifie's smile,
  The lispin' infant prattling on his knee
Does a' his weary kiaugh [4] and care beguile,
And makes him quite forget his labour and his toil.

       ROBERT BURNS (1759–96): *The Cotter's Saturday Night.*

THE SHEPHERD'S KITCHEN

Then round our wee cot though gruff winter should roar,
And poortith [5] glower [6] in like a wolf at the door;
Though our toom [7] purse had barely twa boddles [8] to
    clink,
  And a barley meal scone were the best on our bink,[9]
Yet he wi' his hirsel,[10] and I wi' my wheel,
  Through the howe o' the year [11] we would fen' [12] unco
    weel.[13]

       THOMAS PRINGLE (1789–1834): *The Ewe-buchtin's* [14] *Bonnie.*

Dorothy Wordsworth, in her *Recollections of a Tour Made in Scotland* (1803), describes the kitchen of a primitive Highland cottage, with the fire in the middle of the floor and a hole in the roof in place of a chimney:

[1] Stagger.   [2] Fluttering.   [3] Fire (Gael. *aingeal*).   [4] Anxiety.
[5] Poverty.   [6] Stare.   [7] Empty.   [8] A small copper coin.   [9] Shelves fixed to the wall for holding plates, &c.   [10] A flock of sheep.   [11] The depth of winter [12] Fend.   [13] Very well.   [14] Folding of the ewes.

" The good woman had provided, according to her promise, a better fire than we had found in the morning; and indeed when I sate down in the chimney corner of her smoky biggin' I thought I had never been more comfortable in my life. Coleridge had been there long enough to have a pan of coffee boiling for us. . . . We caressed our cups of coffee, laughing like children at the strange atmosphere in which we were: the smoke came in gusts, and spread along the walls and above our heads in the chimney, where the hens were roosting like light clouds in the sky. We laughed and laughed again, in spite of the smarting of our eyes, yet had a quieter pleasure in observing the beauty of the beams and rafters gleaming between the clouds of smoke. They had been crusted over and varnished by many winters, till, where the firelight fell upon them, they were as glossy as black rocks on a sunny day cased in ice. When we had eaten our supper we sate about half an hour, and I think I had never felt so deeply the blessing of a hospitable welcome and a warm fire."

Modern ranges and modern factory-made furniture and utensils are being gradually introduced into the cottage homes of Scotland to-day, but the old simple ways linger in the Highlands. A hundred years after Dorothy Wordsworth's visit, Mrs. Kennedy-Fraser was entertained in a kitchen of precisely the same type on the tiny island of Eriskay, in the Outer Hebrides.

Her hostess " sat me down on a low three-legged stool by the peat-fire, which was burning brightly on the floor, and seated herself on another. I had learned by the experience of semi-suffocation to prefer those low stools to the high deal chair which was always politely brought from behind the partition for the stranger's use. On the low stool one was free from the smoke, which, when it reached a certain height, wandered at its own sweet will and escaped as best it might by the chinks in the ' drystane ' walls or the crevices in the roof. The interior of the old hut was really beautiful in the morning light, which slanted down from the small, deep-set windows on the dear old woman by the fire." And in a neighbouring cottage "a little clean sanded kitchen, with its tiny home-made dresser, adorned with fine old painted bowls and jugs, its two wooden benches along the walls with accommodation below for peats, its barrel of flour topped with the baking-board (serving as a kitchen table), and its bag of oatmeal by the fire, was the recognized rendezvous of the island ".

Though the Gael [1] does not sing the praises of

---

[1] To speak of the Highlander as a Gael in contradistinction to the Lowlander is a mere *façon de parler*, for it is now generally accepted that *racially* the basis of the whole Scottish race is Celtic. *Culturally*, however, there is a real distinction, as even these few extracts indicate. Morley has spoken of Gladstone as a Highlander in the

his kitchen in the simple homely way of the vernacular poets, he has a store of songs which are identified with the various domestic tasks. In the *Songs of the Hebrides*, Mrs. Kennedy-Fraser and Kenneth Macleod have preserved for us some of the ancient churning, quern-grinding, and waulking songs, each composed in a measure suited to the rhythmic motion of the body at work, and in his collection, *Carmina Gadelica*, Alexander Carmichael gives us some old runes and incantations associated with the ritual of domestic life, for to the Highlander the secular and the spiritual were inextricably blended. Very characteristic is the *Beannachadh Beothachaidh*, the Blessing of the Kindling:[1]

I will kindle my fire this morning
In presence of the holy angels of Heaven,
In presence of Ariel of the loveliest form,
In presence of Uriel of the myriad charms,
Without malice, without jealousy, without envy,
Without fear, without terror of anyone under the sun,
But the Holy Son of God to shield me.

custody of a Lowlander; may not the modern Scot be described as a Celt in the custody of a Saxon? There are, however, indications (notably in the Scottish Renascence Movement) of a healthy reaction, and the increasing influence of *An Comunn Gaidhealach* (the Highland Association) testifies that the Scot no longer views with indifference the threatened extinction of Gaelic, but is awakening to the fact that were the ancient tongue to perish, with it would perish a great spiritual heritage.
—F.M.McN.

[1] " The people look upon fire as a miracle of divine power provided for their good —to warm their bodies when they are cold, to cook their food when they are hungry, and to remind them that they, too, like the fire, need constant renewal mentally and physically."—A. C.

The Plenishing of the Kitchen

Without malice, without jealousy, without envy,
Without fear, without terror of anyone under the sun,
But the Holy Son of God to shield me.

God, kindle thou in my heart within
A flame of love to my neighbour,
To my foe, to my friend, to my kindred all,
To the brave, to the knave, to the thrall,
O Son of the loveliest Mary,
From the lowliest thing that liveth,
To the Name that is highest of all.
O Son of the loveliest Mary,
From the lowliest thing that liveth,
To the Name that is highest of all.[1]

In districts where wood is unattainable, the fire
is *smoored* (smothered or subdued) with ashes
that it may smoulder all night. The process was

[1] BEANNACHADH BEOTHACHAIDH

Togaidh mi mo theine an diugh,
An lathair ainghlean naomha neimh,
An lathair Airil is ailde cruth,
An lathair Uiril nan uile sgeimh,
Gun ghnu, gun tnu, gun fharmad,
Gun ghiomh, gun gheimh roimh neach fo'n ghrein,
Ach Naomh Mhac De da m'thearmad.
    Gun ghnu, gun tnu, gun fharmad,
    Gun ghiomh, gun gheimh roimh neach fo'n ghrein,
    Ach Naomh Mhac De da m'thearmad.

Dhe fadaidh fein na m'chridhe steach
Aingheal ghraidh do m'choimhearsnach,
Do m'namh, do m'dhamh, do m'chairde,
Do'n t-saoidh, do'n daoidh, do'n traille,
A mhic na Moire min-ghile,
Bho'n ni is isde crannachaire,
Gu ruig an t'Ainm is airde.
    A mhic na Moire min-ghile,
    Bho'n ni is isde crannachaire,
    Gu ruig an t'Ainm is airde.

beautiful and symbolic, the woman chanting the while:

Smaladh an Teine.	Smooring the Fire.
An Tri numh	The sacred Three
A chumhnadh,	To save,
A chomhnadh,	To shield,
A chomraig,	To surround
A tula,	The hearth,
An taighe,	The house,
An taghlaich,	The household,
An oidhche,	This eve,
An nochd,	This night,
O an oidhche,	O this eve,
An nochd,	This night,
Agus gach oidhche,	And every night,
Gach aon oidhche.	Each single night.
Amen.	Amen.

V

THE TABLE: SOME TYPICAL MEALS

" Cha'n fhiach cuirm gun a còmhradh" (A feast is worth nothing
without its conversation).—Gaelic Proverb.

In the early Scots kitchen the fare consisted of game or fish boiled or seethed in primitive fashion over the peat embers; barley bannocks and oat-cakes baked on the ancient *greadeal*; cheese and butter; wild fruit, wild herbs, and the honey of the wild bee. In the Highlands, in particular, the ancient parsimony was long preserved. " The great heroes of antiquity," says Sir John Sinclair, " lived chiefly on broth. The water in which a piece of mutton or venison was boiled, thickened with oatmeal and flavoured with wild herbs, formed the morning and evening meal in the hall of a Highland chief."[1]

Martin, who visited Skye about two hundred years ago, writes: " Their ordinary diet is butter, cheese, milk, potatoes, coleworts, *brochan*, i.e. oatmeal boiled with water. The latter, taken with some bread, is the constant food of several thousands of both sexes in this and other islands during winter and spring, yet they undergo many fatigues both by sea and land, and are very healthful. This verifies what the poet saith: *Populis sat est Lymphaque Ceresque*, Nature is satisfied with bread and water."

The same frugality prevailed in the Lowlands. An English visitor in 1704 remarks that at Lesmahagow, a village in Lanarkshire, he found the people living on cakes made of pease and barley mixed. " They ate no meat, nor drank anything but water, and the common people go without shoes or stockings all the year round. I pitied their poverty, but observed the people were fresh

[1] " Among the peculiarities of Highland manners is an avowed contempt for the luxuries of the table. A Highland hunter will eat with a keen appetite and sufficient discrimination, but were he to stop in any pursuit because it was meal-time, to growl over a bad dinner or visibly exult over a good one, the manly dignity of his character would be considered as fallen for ever."—Mrs. Grant of Laggan (1807).

and lusty, and did not seem to be under any
uneasiness with their way of living."

Over and over again, in our proverbs and poetry,
the virtue of frugality [1] is lauded:

> Mickle [2] meat, mony maladies.
> Surfeits slay mair than swords.
> He that eats but ae [3] dish seldom needs the doctor.
> Licht suppers mak lang life.

Allan Ramsay writes:

> For me, I can be weel content,
> To eat my bannock on the bent, [4]
>   And kitchen 't [5] wi' fresh air;
> O' lang kail I can mak' a feast,
> And cantily [6] haud up my crest
>   And laugh at dishes rare.

In *The Cotter's Saturday Night*, Burns describes
the simple fare on which he was nurtured:

> But now the supper crowns their simple board,
>   The halesome [7] parritch, [8] chief of Scotia's food;
> The soupe their only hawkie [9] does afford,
>   That yont the hallan [10] snugly chows her cood:
> The dame brings forth, in complimental mood,

---

[1] Scottish frugality is, of course, proverbial. But so, too, is Scottish hospitality.
Thus even the table illustrates what Gregory Smith calls " the Caledonian
antisyxygy ", " the contrasts which the Scot shows at every turn, in his political
and ecclesiastical history, in his polemical restlessness, in his adaptability, . . . in
his practical judgment ". The Aberdonian, in whom both virtues are highly de-
veloped, and who has the rare gift of being able to laugh at himself, delights the
world with a constant stream of jests based on the former attribute, but, characteristi-
cally, leaves the stranger to discover the latter for himself.—F. M. McN.

[2] Much.   [3] One.   [4] In the open.   [5] Give it relish.   [6] Cheerily.
[7] Wholesome.   [8] Porridge.   [9] Cow.   [10] Inner wall (corr. of Gael. *an talan*, *
wooden partition).

To grace the lad, her weel-hained [1] kebbuck;[2] fell
   And aft he 's pressed, and aft he ca's it gude.
The frugal wifie, garrulous, will tell
   How 'twas a twalmont[3] auld, sin' lint was i' the bell.

And elsewhere he writes:

> What though on hamely fare we dine,
>   Wear hodden grey [4] an' a' that?
> Gie fools their silks, an' knaves their wine—
>   A man 's a man for a' that!

Because of that, Fergusson would say.

On siccan [5] food [6] has mony a doughty deed
   By Caledonia's ancestors been done;
By this did mony a wight fu' weirlike [7] bleed
   In brulzies [8] frae the dawn to set o' sun;
'T was this that braced their gardies [9] stiff and strang,
   That bent the deadly yew in ancient days,
Laid Denmark's daring sons in yird [10] alang,
   Gar'd [11] Scottish thistles bang the Roman bays:
For near our crests their heads they doughtna [12] raise! [13]

In the old song, *The Blythesome Bridal*,[14] we have
a complete exposition of the kitchen of the humbler
classes in Scotland in the seventeenth century.

---

[1] Well-preserved.   [2] Cheese (Gael. *cabag*).   [3] Twelvemonth.   [4] Grey home-
spun.   [5] Such.   [6] I.e. Bannocks and kail.   [7] War-like.   [8] Broils
[9] Arms (Gael. *gairdain*).   [10] Earth.   [11] Caused.   [12] Dared not.   [13] Fergusson:
The Farmer's Ingle.

[14] Attributed to Sir Robert Semphill of Beltrees, Renfrewshire (*c.* 1595–*c.* 1660), or
his son Francis.

And there 'll be lang kail [1] and pottage
And bannocks [2] o' barley meal,
And there 'll be guid saut herrin'
To relish a cogue [3] o' guid yill.[4]

. . . .

Wi' siybows [5] and rifarts [6] and carlines [7]
That are baith sodden [8] and raw.

There 'll be tartan,[9] dragen,[9] and brochan,[9]
And fouth [10] o' guid gabbocks [11] o' skate,
Powsowdie,[12] and drammock,[13] and crowdie,[14]
And caller nowt-feet [15] on a plate.
And there 'll be partans [16] and buckies,[17]
And speldins [18] and haddocks enew,[19]
And singit sheep heads and a haggis,
And scadlips [20] to sup till ye 're fou.[21]

There 'll be lapper-milk kebbucks,[22]
And sowens,[23] and farls,[24] and baps,[25]
Wi' swats [26] and weel-scrappit paunches,[27]
And brandy in stoups [28] and in caups; [28]
And there 'll be meal-kail [29] and custocks,[30]
Wi' skink [31] to sup till ye rive,[32]
And roasts to roast on a brander
O' flouks [33] that were taken alive.

Scrapt haddocks, wilks, dulse,[34] and tangle,[34]
And a mill [35] o' guid sneeshin' [36] to prie; [37]
When weary wi' eatin' and drinkin'
We 'll rise up and dance till we dee.

---

[1] Colewort. [2] Round flat cakes. [3] A drinking-vessel. [4] Ale. [5] Young
onions. [6] Radishes. [7] Peas. [8] Boiled. [9] Preparations of meal. [10] Abundance. [11] Mouthfuls. [12] Sheep's-head broth. [13] [14] Preparations of meal.
[15] Fresh ox-feet. [16] Crabs. [17] Winkles. [18] Small fish split and dried. [19] Enough.
[20] Thin broth with barley. [21] Full. [22] Sour-milk cheeses. [23] Flummery.
[24] Oat-cakes. [25] Rolls. [26] New ale. [27] Tripe. [28] Drinking-vessels. [29] Kale
brose [30] Cabbage stalks. [31] A soup. [32] Burst. [33] Flounders. [34] Edible
seaweeds. [35] Box. [36] Snuff. [37] Taste.

Note the abundance of fish and the variety of preparations of oatmeal.

Tartan or tart-an-purry (purée) is a kind of pudding made of chopped kail and oatmeal; brochan is a gruel or porridge, occasionally flavoured with onions and grated cheese; drammock is made of raw meal and water. Crowdie is a thicker variety of the same, sometimes with the addition of butter; or it may be made with butter-milk or with whipped cream. There is no beef except "nowt-feet", and no mutton except "singit sheep heads", tripe, and the pluck contained in the haggis.

In *The Bride of Lammermoor*, Scott gives us an aristocratic menu of a somewhat later period.[1] The worthy Caleb seeks to hide by a ruse the impoverished state of the young Master of Ravenswood's larder, and thus describes the imaginary feast he is about to prepare:

" First course, capons in white broth—roast kid — bacon with reverence[2]; second course, roasted leveret—buttered crabs—a veal florentine;[3] third course, blackcock, plumdamas,[4] a tart, a flam,[5] and some nonsense sweet things—an' that's a'—forbye the apples and pears." Later, describing the imaginary accident that has ruined

---

[1] " The fashionable grace-before-meat at the tables of the Scottish nobility, in the reign of Queen Mary," Chambers tells us, " was *Soli Dei Honor et Gloria*." This legend was carved over many doorways in old Edinburgh.

[2] With its garnishings. [3] A kind of pie. [4] Prunes. [5] A kind of custard. Fr. *flan*

the feast: " The good vivers lying a' aboot—
beef, capons, and white broth—florentine and
flams—bacon wi' reverence—an' a' the sweet
confections wi' whim-whams [1]."

In the same book we read of the preparations
made in a Lowland hamlet for the arrival of the
Master and the Marquis of A.:

" Never had there been such slaughtering of
capons, and fat geese, and barn-yard fowls, never
such boiling of reested [2] hams; never such making of car-cakes [3] and sweet scones, Selkirk
bannocks, cookies, and petticoat-tails—delicacies
but little known to the present generation."

In 1784, the French traveller, Faujas de St.
Fond,[4] tells us, " at the Duke of Argyll's table,
the different courses and the after-meats were
all done as in France, and with the same variety
and abundance. We had delicate water-fowl, excellent fish, and vegetables which did honour to
the Scotch gardeners.

" At the dessert, the cloth and napkins dis-
appeared, and the mahogany table was covered
with brilliant decanters filled with the most
exquisite wines, vases of porcelain and crystal glass
containing comfits, and beautiful baskets replete
with choice fruits, which could scarcely have been

---

[1] A variety of sweet.   [2] Smoked.
[3] Small cakes made with eggs and eaten on Fastern's E'en (Shrove Tuesday):
probably a kind of pancake. Car, from *keren*, to turn or toss.—Jamieson.
[4] Professor of Geology at the Museum of Natural History in Paris.

expected in this cold climate, even with every assistance from art....

" In the drawing-room, tea and coffee were served; but the latter is always weak, bitter, and destitute of its fine aroma."

In eighteenth-century Edinburgh there were many haunts, such as Johnie Dowie's,

> where ye can get
> A crum o' tripe, ham, dish o' pease,
> An egg, or, cauler [1] frae the seas,
> A fluke [2] or whiting.
>
> A nice beef-steak; or ye may get
> A guid buffed [3] herring, reisted [4] skate,
> An' ingins,[5] or (though past its date)
> A cut o' veal.[6]

" The principal taverns of our Old City," we read in the *Annals of the Cleikum Club*, " used to be called Oyster-Taverns, in honour of their favourite viand. . . . ' How many celebrated wits and bon-vivants, now quite chop-fallen,' said Winterblossom, ' have dived into the dark defiles of closes and wynds in pursuit of this delicacy, and of the wine, the wit, the song that gave it zest. I have heard my learned and facetious friend, the late Professor Creech—for it was rather before my day—say that before public amusements were much known in our Presbyterian capital an

---

[1] Fresh. [2] Flounder. [3] Pickled. [4] Smoked. [5] Onions. [6] Chambers *Minor Antiquities.*

(D 994)

Oyster-ploy, which always included music and a little dance, was the delight of the young fashionables of both sexes.' "[1]

And again:

" 'No spot on earth once,' said Mr. Touchwood, ' like the Old Flesh Market Close of Edinburgh, for a spare-rib steak [2]; and I believe it has not yet quite lost its ancient celebrity. I never ate one in perfection but there ': and the old beau related, with much vivacity, the adventures of a night on which he had accompanied to this resort the eccentric Earl of Kellie, and a party of Caledonian bon-vivants of the last age. ' But the receipt?' inquired Redgill, with grave earnestness corre-

---

[1] " The principal oyster-parties, in old times, took place in Lucky Middlemass's tavern, in the Cowgate (where the south pier of the bridge now stands), which was the resort of Fergusson and his fellow-wits—as witness his own excellent verse:

> Whan big as burns the gutters run,
> Gin ye hae catched a droukit skin,
> To Luckie Middlemist's loup in,
> And sit fu' snug
> O'er oysters and a dram o' gin,
> Or haddock lug."

R. Chambers: *Traditions of Edinburgh.*

" The municipal authorities of Edinburgh were wont to pay considerable attention to the ' feast of shells ', both as regarded the supply and the price. . . . At the commencement of the dredging-season, a voyage was boldly taken to the oyster-beds in the Firth of Forth by the public functionaries, with something of the solemnity of the Doge of Venice wedding his Adriatic bride."

—Meg Dods: *Manual of Cookery*, Note.

The fishermen of the Forth used to sing as they trailed the dredging-nets; for as Scott tells us,

> The herring loves the merry moonlight,
> The mackerel loves the wind,
> But the oyster loves the dredging-song
> For he comes of gentle kind.

[2] " In England, the best steaks are cut from the middle of the rump. In Ireland Scotland, and France, steaks that are thought more delicate are oftener cut, like chops from the sirloin or spare-rib, trimming off the superfluous fat, and chopping away the bone."—Meg Dods.

sponding to the magnitude of the subject. ' O!
neither more nor less than that those taverns were,
and are kept by butchers' wives, so that the
primest of the meat found its way there. In the
darksome den into which we dived—Luckie [1]
Middrit's of savoury memory—hungry customers
consumed beef-steaks by wholesale, at all hours
of the night and day, or rather of the perpetual
night. The coal-fire always in prime condition,
and short way between the brander and the
mouth, Doctor, . . . before the collop-tongs had
collapsed in the hands of the cook, in rushed
the red-legged waiting-wench with the smoking
wooden platter. . . . Ay, this is to eat a steak in
perfection.' "

In his *Elegy on Lucky Wood*, Allan Ramsay has
immortalized the landlady of his favourite resort
in the Canongate.

> She gae us aft hale legs o' lamb,
> And didna hain [2] her mutton-ham;
> Then aye at Yule [3] whene'er we cam',
>   A braw goose-pye:
> An' wasna that good belly-baum?
>   Nane dare deny.

Lucky Flockhart,[4] of the Potter's Row, and

---

[1] Mistress, Goody.   [2] Spare.   [3] Christmas.

[4] " Mrs. Flockhart, better known as Luckie Fykie, . . . seems to have been the
Mrs. Flockhart of Waverley. . . . She was a neat, little, thin woman, usually habited
in a plain striped blue gown, and apron of the same stuff, with a white *mutch*, having
a black ribbon round the head, and lappets brought down along the cheeks and
tied under the chin. . . . Her customers were very numerous and respectable,

other eighteenth-century vintners, used to provide a savoury chop-steak stew, known as a *soss*,[1] for their customers who had not been able to breakfast on account of the previous evening's conviviality, and who felt hungry during the forenoon; Dawny Douglas's Tavern [2] in the Anchor Close was noted for its suppers of tripe and rizzared [3] haddocks, minced collops and hashes, which never cost more than sixpence a head; and we read how Professor R. Simpson, Dr. Cullen, and Adam Smith were lured from the tavern where they could have their much loved banquets of hen broth, composed of two or three hcwtowdies,[4] a haggis, a crab pie, with ample punch.[5]

---

including Mr. Dundas, afterwards Lord Melville—Lord Stonefield—Lord Braxfield—Sheriff Cockburn—Mr. Scott, father of Sir Walter—Mr. Donald Smith, banker, and Dr. Cullen. The use and wont of these gentlemen, on entering the shop, and finding Mrs. Flockhart engaged with customers, was to salute her with " Hoo do ye do, mem?" and a *coup de chapeau*, and then walk *ben* to the room, where, upon the bunker-seat of the window, they found three bottles, severally containing brandy, rum, and whiskey, flanked by gingerbread and biscuits. They seldom sat down, but after partaking of what bottle they chose, walked quickly off."

                        —R. Chambers: *Traditions of Edinburgh.*

[1] O. Fr. *sausse.*

[2] Mentioned in *St. Ronan's Well.*

" The guests, before getting to any of the rooms, had to traverse the kitchen—a dark, fiery pandemonium, through which numerous ineffable ministers of flame were constantly flying, like the devils in a sketch of the Valley of the Shadow of Death, in the *Pilgrim's Progress.* Close by the door of the kitchen sat Mrs. Douglas, a woman of immense bulk, dressed out in the most splendid style, with a head-dress of stupendous grandeur, and a coloured silk gown having daisies flowered upon it like sunflowers, and tulips as big as cabbages. She never rose from her seat upon the entry of the guests, either because she was unable from fatness, or that by sitting, she might preserve the greater dignity. She only bowed to them as they passed, and there were numerous waiters and slip-shod damsels, ready to obey her directions. . . . The genius and tongue of his wife had evidently been too much for [Daunie], for she kept him in the most perfect subjection, and he acted only as a sort of head waiter under her."—R. Chambers: *Traditions of Edinburgh.*

[3] Sun-dried.   [4] Pullets.

[5] See Henry Grey Graham: *Social Life in Scotland in the Eighteenth Century.*

Southern visitors, however, often failed to relish our national dishes.

"When shall I see Scotland again?" writes Sydney Smith, the witty English divine, who spent five years (1798–1803) in Edinburgh. "Never shall I forget the happy days I spent there amidst odious smells,[1] barbarous sounds,[2] *bad suppers*,[3] excellent hearts, and the most enlightened and cultivated understandings."

This view was shared by the average peninsular Englishman.[4] One anonymous writer tells us that he was so disgusted at the mere sight of haggis and sheep's head that he could not bring himself to taste them. True, the "honest sonsy face" of the haggis is hardly calculated to inspire an appetite in the uninitiated (though it did inspire Burns to an ode), and a singed sheep's head, to the eye, is no lovesome thing, God wot (though we have Dorothy Wordsworth's word that "Coleridge

---

[1] In former days Edinburgh was a by-word among cities all more or less dirty and smelly. Her congested system of housing—which lingers in the tall high *lands* of the High Street—greatly intensified the evil, and the snell winds that blew up from the Firth were a badly needed antidote to the prevalent stench. It was doubtless the very intensity of the evil that drove her to her sewerage experiments and eventually made her a pioneer in public sanitation.—F. M. McN.

[2] Dunbar in the fifteenth and Fergusson in the eighteenth century complain of the turmoil caused by the street traders, crying their wares.

[3] The italics are mine.—F. M. McN.

[4] In *Humphry Clinker*, an English visitor to Edinburgh remarks: "I am not yet Scotchman enough to relish their singed sheep's head and haggis."

Dean Ramsay, in his *Reminiscences of Scottish Life and Character*, relates how old Lady Perth, offended with a French gentleman for some disparaging remark on Scottish dishes, answered him curtly, "Weel, weel, some fowk like parritch, and some like paddocks."

and I ate heartily of it ") [1]; but Dr. Johnson's comment is more sagacious:

" Their more elaborate cookery, or made dishes, an Englishman, at the first taste, is not likely to approve, but the culinary compositions of every country are often such as become grateful to other nations only by degrees." And Professor Saintsbury,[2] another Englishman, and a distinguished critic of food and wine, as well as of letters, writes:

" Generally speaking, Scotch ideas on food are sound. The people who regard haggis and sheep's head as things that the lips should not allow to enter them, and the tongue should refuse to mention, are, begging their pardon, fools." [3]

Breakfast, however, is the meal upon which we Scots particularly pride ourselves.

" In the breakfast," says Dr. Johnson, " the Scots, whether of the Lowlands or mountains, must be confessed to excel us. The tea and coffee are accompanied not only with butter, but with honey, conserves, and marmalades. If an epicure could remove by a wish in quest of sensual gratification, wherever he had supped, he would breakfast in Scotland." [4]

Sir Walter Scott had, happily, a lively interest

---

[1] *Recollections of a Tour made in Scotland* (1803).

[2] For many years Professor of English in the University of Edinburgh.

[3] " But," he adds, " I cannot forgive them for making sandwiches of mutton."
  —*A Second Scrap Book.*

[4] " Brother, let us breakfast in Scotland, lunch in Australia, and dine in Paris."
  Henry Kingsley.

in the table and with his aid we may easily trace the evolution of the Scottish breakfast.

First, a feudal breakfast from *Old Mortality*:

" The breakfast of Lady Margaret Bellenden no more resembled a modern *déjeuner*, than the great stone hall at Tillietudlem could brook comparison with a modern drawing-room. No tea, no coffee, no variety of rolls, but solid and substantial viands—the priestly ham, the knightly sirloin, the noble baron of beef, the princely venison pasty; while silver flagons, saved with difficulty from the claws of the Covenanters, now mantled, some with ale, some with mead, and some with generous wine of various qualities and descriptions."

In 1729, Mackintosh of Borlum laments the sadly changed times:

" When I come to a friend's house of a morning, I used to be asked if I had had my morning draught yet. I am now asked if I have had my tea. And in lieu of the big quaigh [1] with strong ale and toast, and after a dram of good wholesome Scots spirits, there is now the tea-kettle put to the fire, the tea-table and silver and china equipage brought in, and marmalade and cream."

In *Waverley* there are two descriptions of the Highland breakfast, of diverse types. The period is the eighteenth century.

[1] Gael. *cuach*, a cup or bowl.

" Waverley found Miss Bradwardine presiding
over the tea and coffee, the table loaded with
warm bread, both of flour, oatmeal, and barley-
meal, in the shape of loaves, cakes, biscuits, and
other varieties, together with eggs, reindeer ham,
mutton and beef ditto, smoked salmon, marmalade, and all the other delicacies which induced
even Johnson himself to extol the luxury of a
Scotch breakfast above that of all other countries.
A mess of oatmeal porridge, flanked by a silver jug,
which held an equal mixture of cream and buttermilk, was placed for the Baron's share of this
repast."

Then an *al fresco* breakfast from the same
book:

" Much nearer to the mouth of the cave he
heard the notes of a lively Gaelic song, guided by
which, in a sunny recess shaded by a glittering
birch-tree, and carpeted with a bank of firm white
sand, he found the damsel of the caravan, whose
lay had already reached him, busy, to the best of
her power, in arranging to advantage a morning
repast of milk, eggs, barley bread, fresh butter
and honeycomb. . . . To this she now added a
few bunches of cranberries, gathered in an ad-
jacent morass. . . . Evan and his attendant now
returned slowly along the beach, the latter bearing
a large salmon-trout, the produce of the morning's
sport. . . . A spark from the lock of his pistol

produced a light, and a few withered fir branches were quickly in flame, and as speedily reduced to hot embers, on which the trout was broiled in large slices. To crown the repast, Evan produced from the pocket of his short jerkin a large scallop-shell, and from under the folds of his plaid a ram's horn full of whiskey. Of this he took a copious dram."

In 1784, at the house of Maclean of Torloisk, on the island of Mull, Faujas de St. Fond found the breakfast table " elegantly covered with the following articles: Plates of smoked beef, cheese of the country and English cheese, fresh eggs, salted herrings, butter, milk, and cream; a sort of *bouillie* of oatmeal and water, in eating which, each spoonful is plunged into a basin of cream; milk worked up with yolks of eggs, sugar, and rum; currant jelly, conserve of myrtle, a wild fruit that grows among the heath; tea, coffee, three kinds of bread (sea biscuit, oatmeal cakes, and very thin and fine barley cakes); and Jamaica rum."

" The breakfast!" exclaims Dr. Redgill in Susan Ferrier's *Marriage*, after vigorously abusing the Scottish dinner, " that's what redeems the land—and every county has its peculiar excellence. In Argyllshire you have the Lochfyne herring, fat, luscious, and delicious, just out of the water, falling to pieces with its own richness

—melting away like butter in your mouth. In Aberdeenshire, you have the Finnan haddo' with a flavour all its own, vastly relishing—just salt enough to be piquant, without parching you up with thirst. In Perthshire there is the Tay salmon, kippered, crisp and juicy—a very magnificent morsel—a *leetle* heavy, but that's easily counteracted by a teaspoonful of the Athole whiskey. In other places you have the exquisite mutton of the country made into hams of a most delicate flavour; flour scones, soft and white; oatcakes, thin and crisp; marmalade and jams of every description."[1]

Afternoon tea evolved naturally out of the "four-hours"[2], which was long regarded as a necessary refreshment by all classes in Scotland. Originally ale and claret were the sole beverages served.

Tea appears to have been introduced to Scotland by the beautiful and gracious Mary of Modena, wife of James VII and II, who, while Duke of York, held court at Holyrood in 1681 as

[1] " Beside the ordinary articles of eggs, broiled fish, pickled herrings, Sardinias, Finnans, beef, mutton, and goat hams, reindeer's and beef tongues, sausages, potted meats, cold pies of game, &c., a few stimulating hot dishes are, by a sort of tacit prescription, set apart for the *déjeuner à la fourchette* of the gourmand and sportsman. Of this number are broiled kidneys, calf's and lamb's liver with fine herbs, and mutton cutlets *à la Vénitienne*. . . . Smoked Solan geese are well-known as contributing to the abundance of a Scottish breakfast, though too rank and fishy-flavoured for unpractised palates. They are eaten as whets, or relishes."—Meg Dods.

[2] " *North:* Now, James, acknowledge it—don't you admire a miscellaneous meal?
" *Shepherd:* I do. Breakfast, noony, denner, four-hours, and sooper a' in ane."
—Christopher North: *Noctes Ambrosianae.*

Lord High Commissioner. It was denounced by both medical men and clergy, and its acceptance was slow; but by 1750 its conquest of the women-folk was complete, and wine was reserved for gentlemen.[1]

During the nineteenth century, the Scottish tea-table reached as high a point of perfection as the breakfast-table. Scotland has, of course, always been celebrated for her cakes, but visitors are surprised at the rich store of scones and light tea-bread. The daintiness and variety of the fare, together with the beauty of the decoration, brought the Glasgow tearoom of the early twentieth century a just renown.

If our dinners and suppers remain more distinctive than distinguished, we can reflect with satisfaction that our breakfasts and teas, at their best, are nowhere surpassed.

VI

HOSPITALITY

I saw a stranger yestreen;
I put the food in the eating place,
Drink in the drinking place,
Music in the listening place;
And, in the sacred name of the Triune,

[1] " In 1705 green tea was advertised and sold at 16s. and Bohea at 30s. a pound by George Scott, goldsmith, Luckenbooths."—Chambers: *Traditions of Edinburgh*.

He blessed myself and my house,
My cattle and my dear ones.
And the lark said in her song,
　　Often, often, often,
Goes the Christ in the stranger's guise;
　　Often, often, often,
Goes the Christ in the stranger's guise.

—Old Gaelic Rune recovered by Kenneth Macleod.

Among the ancient Scots it was deemed in-
famous in a man to have the door of his house
shut, lest, as the bards express it, "the stranger
should come and behold his contracted soul".
The free and open hospitality which characterizes
a primitive condition of society survived much
later in Scotland, and particularly in the Highlands,[1] than in the more highly civilized countries
of Europe. Fynes Morison, a graduate of Cam-
bridge, who visited Scotland in 1598, tells us that
he noticed no regular inns with signs hanging out,
but that private householders would entertain
passengers on entreaty or where acquaintance was
claimed. The last statement is interestingly corro-
borated in the account of his journey to Scotland
which that eccentric genius, John Taylor, the
Thames waterman (commonly known as the
Water-poet), printed in 1618. In the course of
what he terms his "Fennyless Pilgrimage, or

[1] Hospitality was one of the virtues emphasized in the rule of Iona. Martin re-
cords that in the isle of Barra all strangers were obliged by the natives to eat "ocean-
meat" on coming off the sea, however recently they might have eaten.

Moneyless Perambulation ", he claims to have depended entirely on private hospitality. Everywhere, indeed, in his progress through Scotland, he appears to have been feasted sumptuously, and liberally supplied with money by hospitable gentlemen who probably found his witty conversation ample recompense. " So much of a virtue comparatively rare in England, and so much plenty in a country which his own people were accustomed to think of as the birthplace of famine, seems," Chambers comments, " to have greatly astonished him."

Defoe (1706–8) and Bishop Pococke (1760) add their testimony; and Pennant, who visited Scotland in 1769 and again in 1772, writes of the Highlanders:

" As for the common people, they were chiefly characterized by good manners, pride, inquisitiveness, and a *genius for hospitality* and religion."[1]

Dr. Johnson, in 1776, was amazed at the scale and magnificence of the hospitality he enjoyed— " veal in Edinburgh, roasted kid in Inverness, admirable venison and generous wine in the castle of Dunvegan ". " Everywhere," he writes, " we were treated like princes in their progress."[2]

[1] Lest they might have under their roof an enemy to whom the laws of hospitality equally applied, it was customary in olden times never to ask the name and business of a stranger until a year and a day had elapsed—an extraordinary effort, says Hugh Miller, for a people so naturally inquisitive.

[2] The lavish hospitality of the Highland chiefs was equalled only by their vanity. ' A great hero was Clarranald," said the old folk. " He would have seven casks

"The last act of manorial hospitality," Scott reminds us in a note to *The Pirate*, "was enacted upon the lawn. On each, in front of the mansion, was a platform of masonry—the loupin'-on stone. Here gentlemen mounted their horses, and were supplied with the doch-an-doruis or stirrup-cup.[1] Drunk from a quaich (a timber bowl with two ears), it was otherwise known as a bonalay."

It was precisely because the tradition of private hospitality was so strong that the development of the inn was so long retarded. The Wordsworths, on their Highland tour in the autumn of 1803, had no Boswell to arrange hospitality, nor did they choose to claim it like the adventurous Water-poet; and, save in one or two Lowland halting-places, the fastidious Dorothy found the standard

of the ruddy wine of Spain in his stable, and if a stranger asked what that was for he would be told that that was the drink for Clanranald's horses. One of the Macneill chiefs, however, went one better than that. Each evening, after dinner, he sent a trumpeter up to his castle-tower to make the following proclamation: Ye kings, princes, and potentates of all the earth, be it known unto you that MacNeill of Barra has dined—the rest of the world may dine now."
—Kenneth Macleod: Note to *The Songs of the Hebrides*.

[1] "A glass of ardent spirits, or draught of ale, given by the host to his guests when about to depart."—Scott: *Guy Mannering*.

"The Poculum Potatorium of the valiant Baron, his blessed Bear, has a proto-type at the fine old Castle of Glammis, so rich in memorials of ancient times; it is a massive beaker of silver, double gilt, moulded into the shape of a lion, and holding about an English pint of wine. The form alludes to the family name of Strathmore, which is Lyon, and, when exhibited, the cup must necessarily be emptied to the Earl's health. The author ought perhaps to be ashamed of recording that he has had the honour of swallowing the contents of the lion; and the recollection of the feat served to suggest the story of the Bear of Bradwardine. In the family of Scott of Thirlstane (not Thirlstane in the Forest, but the place of the same name in Roxburghshire) was long preserved a cup of the same kind, in the form of a jack-boot. Each guest was obliged to empty this at his departure. If the guest's name was Scott, the necessity was doubly imperative."—Scott: *Waverley*, Note

of cleanliness and comfort considerably lower than in English inns.[1]

Two pictures of Highland hospitality, both from real life.

The first is from Boswell's *Tour to the Hebrides* (1786).

"' Mr. McQueen's compliments to Mr. Boswell, and begs leave to acquaint him that, fearing the want of a proper boat, as much as the rain of yesterday, might have caused a stop, he is now at Skianwden with *Macgillichallum's*[2] carriage, to convey him and Dr. Johnson to Rasay, where they will meet with a most hearty welcome, and where Macleod,[3] being on a visit, now attends their motions.' . . .

" It was past six o'clock when we arrived.[4] Some excellent brandy was served round immediately, according to the custom of the Highlands, where a dram is generally taken every day. They call

---

All that is long since altered. For better and for worse, the Highlands are becoming rapidly "civilized". "A generation ago," the writer was told by the proprietrix of a Hebridean inn, "a Highland maid-servant would blush with shame on being offered a tip. Now she looks for it as a matter of course."

The virtue of hospitality is being systematically extirpated in the Highlands by the powers that be. A man who has paid a sum running into four figures for a few weeks' deer-stalking naturally objects to having his day's sport ruined by the appearance of a couple of pedestrians at the moment his gun is levelled at the stag. Therefore in many districts the crofters are not merely discouraged from giving hospitality, but are forbidden under threat of eviction. Thus not only the material but even the spiritual well-being of the native race is sacrificed to the great god Sport.—F. M. McN.

[2] The Highland expression for the Laird of Raasay, a chieftain of the Clan Macleod.

[3] *The* Macleod: chief of the clan.

[4] " We were introduced into the house, which one of the company called ' the *Court* of Rasay ', with politeness which not the Court of Versailles could have thought defective."—Dr. Samuel Johnson: *Letters*.

it a *scalch*.[1] On a sideboard was placed for us, who had come off the sea, a substantial dinner and a variety of wines. Then we had coffee and tea. I observed in the room several elegantly bound books and other marks of improved life. Soon afterwards a fiddler appeared, and a little ball began. *Rasay* himself danced with as much spirit as any man, and Malcolm bounded like a roe. Sandie Macleod, who has at times an excessive flow of spirits, . . . made much jovial noise. Dr. Johnson was so delighted with this scene that he said: ' I know not how we shall get away.' . . . We had a company of thirty at supper, and all was good humour and gaiety, without intemperance."

The second is by Alexander Carmichael, who describes an experience when collecting material for his *Carmina Gadelica* (published in 1900) in the Outer Hebrides:

" The house was clean and comfortable, if plain and unpretending, most things in it being home made. There were three girls in the house, young, comely, and shy, and four women, middle-aged, handsome, and picturesque in their home-spun gowns and high-crowned mutches. Three of the women had been to the moorland pastures with their cattle, and had turned in here to rest on their way home.

[1] Usually skalk (Scott). From Gael. *sgaile*.

"'Hail to the house and household,' said I, greeting the inmates in the salutation of our fathers. 'Hail to you, kindly stranger,' replied the housewife. 'Come forward and take this seat. If it be not ill-mannered, may we ask whence you have come to-day? . . . May the Possessor keep you in his own keeping, good man! You have left early and travelled far, and must be hungry.' With this the woman raised her eyes towards her daughters standing demurely silent, and motionless as Greek statues, in the background. In a moment the three fair girls became active and animated. One ran to the stack and brought in an armful of hard black peats, another ran to the well and brought in a pail of clear spring water, while the third quickly spread a cloth, white as snow, upon the table in the inner room. The three neighbour women rose to leave, and I rose to do the same. 'Where are you going, good man?' asked the housewife in injured surprise, moving between me and the door. 'You must not go till you eat a bit and drink a sip. That indeed would be a reproach to us that we would not soon get over. . . . Food will be ready presently, and in the meantime you will bathe your feet and dry your stockings which are wet after coming through the marshes of the moorland.' Then the woman went down upon her knees and washed and dried the feet of the stranger as tenderly as a mother would those of her child. . . .

" In an incredibly short time I was asked to go ' ben ' and break bread. . . . The table was laden with wholesome food sufficient for several persons. There were fried herrings and boiled turbot fresh from the sea, and eggs fresh from the yard. There were fresh butter and salt butter, wheaten scones, barley bannocks, and oat-cakes, with excellent tea and cream. The woman apologized that she had no ' aran coinnich '—moss bread, that is loaf bread—and no biscuits, they being simple crofter folk far away from the big town.

" ' This,' said I, taking my seat, ' looks like the table for a " reiteach " (betrothal), rather than for one man.' "

Burns, who made a tour of the Highlands in 1787, leaves an enduring tribute to the virtue of hospitality in the race to which he was bound by blood and sentiment:

> When death's dark stream I'll ferry o'er—
>   A time that surely shall come—
> In heaven itself I 'll ask no more
>   Than just a Highland welcome.

RECIPES

A GRACE

" Some hae meat that canna eat,
And some wad eat that want it;
But we hae meat, and we can eat,
And sae the Lord be thankit."

SOUPS

BARLEY-BROTH

" The bland, balsamic barley-broth of Scotland."—Meg Dods.
[In Aberdeen] " At dinner, Dr. Johnson ate several plate of Scotch broth, with barley and peas in it, and seemed very fond of the dish. I said, ' You never ate it before?'—Johnson, ' No, sir; but I don't care how soon I eat it again.'"
Boswell: *Journal of a Tour to the Hebrides with Samuel Johnson* (1786).

(*Meg Dods's Recipe*)

Beef or mutton, barley, peas, carrots, turnips, onions or leeks, parsley or celery, greens, water.

To from three to six pounds of beef or mutton, according to the quantity of broth wanted, put cold water in the proportion of a quart to the pound, a quarter-pound of Scotch barley, or more or less as the meat and the water, and a spoonful of salt, unless the meat is already slightly salted. To this put a large cupful of soaked white pease, or split grey pease, unless in the season when fresh green pease are to be had cheap, a double quantity of which must be put in with the other vegetables, using less barley. Skim very carefully as long as any scum rises; then draw aside the pot, and let the broth boil slowly for an hour, at which time put to it two young carrots and turnips cut in dice, and two or three onions sliced. A quarter of an hour before the broth is ready, add a little parsley picked and chopped, or the white part of three leeks may be used instead of onions, and a head of celery sliced, instead of the parsley-seasoning; but celery requires longer boiling. For beef-broth a small quantity of greens roughly shred, and the best part of four or five leeks cut in inch-lengths, are better suited than turnip, carrot, and parsley, which are more adapted to mutton. If there is danger of the meat being overdone before the broth is properly lithed,[1] it may be taken up, covered for a half-hour, and returned into the pot to heat through before it is dished. Garnish with carrot and turnip boiled in parsley and butter, or a sauce made of pickled cucumbers, or nasturtiums heated in melted butter (sauce), or in a little clear broth, with a teaspoonful of made mustard and another of vinegar. Minced parsley, parboiled for two minutes, may also be strewed over bouilli, or a sprinkling of boiled carrots cut in small dice. Serve the broth in a tureen, removing any film of fat that may gather upon the surface.

The ingredients given in a two-hundred-year-old recipe are: a chopped leg of beef, a fowl, carrots, barley, celery, sweet herbs, onions, parsley, and *a few marigolds*! See *A New and Easy Method of Cookery*, by Elizabeth Cleland (Edinburgh, 1759).

In the eighteenth century, Faujas de St. Fond was regaled in Mull with " a large dish of Scots soup, composed of broth of beef, mutton, and sometimes fowl, mixed with a little oatmeal, onions, parsley, and a considerable quantity of peas. Instead of slices of bread as in France, small slices of mutton and giblets of fowl are thrown into this soup."

In Caithness and elsewhere, *shilling broth* was made from shilled corn, i.e. freed from the husk (Gael. *silleanan* ,seeds of corn).

HOTCH POTCH

> Then here 's to ilka kindly Scot
> Wi' mony gude broths he boils his pot,
> But rare hotch-potch beats a' the lot,
> It smells an' smacks sae brawly.
> —Sheriff Bell.

(*Old Family Recipe*)

Neck of lamb, carrots, turnips, cauliflower, lettuce, green peas, broad beans, spring onions, parsley, or any other young fresh vegetables, salt, pepper, water.

Put three pounds of neck of lamb [2] into a saucepan with two and a half quarts of cold water and a little salt. Bring to the boil and skim carefully. Shell a pint and a half of fresh green peas; shell and skin half a pint of broad beans; pare six young

---

[1] To *lithe*: to thicken, to mellow. A.S. *lith-ian*, to mitigate.—Jamieson. A Scottish culinary term.

[2] Mutton, beef, or a marrow bone may be used in place of lamb.

turnips, scrape six young carrots and cut both into dice; cut
six spring onions into small pieces. Retain half a pint of peas
and put the rest of the prepared vegetables into the boiling
liquor. Draw to the side and simmer slowly for three or four
hours or longer. It can hardly be cooked too slowly or too
long.[1] Meanwhile put a cauliflower and a lettuce into water
with a little salt and let them lie for half an hour. Then break
the cauliflower into sprigs and chop the lettuce, and, half an
hour before serving, put them into the pot with the remainder
of the peas and a handful of chopped parsley. The soup should
be nearly as thick as porridge. When ready, remove the mutton,
season, and serve in a hot tureen.

This makes a famous hot dish after a chilly day on the hill.

The excellence of this dish depends mainly on the meat, whether beef or mutton
being perfectly fresh, and the vegetables being all young, and full of sweet juices,
and boiled till of good consistence. The sweet white turnip is best for hotch-potch,
or the small, round, smooth-grained yellow kind peculiar to Scotland, and almost
equal to the genuine *navet* of France.—Meg Dods.

Almost any vegetables that are in season may be added with improvement. The
meat may be cut up and served in the soup, but this is rarely done nowadays.—Ed.

It is related of the late Prince Consort that whilst crossing one of the Scottish
lochs in a steamer, on approaching the galley he was attracted by the delicious odour
of hotch-potch.

" How is it made?" he asked of the cook, who failed to recognize him.

" Weel, there's mutton intill't and neeps intill't and peas intill't . . ."

" What is intill't?"

" I'm tellin' ye, there's mutton intill't, and neeps intill't, and . . ."

" Yes, but what's *intill't*?"

" Gudesake, man, am I no thrang tellin' ye what's intill't? There's *mutton* intill't ..."

The timely arrival of a member of the Prince's suite put an end to the confusion.
He explained that that important ingredient *intill't*, meant " into it " and nothing
more!—F. M. McN.

POWSOWDIE,[2] OR SHEEP'S HEAD BROTH

(*Meg Dods's Recipe*)

*Sheep's head and trotters, mutton, barley, peas, carrot,
turnips, onions, parsley.*

Choose a large, fat, young head. When carefully singed by
the blacksmith, soak it and the singed trotters for a night, if
you please, in lukewarm water. Take out the glassy part of

[1] Eight hours is not too much.—Lady Harriet St. Clair.
[2] From *pow*, the head, and *sowdie*, sodden or boiled.

the eyes, scrape the head and trotters, and brush till perfectly clean and white; then split the head with a cleaver, and lay aside the brains, &c., clean the nostrils and gristly parts, split also the trotters, and cut out the tendons. Wash the head and feet once more, and let them blanch till wanted for the pot.

Take a large cupful of barley, and about twice that quantity of soaked white, or old, or fresh green pease, with a gallon or rather more of water. Put to this the head, and from two to three pounds of scrag or trimmings of mutton, perfectly sweet, and some salt. Take off the scum very carefully as it rises, and the broth will be as limpid and white as any broth made of beef or mutton. When the head has boiled rather more than an hour, add sliced carrot and turnip, and afterwards some onions and parsley shred. A head or two of celery sliced is admired by some modern gourmands, though we would rather approve of the native flavour of this really excellent soup. The more slowly the head is boiled, the better will both the meat and soup be. From two to three hours' boiling, according to the size of the head and the age of the animal, and an hour's simmering by the side of the fire, will finish the soup. Many prefer the head of a ram to that of a wether, but it requires much longer boiling. In either case the trotters require less boiling than the head. Serve with the trotters and sliced carrot round the head. Sheep's head, not too much boiled, makes an excellent ragout or hash of higher flavour than calf's head ragout.

The sauces ordered for boiled mutton and cow-heel are well adapted to this dish, if sauce must be had where it is so little required. For ragout, a sauce may be made of the broth thickened with butter and flour.

"The reviewer of the first edition of this work * in *Blackwood's Magazine* suggests that there should be two heads and eight trotters, which admirable emendation certainly more than doubles the value of the receipt."—M. D.

        * Meg Dods's *Manual*.

Powsowdie is mentioned by Scott in *The Antiquary*.

"This national preparation was wont to be a favourite Sunday dinner dish in many comfortable Scottish families. Where gentlemen ' killed their own mutton ', the head was reserved for the Sunday's broth; and to good family customers, and to *victuallers*, a prime *tup's* head was a common Saturday's gift from the butchers with whom they dealt. By the way, nationally speaking, we ought to say fleshers, as our countrymen would, till very lately, have been mortally offended at the designation of ' butcher '.

Soups 89

" Sheep s head broth is reckoned medicinal in certain cases; and was frequently prescribed as an article of diet by the celebrated Dr. Cullen.

" This dish has furnished whole pages to Joe Miller and his right witty contemporaries. In one of the most pleasing pieces of biography that ever was written, ' The Life of Lady Grizel Baillie ', there is an amusing ' sheep's head anecdote ', which at once affords a glimpse of the simplicity of the national manners, and of the dexterity and good sense of the affectionate and very juvenile heroine. Her father, Sir Patrick Home, proscribed after the Restoration, was hidden near his own mansion—his lady and his daughter Grizel being alone privy to his place of concealment. It was the duty of this young girl, not only to carry food to her father during the night, but to abstract these supplies from the dinner-table, so that neither the servants nor younger children might be aware that there was an invisible guest to feed. Her inordinate appetite and stratagems to procure food became the cause of many jokes at table; and one day, when a sheep's head—a favourite dish with Sir Patrick —was produced, she had just conveyed nearly the whole into her lap, when her young brother, afterwards Earl of Marchmont, looked up and exclaimed, ' Mother, Mother, look at Grizel; while we have been taking our broth, she has eaten up the whole sheep's head!'

" The consternation of young Home could not, however, exceed that of a learned gentleman, who at present fills a chair in Edinburgh University, upon a somewhat similar occasion. Before filling his present honourable situation, Professor —— was for some years a professor in S—— College; and, as might have been surmized, in the lapse of those three years of exile, experienced a natural and national longing for that savoury food which, to a Scotsman, is like his mother's milk. A sheep's head was accordingly procured by his orders, and sent to the blacksmith's to be singed. The hour of dinner arrived; the chops of the learned professor watered with expectation; when lo! to his disappointment and horror, the fleshless skull was presented; and, doubly worse, accompanied with the sauce of a bill, setting forth, ' To polishing a sheep's head for Professor ——, one shilling and four pence ' !—thus making the unfortunate philosopher come down with sixteen shillings, Scots money, for being deprived of the exquisite pleasure which he had anticipated in polishing the skull himself."—Meg Dods: *Manual of Cookery*, Note.

A singed sheep's head is a special dish on St. Andrew's Day.

SKINK: AN OLD SCOTS STEW SOUP

" A spoonfu' o' stink will spoil a patfu' o' skink."
(One ill weed will spoil a mess of pottage.)
—Old Scots Proverb.

(Meg Dods's Recipe)

Beef, mixed vegetables, water, pepper, and salt.

Take a leg of beef, put it on with a gallon of water; let it boil for six hours, taking care to skim the soup well all the time, as the gravy should be very clear and bright; then strain the liquor from the meat, take the sinewy part of the meat and lay it aside till your soup is ready to serve up. Cut the sinews about an inch long. Have some vegetables cut, such as carrots, turnips, leeks, onions, celery, lettuce, cabbage shred small, and green pease, when to be had. Blanch the whole in boiling water for ten minutes. Put the whole into the soup and boil till quite tender. Serve up the sinews in the tureen with the soup. Season the soup with salt and pepper before dishing it.

" Herbs may be used in these soups; and white pease (boilers) are by many thought an improvement. Both are cheap and excellent family dishes."—M. D.

THE OLD SCOTS BROWN SOUP

(*Meg Dods's Recipe*)

Beef, meat trimmings, carrot, celery, onions, leek, turnip, water, catsup, salt, pepper, cayenne, sippets.

Have eight pounds of a shin of beef chopped across in two places, and a knuckle of veal or a scrag or some shanks of mutton with any fresh trimmings the larder can furnish, and a piece of ham, if the ham flavour is admired. Heat and rub hard a nicely tinned stew-pot; melt in it some butter, or rub it with marrow. Let the meat, with a slice of carrot, a head of celery, onions, the white part of two leeks, and a turnip, sliced, *catch*, but not burn, over a quick fire (let it be nicely browned); then add four quarts, or better, of soft water. Carefully skim. When it is once skimmed, throw in a pint of cold water to refresh it, and take off what more scum is detached till it become quite limpid. Let the stew-pot simmer slowly by the fire for four hours, without stirring it any more from the bottom, till all the strength is obtained, but not so long as to cause the soup to become ropy. Take it off and let it settle; skim off the fat, and strain off gently what flows freely through a fine search. When ready, put to it two pounds of rump-steaks, cut rather small and nicely browned in the frying-pan, but drained from the frying-fat. Simmer the steaks in the soup for an hour; strain it; add a small glassful of catsup, with salt, pepper, and cayenne; slip toasted sippets into the tureen and skimming off the filmy fat, serve the soup with the steaks in it. Without the steaks, which one now rarely sees, this is plain *brown soup*.

THE OLD SCOTS WHITE SOUP OR SOUP À LA REINE

(*Meg Dods's Recipe*)

Veal, fowl, bacon, lemon-thyme, onions, carrot, turnip, celery, peppercorns, mace, macaroni or vermicelli or French roll, water.

Take a large knuckle of the whitest veal, well broken and soaked, a white fowl skinned, or two chickens, a quarter-pound of well-coloured lean undressed bacon, lemon-thyme, onions, carrot, celery, and a white turnip, a few white peppercorns, and two blades of mace. Boil for about two hours; skim repeatedly and carefully during that time. When the stock is well tasted, strain it off. It will form a jelly. When to be used, take off the surface fat, clear off the sediment, and put the jelly into a tin saucepan or stewpan well tinned; boil for half an hour, and serve on a couple of rounds of a small French roll; or with macaroni, previously soaked, and stewed in the soup till perfectly soft, or vermicelli. This is plain white soup.

LORRAINE SOUP [1]

(*Meg Dods's Recipe*)

The old Scots white soup (q.v.), sweet almonds, eggs, cold roast fowl, bread-crumbs, lemon-peel, nutmeg, cream.

The old Scots white soup is raised to Lorraine soup as follows: Take a half-pound of sweet almonds, blanched (that is, scalded and the husks rubbed off), the hard-boiled yolks of three eggs, and the skinned breast and white parts of cold roast fowl; beat the almonds to a paste in a mortar with a little water to prevent their oiling; mince very finely the fowl and eggs and some bread-crumbs. Add to this hash an English pint or more of

[1] Probably named after Mary of Lorraine or Guise, wife of James V of Scotland and mother of Mary Stuart.—F. M. McN

the stock, lemon-peel, and a scrape of nutmeg; bring it to the boil and put to it a pint of boiling sweet cream and the rest of the stock. Let it be for a considerable time on the very eve of boiling that it may thicken, but take care it does not boil, lest the cream curdle. Strain through a sieve. Yolks of eggs will do for half the cream.

POTAGE À LA REINE
(THE FASHIONABLE WHITE SOUP)

(Meg Dods's Recipe)

Fowls, veal, veal-broth, parsley, bread-crumb, almonds (sweet and bitter), cream.

Take a couple of large or three small fat pullets; clean and skin them; take also two pounds or more of veal cut into pieces; put these together into a very nicely tinned stewpan with parsley, and moisten them with clear boiling veal-broth. Let this stew softly for an hour; then soak in the broth the soft part of a penny loaf; cut the flesh off the breasts and wings of the chickens; chop and pound it in a mortar with the hard yolks of four eggs, the soaked crumbs, ten sweet almonds and three bitter, all blanched. Rub the compound into the soup; strain the whole, and add gradually a quart of sweet cream brought to boil by itself; the beat yolks of three or four eggs may be substituted for two-thirds of the cream. Cow-heel or calf's feet will make a good white soup. Rabbits may be economically substituted for chickens, and lean beef for the veal.

FRIAR'S CHICKEN [1]

" A dish invented by that luxurious body of men."—Sir John Sinclair.

(Mrs. Dalgairns' [2] Recipe)

Chicken, veal, eggs, salt, pepper, parsley, water.

[1] Mrs. Glasse (a Londoner) calls it *Scots chicken* in her *Art of Cookery* (1747), and adds " This is also a very pretty dish for sick people, but the Scotch gentlemen are very fond of it." According to Scott, in *The Fortunes of Nigel*, it was a favourite of James VI and I.

[2] From *The Practice of Cookery*, by Mrs. Dalgairns (Edinburgh, 1829).

Put two pounds of knuckle of veal into a pan with some water; boil for two hours; strain; cut a young fowl into joints, skin it, and add it to the boiling broth; season with white pepper and salt; let it boil for a little, then add a tablespoonful of chopped parsley. When the chicken is boiled tender, add three well-beaten eggs; stir them quickly into the broth one way, and remove immediately from the fire.

Friar's chicken is served (old style) with the carved chicken in the soup. Meg Dods recommends the addition of a little mace, and adds: " The stock may be simply made of butter, and the meat may be nicely browned in the frying-pan before it is put to the soup. Rabbits make this very well. Some like the egg curdled, and egg in great quantity, making the dish a sort of *ragout* of eggs and chicken." Another old recipe gives a flavouring of cinnamon.—F. M. McN.

NETTLE BROTH

(*Highland*)

Chicken stock, barley, nettles, pepper, salt.

Gather young nettles from the higher part of the wall where they are clean. Wash the tops in salted water and chop very finely. Have some good stock boiling—chicken stock is best— in which you have cooked a sufficient quantity of barley. Add the nettles, simmer till tender, and season to taste.

Nettles also combine well with potatoes.

NETTLE SOUP

(*Highland*)

Nettles, milk, water, butter, pepper, salt, potato- or corn-flour.

Prepare the nettles as above and steam in a little water. Add milk, a small piece of butter, pepper and salt, and thicken with cornflour, potato-flour, or a little mashed potato.

FEATHER FOWLIE[1]

(A LUNCHEON SOUP)

(*Lady Clark of Tillypronie's Recipe*)

Fowl, ham, celery, onion, thyme, parsley, mace, salt, eggs, cream.

Take a fresh fowl; joint and let the pieces soak for half an hour in cold water to which you have added a dessertspoonful of salt, then wash it well under the tap and put it into a stew-pan with a slice of ham, a stick of celery cut small, a sliced onion, thyme, parsley, and a bit of mace. Cover with a quart of cold water, put the lid on, and bring it to the boil; then draw it to the side and let it cook gently for an hour and a half; strain, and immediately clear off all the grease with paper. Put it into another stew-pan and add a dessertspoonful of chopped parsley and a ladleful of first stock. Let it heat up for fifteen minutes and add the minced white meat of the fowl. Remove from the fire, stir in three strained yolks of egg and a dessert-spoonful of warmed cream. Pour into a heated tureen.

COCK-A-LEEKIE [2]

The King (James VI and I): " And, my lords and lieges, let us all to dinner, for the cockie-leekie is a-cooling."—Scott: *Fortunes of Nigel*, last line.

(*Mrs. Dalguirns' Recipe*)

A cock or fowl, beef or veal stock, leeks, prunes, Jamaica pepper, salt.

Cut off the roots and part of the heads of two or three bunches of large winter leeks.[3] Cut in pieces an inch long (which may be

---

[1] Corruption of *Œufs filés*.

[2] Fynes Morison, who visited Scotland in 1598, was regaled at a knight's house with " a Pullet with some prunes in the broth ".

[3] " The leek is one of the most honourable and ancient of pot-herbs. It is called *par excellence* the herb; and learned critics assert that our word porridge or pottage is derived from the Latin *porrus*, a leek. ' From Indus to Peru ', the adoration of the garlic, onion, and leek is universal. The leek is the badge of a high-spirited, honourable, and fiery nation—the Ancient Britons. In the old poetry of the northern nations, where a young man would now be styled the *flower*, he was called ' the *leek* of his family, or tribe ', an epithet of most savoury meaning."

—Meg Dods's *Manual*, Note.

split). Wash well in three waters, and, if old and strong, boil for ten minutes in water. Put them in a close stew-pan with some beef or veal stock and a trussed fowl or cock, with Jamaica pepper, and salt. Let the whole simmer very gently at the side of the fire for four hours, keeping it well skimmed. Half an hour before serving add a dozen or so of prunes, unbroken. When ready to serve, take out the cock or fowl and cut it in pieces, place it in the tureen, and pour broth over it. The prunes may be omitted.[1]

POACHER'S SOUP
(OR SOUP À LA MEG MERRILIES)

" Of the ruder and more national form (which is also, I think, the best) of grouse soup, the celebrated stew whereof Meg Merrilies made Dominie Sampson partake was probably a variety, though the authority said that moor-game were not the only ingredient of that soup or broth or stew. (See p. 127.) . . . For the really hungry man, this is, no doubt, the best way of all, but as a dinner dish it is perhaps, as has been hinted, too solid for the mere overture to which we have now reduced soup. In the days of our ancestors they ate it late instead of early in the order of dishes, and I am not certain that they were wrong."—Professor Saintsbury

(Meg Dods's Recipe)

Venison, beef or mutton, game, celery, carrots, turnips, potatoes, cabbage, onions, parsley, peppercorns, spices, salt, red wine, mushroom catsup, water.

This savoury and highly relishing new stew-soup may be made of any or every thing known by the name of game. Take from two to four pounds of the trimmings or coarse parts of venison, shin of beef, or shanks or lean scrag of good mutton —all fresh. If game is plenty, then use no meat. Break the bones and boil this with celery, a couple of carrots and turnips, four onions, a bunch of parsley, and a quarter-ounce of pepper-corns, the larger proportion Jamaica pepper. Strain this stock when it has boiled for three hours. Cut down and skin a black-

---

[1] " *Shepherd*: Speakin' o' cockyleekie, the man was an atheist that first polluted it with prunes.

" *North*: At least no Christian.

" *Shepherd*: Prunes gie't a sickenin' sweetness till it taste like a mouthfu' o' a cockney poem."—Christopher North: *Noctes Ambrosianae*.

cock or woodcock, a pheasant, half a hare or a rabbit, a brace of partridges or grouse, or one of each (whichever is obtained most easily), and season the pieces with mixed spices. These may be floured and browned in the frying-pan; but as this is a process dictated by the eye as much as the palate, it is not necessary in making this soup. Put the game to the strained stock with a dozen of small onions, a couple of heads of celery sliced, half a dozen peeled potatoes, and, when it boils, a small white cabbage quartered, black pepper, allspice, and salt to taste. Let the soup simmer till the game is tender, but not overdone; and, lest it should, the vegetables may be put in half an hour before the meat.

" This soup may be coloured and flavoured with red wine, and if two spoonfuls of mushroom catsup is mixed should not be salted till that ingredient is added, as catsup contains so much salt itself."—M. D.

" The Club were at variance on [Meg Dods's] receipt. Jekyl declared for the simple racy flavour of the rude sylvan cheer; Winterblossom liked the addition of forcemeat-balls and catsup; and the Doctor—hovering between the tureens like Macheath between his rival charmers—laid his ears deeply in both, but when compelled to decide, from an habitual reverence to soups as they are, voted for the plain soup, as originally swallowed with so much unction by Dominie Sampson."
—*Annals of the Cleikum Club.*

SUPERLATIVE GAME SOUP

" *Tickler* : But oh! my dear North, what grouse-soup at Dalnacardoch! You smell it on the homeward hill, as if it were exhaling from the heather."
Christopher North: *Noctes Ambrosianae.*

(*Meg Dods's Recipe*)

Game, venison or rabbits, ham, onions, carrots, parsnips, celery, parsley, Jamaica pepper, cloves, veal or beef stock.

This soup is made of all sorts of black or red game, or of venison or wild rabbits. Skin the birds, carve and trim them neatly, and fry the pieces along with a few slices of ham, sliced onions, carrots, and parsnips, a little of each. Drain and stew this meat gently for an hour in good fresh veal or beef stock-broth, with a head of celery cut in nice bits, a little minced parsley, and what seasonings you like. Very small steaks of venison may be fried as the birds, and stewed in the broth;

and if the stock is made of any venison trimmings, it will be an advantage both in flavour and strength.

"Jamaica pepper and cloves are suitable seasonings; celery, from its nutty flavour, is a proper vegetable for hare and game soups. Take out the ham before dishing."
—M. D.

SCOTS HARE SOUP

" Hare soup, sir, I will candidly own, is only understood in Scotland."
—Dr. Redgill: *Annals of the Cleikum Club.*

(*Old Family Recipe*)

Hare, beef, turnips, carrots, onions, sweet herbs, celery, water, peppercorns, rice flour or arrowroot, mushroom catsup, port wine.

Skin and clean the hare thoroughly, holding it over a large basin to catch all the blood, which contains much of the flavour of the hare. Wipe it carefully with a damp cloth to remove any small hairs that may be sticking to it. Cut a dozen or so of very small steaks from the back, shoulders, and rump. Put all that remains of the hare into a large pot with four pounds of fresh shin or neck of beef and four quarts of water. When the liquor boils, add two turnips, two carrots, and six onions (all cut up), a large head of celery, a faggot of sweet herbs, half an ounce of black and Jamaica peppercorns, and an ounce of salt. Simmer for three hours and strain. Flatten and season the steaks, dredge them with flour, and brown them nicely in a saucepan. Add the strained stock and simmer for one and a half hours. Strain the blood, rub it with two ounces of rice flour or arrowroot and half a pint of soup as if making starch; add more hot soup and stir the whole into the soup, which must be kept only at the point of boiling for ten minutes, lest the blood curdle. The soup may be further thickened with the parboiled liver pounded in a mortar with the pieces of hare boiled for stock. When done enough, skim, put in a glass of mushroom ketchup and one or more of port wine. Add any more salt, pepper, or cayenne that may be required. Serve with the hare steaks in the tureen. A boiled potato should be served separately for each person.

A knuckle of veal, or a veal bone and a ham bone, may be used in place of beef.

" Red wine, in the proportion of a quarter-pint to a tureen of soup, is reckoned an improvement by some gourmands; and those of the old school still like a large spoonful of currant jelly dissolved in the soup.

" You may lay aside as much of the fleshy part of a good hare as will make a handsome dish of hare-cakes, or minced collops, garnished with sippets, or as will make forcemeat balls for the soup."—Meg Dods.

For a less expensive soup use two pounds of shin of beef instead of four, or a knuckle of veal, or a veal or ham bone in place of beef. The sweet herbs and the port wine may be omitted, and fewer vegetables used. A very few cloves, stuck into an onion, improve the flavour. Many gudewives thicken hare soup with oatmeal (using about three handfuls), which should be added after the soup has first come to the boil. (Oatmeal, incidentally, is particularly good as a thickening for tomato soup.)

PLAIN SCOTS FISH-AND-SAUCE

(*Meg Dods's Recipe*)

Haddocks or other fish, green onions, parsley, chives, pepper, butter, flour, catsup.

This is, in fact, just a fish soup. Make a stock of the heads, points of the tails, fins, &c., or where fish is cheap and fresh, cut down one or two to help the stock. Boil green onions, parsley, and chives in this, and some whole pepper. When all the substance is obtained, strain it. Thicken with butter kneaded in browned flour, but only to the consistence of a soup, and put in the fish (generally haddocks), cut in three or divided. Boil the fish ten minutes, add catsup, and serve them and the sauce together in tureen or soup dish.

CULLEN SKINK

(*A Cottage Recipe from the Shores of the Moray Firth*)

Findon haddock, onion, mashed potatoes, butter, milk, pepper, and salt.

Skin a Findon haddock and place it in a pan with sufficient boiling water to cover it (no more). Bring to the boil and add a chopped onion. When the haddock is cooked, take it out and remove all the bones. Flake the fish and return all the bones to the stock. Boil for one hour. Strain the stock

and again bring to the boil. Boil about a pint of milk separately
and add it to the stock with the flaked fish and salt to taste.
Boil for a few minutes. Add enough mashed potato to make
the soup a nice consistency, with a tablespoonful of butter,
and pepper to taste, and serve.

PARTAN BREE[1]
(CRAB SOUP)

(*Lady Clark of Tillypronie's Recipe*)

Crabs, rice, white stock, salt, pepper, anchovy, cream.

Pick all the meat from two cooked crabs and set aside that
from the large claws. Boil five or six ounces of rice in milk till
soft and pass it with the crab-meat through a tammy into a
basin. Stir it with a wooden spoon till perfectly smooth and
add to it, very gradually, sufficient white unseasoned stock for
a party of twelve or fourteen people. Do not make it as thick
as a purée. Season with salt, white pepper, and anchovy. Put
it all into a pan and stir it over the fire until quite hot, but do
not let it boil. Add pieces of meat from the claws, and, just
before serving, stir in half a pint of cream.

MUSSEL BROSE

At Musselbrough and eke [2] Newhaven
The fisher-wives will get top livin
When lads gang [3] oot on Sunday's even
    To treat their joes,[4]
An' tak o' fat pandours a prieven [5]
    Or mussel brose.
                              —Fergusson.

(*Traditional Recipe*)

Mussels, oatmeal, stock or milk-and-water.

Wash the shells in several waters, scraping them well, then
put them into a colander and run cold water on them until it

---

[1] From Gael. *partan*, a crab, and *brigh* (pron. bree), juice or gravy.
Also.   [2] Go.   [4] Sweethearts.   [5] Tasting.

runs away quite clear and free of sand, after which put them
to steep for two hours. Drain them, put them on the fire in
an iron stew-pan, closely covered, shake them occasionally
until the shells open, and remove immediately from the fire.
Strain the liquor into a basin, take the mussels out of the shells,
and remove the beards and black parts. Put the liquor on with
some fresh fish stock or some milk-and-water. Bring to the
boil, add the mussels, and boil for ten minutes in all. Have
some oatmeal toasting before the fire. Put a handful or so in
a bowl and dash a cupful of the boiling bree over it. Stir up
quickly so as to form knots, return to the pan for a minute
or two, and serve very hot.

Cockles may be used in the same way.

Mussels, "the oyster's poor relation", were conceivably consumed in the burgh
of that name as early as the Roman period, for this was originally a Roman station,
and owes its name to the shell-fish.—F. M. McN.

WINKLE SOUP

(*Hebrides*)

Winkles, oatmeal, fish stock or milk, water.

Gather a small pailful of winkles on the rocks at low tide.
Put them into a pot, cover them with water, and bring them to
the boil. Take out the winkles (reserving the liquor) and pick
the fish out of the shells with a long pin. Strain carefully the
water they were boiled in, as it is often sandy, and return it
to the pot. It will probably be too salt, so it is an advantage to
use equal proportions of the liquor and water in which fresh
fish has been boiled; but if this is not available, a little milk
and fresh water will do. When it comes to the boil, add enough
oatmeal to make it of the consistency of thin gruel. The meal
should be allowed to fall in a steady rain from the left hand,
whilst you stir it with a porridge stick or wooden spoon. When
the oatmeal is nearly cooked (which takes about twenty minutes),
put back the winkles and boil for ten minutes longer.

SHELL-FISH SOUP

(*Hebrides*)

Cockles, mussels, or razor-fish, fresh fish stock, milk, cornflour, butter, pepper, salt.

Proceed as for winkle soup, adding milk to part of the liquor. Put in a morsel of butter, thicken with cornflour, and season to taste. Use plenty of pepper. Razor-fish should be chopped small before being added.

" As much of the flavour of delicate shell-fish is lost in washing them free of sand, the washings may be kept, strained repeatedly, and put to the stock; but where shell-fish are in plenty this is idle."—Meg Dods.

FAT BROSE

The Monks of Melrose made fat brose
On Fridays when they fasted.—*A Godly Song*.

(*Meg Dods's Recipe*)

Ox head or heel, or sheep's head or skink of beef, oatmeal, water, salt.

Boil an ox head, sheep's head, ox heel, or skink of beef till an almost pure oil floats on the top of the pot. Have some oatmeal well toasted before the fire, as in making haggis; put a handful of the meal into a basin with salt and, pouring a ladleful of the fat broth over it, stir it quickly up so as not to run into a doughy mass, but to form *knots*.

Yule Brose.—In olden times, all, gentle and simple, had fat brose on Yule Day morning.

KAIL BROSE

When I see our Scots lads,
Wi' their kilts and cockades,
That sae aften hae lounder'd [1] our foes, man;
I think to mysel',
On the meal and the *yill*,[2]
And the fruits o' our Scottish kail brose, man.
        —Andrew Shirrefs (1762–1800): *A Cogie o' Yill*.

(*Old Cottage Recipe*)

Ox head or cow heel, green kail, oatmeal, salt, water.

[1] Beaten severely.   [2] Ale.

Put half an ox head or a cow heel into a goblet with three quarts of water. Boil till the fat floats on the top. Take a good stock of kail, wash it carefully and pick it down very small, and put it into the broth. Now take a teacupful of toasted oatmeal, put it into a bowl with a little salt, dash upon it a teacupful of the fat broth, and stir it up like oatmeal brose into knots. Put this into the pot for a moment or two before lifting off the fire. Stir well and serve.

GREEN KAIL [1]

> The Friars of Faill,[2] they made gude kail
>> On Fridays when they fasted;
> They never wanted gear eneuch
>> As lang as their neighbours' lasted.
>> —Old Song.

(Old Cottage Recipe)

Greens, oatmeal, pepper, salt, cream, water.

Put into a pot as much water as will cover your greens. Remove the strong shanks (this is " ribbing " them) and put them in when the water is boiling. Boil for an hour, leaving them uncovered. Take them out, squeeze them free of the liquor, and chop them finely or squeeze them through a sieve. Sprinkle with oatmeal and put back into the pot with the stock. Add a little warmed cream, with pepper and salt to taste. Stir, boil up for a few minutes, and serve with thin oatcakes.

MUSLIN [3] KAIL

> I 'll sit down o'er my scanty meal,
> Be 't water brose or muslin-kail,
>> Wi' cheerfu' face,
> As lang 's the muses dinna fail
>> To say the grace.
>> Burns: *Epistle to James Smith.*

" A purely vegetable soup, without animal ingredients of any kind, and composed of shelled barley, greens, onions, &c."
—C. Mackay.

---

[1] Called also Pan Kail and Lenten Kail.
[2] Faill was a small monastery in the parish of Torbolton, near Mauchline, Ayrshire.
[3] Meslin or mashlum (mixed).

BARLEY KAIL

(*Old Cottage Recipe*)

Hough, barley, kail, pepper and salt, water.

Put two pounds of hough and a teacupful of barley into a goblet with about three quarts of cold water. Bring it to the boil and remove the scum. Let it boil for three hours. Have ready a cullender full of kail, which you have washed carefully, and picked down very fine with the fingers. Boil till tender. Add salt and pepper to taste. Serve with oatcakes.

Two or three leeks, sliced, may be added with the greens.

KILMENY KAIL

(*Fife*)

Rabbit, pickled pork, greens, salt, water.

Take a rabbit, clean it well, and cut it into pieces. Put them into a pot with a piece of pickled pork and sufficient cold water to cover them. Take two heads of greens, pick down with the fingers, and wash free from sand. Add to the broth and boil for three hours. If the pork is very salt, do not add more salt. Serve with oatcakes.

DISHES OF FISH

TO DRESS A COD'S HEAD AND SHOULDERS
(Scots Fashion)

(Meg Dods's Recipe)

Cod, lobster, oysters, eggs, bread-crumbs, lemon, pepper,
salt, flour, butter, parsley, vinegar, stock, Madeira or sherry.

This was a great affair in its day. It is still a formidable, nay
even a respectable-looking dish, with a kind of bulky magnificence which appears imposing at the head of a long board.
Have a quart of good stock ready for the sauce, made of beef
or veal, seasoned with onion, carrot, and turnip. Rub the
fish with salt over night, taking off the scales, but do not wash
it. When to be dressed wash it clean, then quickly dash hot
water over the upper side, and with a blunt knife remove the
slime which will ooze out, taking great care not to break the
skin. Do the same to the other side of the fish; then place it
on the strainer, wipe it clean, and plunge it into a turbot-kettle
of boiling water with a handful of salt and a half-pint of vinegar.
It must be entirely covered, and will take from thirty to forty
minutes' slow boiling. Set it to drain, slide it carefully on a
deep dish, and glaze with beat yolks of eggs, over which strew
fine bread-crumbs, grated lemon-peel, pepper, and salt. Stick
numerous bits of butter over the fish and set it before a clear
fire, strewing more crumbs, lemon-peel, and minced parsley
over it and basting with the butter. In the meanwhile thicken
the stock with butter kneaded in flour and strain it, adding to
it half a hundred oysters nicely picked and bearded, and a
glassful of their liquor, two glasses of Madeira or sherry, the
juice of a lemon, the hard meat of a boiled lobster cut down,
104

Dishes of Fish

and the soft part pounded. Boil this sauce for five minutes
and skim it well; wipe clean the edges of the dish in which
the fish is crisping, and pour the half of the sauce around it,
serving the rest in a tureen. Garnish with fried oysters, small
fried flounders, and pickled samphire, or slices of lemon.

" Cod's head is also dressed with brown sauce made of the stock with butter nicely
browned, and a little mushroom-catsup. This sauce is generally made more piquant
than white, by the addition of a few boned anchovies."—M. D.

This Scotch mode of dressing cod is nearly the same as the French *Cabillaud à la
Sainte Menehould*, only the cod is then stuffed with either meat or fish forcemeat.
Cod may be parboiled and finished in the oven with the above sauce. Oysters, mussels,
or cockles may supply the place of lobster.—F. M. McN.

CABBIE-CLAW

" Cod-fish salted for a short time and not dried in the manner
of common salt fish,[1] and boiled with parsley and horse-radish.
They eat it with egg-sauce, and it is extremely luscious and
palatable."—An anonymous English visitor to Edinburgh at the
end of the eighteenth century.

I have been unable to find precise details of this old Scottish dish. The fish was
probably wind-blown in the traditional manner. See p. 118.—F. M. McN.

" Cod-fish served with horse-radish and egg-sauce."—Rogers.

TO DRESS AND KEEP DRY SALTED TUSK, LING,[2] OR COD FISH

(*Mrs. Dalgairns' Recipe*)

Cut in square bits, or put one large piece in water overnight;
wash it clean in fresh water, and put it on to boil in cold for
one hour and a half; then cool the water, so that the fish may
be easily handled; take it out of the saucepan and pick out the
loose bones and scrape it clean without taking off the skin.
Put it on in boiling water, and if the fish is too fresh add a little
salt with it and let it boil gently from one hour to one and a
half. The very thick part will take this time, the thin bits less,

[1] In the Shetland dialect, a young cod is a *kabbilow*. Cf. Fr. *cabillaud* and
Dutch *kabeljaauw*.—F. M. McN.

[2] There is a Gaelic saying that ling would be the beef of the sea if it had always
salt enough, butter enough, and boiling enough.

to dress. When dished, garnish with hard-boiled eggs and parsley.

Plain boiled parsnips and a butter tureen of egg sauce are served with it.[1]

When the fish is put on the second time some people prefer boiling it in milk and water. To keep any of this sort of fish for winter use it ought to be cut or sawed in pieces, and when perfectly dry, laid in a small cask or wooden box with oatmeal, oatmeal seeds, or malt dust between each layer.

DRIED FISH PUDDING

(*Mrs. Dalgairns' Recipe*)

Fish, potatoes, milk, butter.

Boil the fish, take off the skin and take out the bones, pound it, and add to it an equal quantity of mashed potatoes moistened with good milk and a bit of butter;[2] put it in a dish, smooth it with a knife, and stick here and there little bits of butter and brown it in a Dutch oven; serve it with egg sauce.

HADDOCKS .IN BROWN SAUCE
(An Excellent Scots Dish)

Haddies, caller haddies,
Fresh an' loupin' in the creel!
—*Old Edinburgh Street Cry.*

(*Meg Dods's Recipe*)

Clean, cut off the heads, tails, and fins, and skin from six to eight middle-sized haddocks.[3] Take the heads, tails, and trimmings, with two or three of the fish cut down, and boil them in a quart of water or broth, with a couple of onions, some

---

[1] In Morayshire, dried fish were served with home-made mustard, the seeds, freshly gathered in the cottage garden, being pounded in a mortar.

[2] A teaspoonful or more of made mustard may be added.—F. M. McN.

[3] " A January haddock an' a February hen
Are no' to be marrowed in the ither months ten."
—*A Morayshire Saying.*

sweet herbs, and a piece of lemon-peel; thicken with plenty of butter and browned flour, and season highly with mixed spices and mushroom catsup; strain the sauce, and when it boils and is skimmed, put in the fish cut into neat pieces, and, if you choose, previously browned in the frying-pan. If there be too little sauce, add some good beef-gravy; put in, if you like, a quarter-hundred of oysters and a glass of their liquor, or some mussels and a little wine. Take out the fish, when ready, with a slice, and pour the sauce, which should be brown, smooth, and thick, around them.

CRAPPIT HEIDS[1]

Formerly a favourite supper dish all over Scotland. It is mentioned in *Guy Mannering*. Called also *Stappit Heids*.

"Run up to Miss Napier's upo' the Squaur, and say I wad be sair obleeged till her gin she wad len' me that fine receipt o' hers for crappit heids."
—George MacDonald: *Robert Falconer*.

(Meg Dods's Recipe)

Heads of haddocks, forcemeat.

The original Scotch farce was simply oatmeal, minced suet or butter, pepper, salt, and onions made into a coarse forcemeat for stuffing the heads of haddocks and whitings. Modern crappit heads are farced with the fleshy parts of a boiled lobster or crab, minced, a boned anchovy, the chopped yolk of an egg, grated bread or pounded biscuit, white pepper, salt, cayenne, a large piece of butter broken down into bits, with beat eggs to bind, and a little oyster liquor. A plainer and perhaps as suitable stuffing may be made of the roe of haddock or cod parboiled, skinned, and minced, mixed with double its bulk of pounded rusks or bread-crumbs, a good piece of butter, shred parsley, and seasonings, with an egg to cement the forcemeat. Place the crappit or stuffed heads on end in the bottom of a buttered stew-pan, pour the fish-soup gently over them, cover and boil a half-hour.

[1] "To *crap*: to fill, to stuff. Teut. *kroppen*."—Jamieson.

CRAPPIT HEIDS [1]

(Isle of Lewis)

"A sort of piscatorial haggis."—Hislop's *Scottish Anecdotes.*

The heads and livers of fresh haddocks, oatmeal, pepper, salt, milk.

Take half a dozen haddock heads and livers. Chop the livers, which must be perfectly fresh, mix them with an equal quantity of raw oatmeal, add pepper and salt, and bind with milk. Stuff the heads with this mixture, and boil them with the fish. The liquor makes good stock for fish soup.

A similar stuffing is made with cods' livers, but the body, not the head, is stuffed, through the gullet.

Some Shetland fish-liver dishes

Haggamuggi. The stomach of a fish filled with hashed livers and sunds (air-bladders) and boiled.

Krampus. Sillock livers melted in a frying-pan and mixed with bere burston.[2]

Kroppen. Fish liver and meal thoroughly mixed and seasoned, stuffed into a fish head, and boiled. Cf. *Crappit Heids.*

Krus, or *Liver-krus.* A piece of dough (oatmeal and water, with a pinch of salt) made in the shape of a cruse (small earthenware bowl), filled with livers, and baked on the hearth. Cf. *Cropadeu.*

Liver-flakki. "Two speldit, suket piltiks,[2] laid together with livers between them, and roasted on the hearth."

Mugildens. "Piltiks or silliks roasted with their livers inside them."

Sangster. "A *brüni* (bannock) made of sillik livers and bere burston."[2]

—From *A Glossary of the Shetland Dialect,* by J. S. Angus.

CROPADEU [4]

Oatmeal, water, haddock liver.

Take oatmeal and water, make a dumplin; put in the middle a haddock's liver, season it well with pepper and salt; boil it well in a cloth as you do an apple dumplin. The liver dissolves in the oatmeal and eats very fine.

---

[1] This is an Hebridean version of Crappit Heids. The livers make a rich and nourishing stuffing. In Shetland, where they are much used, a special utensil called a pannabrad (Isl. *panna,* kettle, and *brad,* melting) is used for melting fish livers, and the oil obtained is stored for winter use.

[2] See p. 203.   [3] See *Wind-blown Fish,* Note, p. 118.

[4] A Scots dish from Mrs. Glasse's *Art of Cookery* (Edinburgh, 1781).

COD-LIVER BANNOCK
(Bonnach Grùan)
(Isle of Barra)

A cod's liver, pepper, salt, baking-soda.

Take the liver of a fair-sized cod, fresh from the sea, and let it lie overnight in salted water. Mince roughly, or, better, tear up with the fingers, removing all the stringy bits. Mix in a bowl with a tablespoonful of oatmeal, add a pinch of baking soda, and season with pepper and salt. Form into a bannock (a flat round), put it on a plate, and place in a pot of boiling water. Put the fish over it, and let it cook slowly till ready. Or the cod's gullet may be stuffed with the mixture.

In Skye this dish is called *Bonnach Donn* (Brown Bannock). A recipe obtained there adds " a small onion chopped ", but omits baking-soda, and the liver is not steeped overnight, but merely washed well.

TO SMOKE FINNAN[1] OR ABERDEEN HADDOCKS

(Mrs. Dalgairns' Recipe)

Clean the haddocks thoroughly and split them, take off the heads, put some salt on them, and let them lie two hours, or all night, if they are required to keep more than a week; then, having hung them two or three hours in the open air to dry, smoke them in a chimney over peat or hardwood sawdust.

" When kept above twenty-four hours, they lose much of their delicacy."
—Meg Dods.

" A Finnan haddock dried over the smoke of the sea-weed and sprinkled with salt-water during the process, acquires a relish of a very peculiar and delicate flavour, inimitable on any other coast than that of Aberdeenshire. Some of our Edinburgh philosophers tried to produce their equal in vain. I was one of a party at a dinner where the philosophical haddocks were placed in competition with the genuine Finnan-fish. These were served round without distinction whence they came; but only one gentleman out of twelve present espoused the cause of philosophy."
—Sir Walter Scott: Note to Boswell's *Tour to the Hebrides.*

[1] Finnan or Findon Haddocks are so named from a hamlet in Kincardineshire, about six miles south from Aberdeen.

When there is not a chimney suitable for the purpose they may be done in an old cask open at both ends, into which put some sawdust with a red-hot iron in the midst; place rods of wood across the top of the cask, tie the haddocks by the tail in pairs, and hang them on the sticks to smoke; the heat should be kept as equal as possible, as it spoils the fish to get alternately hot and cold; when done, they should be of a fine yellow colour, which they should acquire in twelve hours at furthest. When they are to be drest, the skin must be taken off. They may be boiled or broiled, and are generally used for breakfast.

TO DRESS SMOKED HADDOCKS

(From an old coverless book on Cottage Cookery)

Findon, Aberdeen, and St. Andrews highly-smoked split haddocks: broil over or cook in front of a quick clear fire; when ready rub butter well into them and serve piping hot.

Arbroath and Auchmittie highly-smoked closed haddocks: heat on both sides, open them out, take out the backbone, spread with butter, close up, place in the oven a few minutes, and serve.

Eyemouth and Montrose lightly-smoked haddocks: cook in a frying-pan with bacon or smoked pork and a little water, with a lid on to keep in the steam.

(Another way)

Skin a Finnan haddock and cut it into pieces. Lay these in a stew-pan with a dessertspoonful of butter. Put on the lid closely and steam for five minutes. Now break a teaspoonful of cornflour with a little milk and add more milk—about a breakfast-cupful in all. Pour over the fish and butter, bring it to the boil, and boil for a minute. Take out the pieces of fish, lay them nicely on a dish, and pour the sauce over them.

TO FRY HERRINGS
(Scots Fashion)

Wha 'll buy my caller herrin'?
They 're bonnie fish and dainty fairin'.
Wha 'll buy my caller herrin',
   New drawn frae the Forth?
          —Lady Nairne: *Caller Herrin'* [1].

Fresh herring, oatmeal, pepper, salt, dripping.

Cleanse and dry the herrings. Sprinkle with pepper and salt
and toss on coarse oatmeal on a sheet of kitchen paper until
they are thoroughly coated. An ounce of oatmeal and the
same quantity of dripping should be allowed for every two herrings. Put the dripping in a frying-pan and when smoking hot
put in the herrings and brown them nicely on both sides. They
should be ready in ten minutes. Drain them on paper, place
on an ashet, and serve very hot. They may be garnished with
parsley and cut lemon.

(Another way)

Split and bone the herrings, flatten them with care, and
proceed exactly as above. Cook for five minutes.

POTTED HERRING

Though the casual Govan herring
Warns us by a sense unerring
That the dead need but interring—
   Pisces Benedicte.

Taken fresh and all unspotted,
Rolled in vinegar and potted,
O, it tickles the parotid—
   Pisces Benedicte.
        —Parvus [2] (in Glasgow University Magazine):
              Sistetie to Fish.

*Fresh herring, salt, pepper, peppercorns, bay leaves (or
mace or cloves), vinegar, water.*

---

[1] The old cry " Caller Herrin'!" rang for centuries through the streets of Edinburgh. The Newhaven fish-wives in their picturesque garb still ply their wares in
the residential quarters of the city, but the cry is rarely heard.
[2] Major Walter Elliot, M.P.

Cleanse, split, and bone six fresh herrings. Sprinkle them with salt and pepper, and roll up inside out, beginning at the tail. Pack them neatly into a small pie-dish and pour over them a teacupful of vinegar and water mixed in equal quantities. The fish should be just covered. Add a dozen black peppercorns and two bay leaves (or three cloves or three blades of mace if preferred). Bake for about forty-five minutes in a moderate oven.[1]

PICKLED HERRING

(*Mrs. Dalgairns' Recipe*)

Salt herring, onions, brown sugar, pepper, salt, vinegar.

Take half a dozen Lochfyne herring out of brine. Split them down the back and soak them in cold water overnight. In the morning clean them nicely and cut them crosswise into strips of half an inch in width. Put them into a deep dish with six onions sliced thin. Sprinkle them with pepper and salt and three tablespoonfuls of brown sugar. Pour on enough vinegar to cover them. They will be ready to use in time for supper, and will keep for a week or more in a cool place.

TO KIPPER HERRING

(*Traditional Recipe*)

Kippers are taken while fresh, and split up. They are then cleaned and thrown into vats with plenty of salt, where they are allowed to lie for a few minutes. Finally they are spread out on tenterhooks or racks, and hung up for eight hours' smoking.

To Dry Herring without Salt (Old Hebridean Method). " The Natives preserve and dry their Herring without Salt, for the space of eight months, provided they be taken after the tenth of September; they use no other art in it, but take out their Guts, and then, tying a rush about their Necks, hang them by pairs upon a rope made of Heath, cross a House, and they eat well, and free from Putrefaction."
    —Martin: *Description of the Western Islands* (1703).

[1] Mrs. McIver (1773) says: Pot herring for four hours in a slow oven.

Dishes of Fish

TO DRESS RED HERRINGS, SARDINIAS, AND BUFFED (PICKLED) HERRINGS

(*Meg Dods's Recipe*)

Red herrings, oil or butter.

Skin, open, and trim red herrings. If old and dry, pour some hot small beer or water over them and let them steep a half-hour, or longer if hard. Broil them over a clear fire at a considerable distance, or before the fire; rub them with good oil or fresh butter while broiling, and rub on a little more when they are served. Serve them very hot with cold butter, or with melted butter and mustard, and mashed potatoes or parsnips.

" Steep pickled herrings from one to two days and nights, changing the water if they be very salt. Hang them up on a stick pushed through the eyes, and broil them when wanted. These are called *buffed* herrings in Scotland, and are used at breakfast or supper."—M. D.

TATTIES AN' HERRIN'

(*Old Cottage Dish*)

Salt herring, potatoes, water.

Fill a three-legged pot nearly full with peeled or unpeeled potatoes. Half-fill it with water. Wash some salt herring and lay them on the top of the potatoes. Cover close, bring to the boil, and hang high on the chain over a peat fire for an hour or till ready.

This dish may be allowed to simmer gently in an ordinary pot at the side of an ordinary range.

FRIAR'S FISH-IN-SAUCE

(*Meg Dods's Recipe*)

Red or other trout, or carp, or perch; salt, mixed spices, onions, cloves, mace, black and Jamaica peppercorns, claret or Rhenish wine, anchovy, lemon, cayenne, flour, butter, stock.

Clean the fish very well; if large, they may be divided or split. Rub them inside with salt and mixed spices. Lay them in the stew-pan and put in nearly as much good stock as will cover them, with a couple of onions and four cloves stuck in them, some Jamaica and black peppercorns, and a bit of mace; and when the fish have stewed a few minutes, a couple of glasses of claret or Rhenish wine, a boned anchovy, the juice of a lemon, and a little cayenne. Take up the fish carefully when ready, and keep them hot. Thicken the sauce with butter kneaded in browned flour; add a little mushroom catsup and a few pickled oysters, if approved: the sauce, though less piquant, is more delicate without catsup. Having skimmed and strained, pour it over the fish.

TO BOIL SALMON

(*Meg Dods's Recipe*)

Scale or clean the fish without any unnecessary washing or handling, and without cutting it too much open. Have a roomy and well-scoured fish-kettle, and if the salmon be very large and thick, when you have placed it on the strainer and in the kettle, fill up and amply cover it with cold spring water, that it may heat gradually. If only a jole or quarter is boiled, it may be put in with warm water. In both cases take off the scum carefully, and let the fish boil slowly, allowing ten minutes to the pound; if the piece is not heavier than five or six pounds, then the time must be less; but it is even more difficult to fix the time that fish should boil than the length of time that meat requires. Experience, and those symptoms which the eye of a practised cook alone can discern, must fix the point, and nothing is more disgusting and unwholesome than underdone fish. It may be probed. The minute the boiling of any fish is completed, the fish-strainer must be lifted and rested across the pan, to drain the fish. Throw a soft cloth or flannel in several folds over it. It would become soft if permitted to soak in the hot water. Dish on a hot fish-plate with a napkin under.

" Besides the essences to be used at discretion, which are now found on every sideboard of any pretension, shrimp, anchovy and lobster sauce are served with salmon; also plain melted butter; and where the fish is got fresh, and served in what is esteemed by some as the greatest perfection—crisp, curdy, and creamy— it is the practice to send up a sauce tureen of the plain liquor in which it was boiled.

Fennel and butter are still heard of for salmon, but are nearly obsolete. Sliced cucumber is often served with salmon, and indeed with all boiled fish. Mustard is considered an improvement to salmon when over-ripe—beginning to spoil, in short; salmon may then be boiled with horse-radish. *Garnish* with a fringe of curled green parsley and slices of lemon. The carver must help a slice of the thick part with a smaller one of the thin, which is the fattest and the best liked by those in the secret. *Carême* skins salmon—a bad practice."—M. D.

" A kettle of fish is a *fête-champêtre* of a particular kind, which is to other fête-champêtres what the piscatory eclogues of Brown or Sannazario are to pastoral poetry. A large caldron is boiled by the side of a salmon river, containing a quantity of water, thickened with salt to the consistence of brine. In this the fish is plunged when taken, and eaten by the company *fronde super viridi*. This is accounted the best way of eating salmon by those who desire to taste the fish in a state of extreme freshness. Others prefer it after being kept a day or two, when the curd melts into oil, and the fish becomes richer and more luscious. The more judicious gastronomes eat no other sauce than a spoonful of the water in which the salmon has been boiled, together with a little pepper and vinegar."—Scott: *St. Ronan's Well*, Note.

Scene: The Parlour, Tibbie Shield's Inn, Selkirkshire, 1834.

" *Shepherd*: Tibbie was for cuttin't in twa cuts, but I like to a sawmon served up in its integrity.

" *Tickler*: And each slice should run from gill to tail.

" *Shepherd*: Alang the shouthers and the back and the line, in that latitude, for the thick; and alang the side and the belly and the line, in that latitude, for the thin; but nae short-curd till in the mouth. . . . The kyeanne pepper—the mustard—the vinegar—the catshop—the Harvey sass—the yest—the chovies! Thank ye, Dolly, my dear. Mair butter, Tickler. North—put the mashed potatoes on the part o' my plate near the saut—and the roond anes a bit ayont. Tappy—the breid; and meanwhile, afore yokin' to our sawmon, what say ye, sirs, to a bottle o' porter?"
—Christopher North: *Noctes Ambrosianae*.

TO KIPPER SALMON

(*Meg Dods's Recipe*)

Salmon, salt, sugar, saltpetre.

The fish must be cut up at the back, cleaned, and scaled but not washed, and have the bone taken neatly out. Rub with equal proportions of salt and Brazil or fine raw sugar, with a little saltpetre.[1] Let the fish lie for two days, pressing it with a board on which weights are placed, then hang it up,[2] or, what is much better, smoke it. Lest the folds gather mustiness and spoil, it is a good plan, when the fish is hung, to stretch it open

---

[1] Say half an ounce of saltpetre to a handful of salt and one of sugar.

[2] Where the sun will not strike upon it. It will be fit for use in two days. Sprinkle with pepper and broil.—F. M. McN.

with pieces of stick that it may dry equally. Peppers in powder may be added to the salt.[1] This forms a favourite addition to a Scotch breakfast, and nothing indeed can be more relishing than fresh kipper, though it soon hardens. Kipper is generally dressed by cutting it into slices and broiling, though we have seen it fried. If long hung the slices may be soaked in water a quarter of an hour, which will soften and improve the quality of the fish. If the fresh fish is very large and rich it may be rubbed with salt and drained for a day before it gets the final salting.

" These fish, dried in the turf smoke of their cabins, or shielings, formed a savoury addition to the mess of potatoes, mixed with onions, which was a principal part of their winter food."—Scott: *Guy Mannering*.

" A salmon-bone, with some rough pickings left, makes an admirable *devil*. The bone cut out of a kippered salmon should be left rough for this purpose. Seasoned with pepper and salt, broiled and buttered, it is quite an epicure's breakfast morsel."
—Meg Dods.

PICKLED SALMON

(*Mrs. Dalgairns' Recipe*)

Salmon, pepper, salt, allspice, mace, vinegar, water, sweet oil.

Cut the salmon into pieces, boil it as for eating, and lay it on a dry cloth until the following day. Boil two quarts of good vinegar with one of the liquor the fish was boiled in, one ounce of whole black pepper, half an ounce of allspice, and four blades of mace. Put the salmon into something deep and pour over it the prepared vinegar when cold. A little sweet oil put upon the top will make it keep a twelvemonth.

SPICED SALMON

(*Mrs. Dalgairns' Recipe*)

Salmon, salt, pepper, cinnamon, vinegar, water.

Mix together, in the proportion of one-third of salt and water to one pint of vinegar, one ounce of whole black pepper, and one ounce of cinnamon. Cut the salmon into slices and boil

[1] " Use plenty of black pepper," says another old recipe.

it in this; when cold pack it close in a pan and pour over it
the liquor it was boiled in, with the spices, so as to cover it
completely; cover the pan closely to exclude the air.

POTTED SALMON ROE

(*Old Tweedside Recipe*)

Salmon roe, milk, water, salt, saltpetre, spirit of nitre, lard.

Take the roe from a fish as nearly spawning as possible.
Wash the roe well in milk-and-water, and then in cold water,
till it come clean off. Afterwards put the roe in a sieve and
drain fifteen minutes. To salt them take eight ounces of salt
to three pounds of spawn and let them lie in the brine forty-
eight hours. Lay them on a board about three-fourths of a
yard from the fire, letting them remain there about half a day.
Bruise them well with a roller, then put them into a pot and
press them well down. Put on them in the proportion of eight
drops of spirit of nitre and as much saltpetre as will lie upon
a sixpence to every pound of spawn. Cover them with a piece
of writing-paper upon which lay a coating of hog's lard as cold
as it will spread, then tie over all a piece of dressed sheep-
skin, and keep in a warm place summer and winter.

SALMON FRITTERS

(*Mrs. Dalgairns' Recipe*)

Salmon, potatoes, cream, egg, lard or beef dripping.

Cut small some cold boiled salted salmon; pound some
boiled potatoes, moistened with cream and the yolk of an egg
beaten; mix them together and make it into small fritters and
fry them of a light brown in fresh lard or beef dripping; serve
them with hard-boiled eggs, cut in quarters. For sauce, melt
two ounces of butter with a little cream and flour mixed, and
add, when it is hot, a dessertspoonful of soy and two of mushroom catsup.

WHITINGS IN THE SCOTS WAY

(*Lady Harriet St. Clair's Recipe*)

Whitings, flour, butter, parsley, green onions or chives, broth, cream.

Choose small, perfectly fresh fish; rub them in flour till it adheres; lay them in a frying-pan with a good bit of butter; sauté them very slowly. They should not be dry or coloured. Mince some parsley and green onions or chives very finely; put them into some good broth and about two tablespoonfuls of cream; mix it well together and pour it over the whitings before they are quite finished cooking; move them about very gently, not to break them, till they are done. They are very delicate and excellent done in this way, which, though simple, requires great care. No butter should be used but what is required to fire them.

WIND-BLOWN FISH

(*Traditional Method*)

Obtain the fish as fresh as possible, clean and skin them, take out the eyes, cover the fish over with salt, immediately after which take them out and shake off the superfluous salt, pass a string through the eye-holes, and hang them up to dry in a passage, or some place where there is a current of air; the next morning take them off, just roll them lightly in a little flour, broil them gently over a slow fire, and serve very hot, with a small piece of fresh butter rubbed over each, or serve quite dry, if preferable.

" Of all the modes of preparing and dressing whitings for breakfast I cannot but admire and prize the system pursued by the Scotch, which renders them the most light, wholesome, and delicious food that could possibly be served for breakfast."
—A. Soyer.

The small whiting, hung up with its skin on, and broiled without being rubbed in flour, is excellent. *Rizzard haddocks* are prepared in much the same manner,

Dishes of Fish

but are usually sprinkled with salt inside and outside, and allowed to lie thus for twelve hours before being hung up in the open air, preferably in the wind and always out of the sun. A wooden frame, called a *hake*, is used for drying fishes. In Orkney cuiths [1] (which in Shetland they call piltocks and in the Hebrides cuddies) are prepared in this way, care being taken that the fish are perfectly fresh, newly gutted, and thoroughly cleaned, and that the salt is rubbed well in along the bone from which the guts have been removed. They may be either boiled or brandered—if boiled, they are eaten with butter, melted. They are particularly good with buttered bere bannocks or wheaten meal scones and tea.—F. M. McN.

TO DRY SILLOCKS

(*Orkney and Shetland*)

Sillocks are the fry of the saith or coal-fish (a variety of cod). Clean the fish, wash them well in salt water, and hang them up in bunches outside. Leave them till they are quite hard. They are eaten uncooked, and are very popular with the school-bairns of Ultima Thule as a relish with their midday " piece " of oatcake or bere bannock.

LOBSTER, HAUT GOÛT

(*Supplied to the Cleikum Club by H. Jekyl, Esq.*)

Lobster, white pepper, cayenne, mace, cloves, nutmeg, salt, gravy, butter, soy or walnut catsup or vinegar, red wine.

Pick the firm meat from a parboiled lobster or two and take also the inside, if not thin and watery. Season highly with white pepper, cayenne, pounded mace, and cloves, nutmeg, and salt. Take a little well-flavoured gravy—for example, the jelly of roast veal—a few tiny bits of butter, a spoonful of soy or walnut catsup, or of any favourite flavoured vinegar, and a spoonful of red wine. Stew the cut lobster in this sauce for a few minutes.

" This is one of those delicate messes which the gourmand loves to cook for himself in a silver dish held over a spirit-lamp, or in a silver stew-pan; the preparation of the morsel being to him the better part of it."—H. J.

[1] The coal-fish in its second season.

PARTAN PIE

(*Meg Dods's Recipe*)

Partan (crab), salt, white pepper, nutmeg, butter, bread, vinegar, mustard (optional).

Pick the meat out of the claws and body; clean the shell nicely and return the meat into it, first seasoned with salt, white pepper, and nutmeg; with a few bits of fresh butter and some bread-crumbs. A half-glass of vinegar, beat and heated up with a little made mustard, may be added, and a small quantity of salad-oil substituted for the butter. Brown the meat when laid in the shell with a salamander.

OYSTERS STEWED IN THEIR OWN JUICE
(Scots Fashion)

Come prie,[1] frail man, for gin [2] thou 'rt sick,
The oyster is a rare cathartic
As ever doctor patient gart [3] lick
To cure his ails;
Whether you ha'e the head or heart ache,
It aye prevails.
—R. Fergusson.

(*Lady Harriet St. Clair's Recipe*)

Oysters, salt.

This is an excellent method of dressing them. Take the largest you can get; wash them clean through their own juice; lay them close together in a frying-pan; sprinkle them with a little salt. Do not put one above another. Make them a fine brown on both sides. If one pan is not sufficient, do off more. When they are all done, pour some of their liquor into the pan, mixing it with any that may be left from their cooking. Let it boil for a minute or two. Pour it over the oysters and serve very hot.

[1] Taste.　　　[2] If.　　　[3] Caused.

LIMPET STOVIES

(Isle of Colonsay)

Limpets, potatoes, water, pepper, salt, butter.

Gather two quarts of limpets on the rocks at low tide. Put them in a pot, cover them with water, and bring to the boil. Take out the limpets, remove them from the shells, and remove the eyes and the sandy trail. Take three times their quantity of peeled potatoes, put a layer in the bottom of a large round three-legged pot, add a layer of limpets, season with pepper and a little salt, and repeat the operation until they are all used up. Then add two cupfuls of the liquor in which the limpets were scalded and put pieces of butter over the top, using about half a pound for that quantity. Cover it all with a clean white cloth well rolled in round the edges, bring to the boil, and hang it high up on the crook above a peat-fire. Let it simmer slowly for at least an hour.

The contributor of the above recipe, who is a native of Colonsay, writes: " I have never seen or heard of the above but in Colonsay, nor have I tasted anything better. They also used to have a dish of fancy seaweed, but the recipe was a secret. I never found out, but a Colonsay woman used to make it for some club in Edinburgh."

" The Limpet being parboil'd in a very little quantity of water, the Broth is drank to increase Milk in Nurses, and likewise when the Milk proves astringent to the Infants. The Broth of the Black Periwinkle is used in the same cases. It is observed that limpets being frequently eaten in June, are apt to occasion the Jaundice. . . . The tender yellow part of the Limpet which is next to the Shell, is reckoned good nourishment and very easie of digestion."

—Martin: *Description of the Western Islands* (1703)

DISHES OF GAME AND POULTRY

TO ROAST RED DEER OR ROE

(An Old Holyrood Recipe,[1] supplied to the Cleikum Club by P. Winterblossom, Esq.)

> *Venison, spices, claret, vinegar or lemons, butter, walnut catsup.*

Season the haunch highly by rubbing it well with mixed spices. Soak it for six hours in claret and a quarter-pint of the best vinegar or the fresh juice of three lemons; turn it frequently and baste with the liquor. Strain the liquor in which the venison was soaked; add to it fresh butter melted, and with this baste the haunch during the whole time it is roasting. Fifteen minutes before the roast is drawn remove the paper, baste with butter, and dredge lightly with flour to froth and brown it.

For sauce.—Take the contents of the dripping-pan, which will be very rich and highly flavoured, and a half-pint of clear brown gravy, drawn from venison or full-aged heath mutton. Boil them up together, skim, add a teaspoonful of walnut catsup, and pour the same round the roast. Instead of the walnut catsup, lemon juice or any of the flavoured vinegars most congenial to venison, and to the taste of the gastronome, may advantageously be substituted.

---

[1] " This was one of those original receipts on which our old beau plumed himself not a little. This mode of dressing venison, he said, had been invented by the Master of the Kitchen to Mary of Guise, and had been ever since preserved a profound secret by the noble family of M——, till the late Earl communicated it to himself."—*Annals of the Cleikum Club.*

TO FRY VENISON COLLOPS

(Supplied to the Cleikum Club by P. Winterblossom, Esq.).

Venison, gravy, lemon or orange, claret, pepper, salt, cayenne, nutmeg.

Cut oblong slices from the haunch, or slices neatly trimmed from the neck or loin. Have a gravy, drawn from the bones and trimmings, ready thickened with butter rolled in lightly browned flour. Strain into a small stew-pan, boil, and add a squeeze of lemon or orange and a small glass of claret, pepper to taste, a saltspoonful of salt, the size of a pin's head of cayenne, and a scrape of nutmeg. Fry and dish the collops hot, and pour this sauce over them.

" A still higher goût may be imparted to this sauce by eschalot wine, basil wine, or Tarragon vinegar, chosen as may suit the taste of the eater. If those flavours are not liked, some old venison-eaters may relish a very little pounded fine sugar and vinegar in the gravy, and currant jelly may be served in a sweetmeat glass. Garnish with fried crumbs. This is a very excellent way of dressing venison, particularly when it is not fat enough to roast well."—P. W.

" The learned in cookery dissent from the Baron of Bradwardine, and hold the roe venison dry and indifferent food, unless when dressed in soup and Scotch collops."
—Scott: *Waverley*, Note

VENISON PASTY

" The princely venison pasty."—Scott: *Old Mortality*.

(Meg Dods's Recipe)

Venison, gravy, pepper, salt, mace, allspice, claret or port, eschalot vinegar, onions (optional), pastry.

A modern pasty is made of what does not roast well, as the neck, the breast, the shoulder. The breast makes a good pasty. Cut into little chops, trimming off all bones and skins. Make some good gravy from the bones and other trimmings. Place fat and lean pieces of the meat together, or, if very lean, place thin slices from the firm fat of a leg or a neck of mutton along with each piece. Season the meat with pepper, salt, pounded mace, and allspice. Place it handsomely in a dish and put in the drawn gravy, a quarter-pint of claret or port, a glassful of eschalot vinegar, and, if liked, a couple of onions very finely shred. Cover the dish with a thick crust.

VENISON PASTY CRUST

Flour, butter, eggs, hot water.

Make a paste in the proportion of two pounds of flour to more than a pound of butter, with six beat eggs and hot water. Roll it out three times, double it, and the last time let the part intended for the top crust remain pretty thick.

"This is a dish in which ornament is not only allowable but is actually expected. The paste decorations are, however, matters of fancy. Before the pasty is served, if the meat be lean, more sauce made of a little red wine, gravy, mixed spices, and the juice of a lemon, may be put in hot. A common fault of venison pasty is being over-done. An hour and a half in a moderate oven is fully sufficient for baking an ordinary-sized pasty—an hour will do for a small one."—M. D.

VENISON SAUCES

Venison may have a sweet, a sharp, or a savoury sauce.

(Meg Dods's Recipes)

Sharp Sauce.—A quarter-pound of the best loaf-sugar, or white candy-sugar, dissolved in a half-pint of Champagne vinegar, and carefully skimmed.

Sweet Sauce.—Melt some white or red currant jelly with a glass of white or red wine, whichever suits best in colour; or serve jelly unmelted in a small sweetmeat-glass. This sauce answers well for hare, fawn, or kid, and for roast mutton to many tastes.

Gravy for Venison.—Make a pint of gravy of trimmings of venison or shanks of mutton thus: broil the meat on a quick fire till it is browned, then stew it slowly. Skim, strain, and serve the gravy it yields, adding salt and a teaspoonful of walnut pickle.

DEER HAGGIS

(From the Kitchen of a Highland Chief)

Deer's heart, liver, and suet, coarse oatmeal, onions, black pepper, salt, paste.

Boil the heart and a piece of the liver of a deer. When cold, mince the heart very fine and grate a teacupful of the liver. To these add a teacupful of coarse oatmeal, previously toasted in the oven or before the fire, three finely chopped onions, a tablespoonful of salt, and a strong seasoning of black pepper. Mix all well together. Put into a pudding-basin, cover with paste as for a beef-steak pudding, and boil for four hours. Serve in the basin, very hot.

TO PREPARE GROUSE

" While nearly all the game-birds are good, and some eminently good, grouse seems to me to be the best, to possess the fullest and at the same time the least violent flavour —to have the best consistency of flesh, and to present the greatest variety of attractions in different parts."—Professor Saintsbury.

Of the varieties of grouse—wood grouse (capercailzie), black grouse, red grouse, and white grouse (ptarmigan)—the red has the most exquisite flavour. It is a native of Scotland and the north of England, and is not to be found elsewhere. It weighs about nineteen ounces, and should hang for from three to ten days, according to its age and the weather.[1] Young birds do not keep so well as old ones. Soft, downy plumes on the breast and under the wings; pointed wings and rounded spurs are signs of youth.

Pluck the birds carefully so as to avoid breaking the delicate skin, do not wash them, but draw and wipe inside and out with a damp cloth.

ROAST GROUSE
(Scots Fashion)

Prepare as directed above. Put an ounce or two of butter, into which you have worked a little lemon-juice, pepper, and salt, into each bird, but not in the crop. Some cooks stuff the birds with red whortleberries or cranberries, which brings out the flavours well and keeps them as moist as butter does. It is essential to avoid dryness. Wrap the birds well with fat bacon and enclose this with greaseproof paper till ten minutes before serving; then remove the wrappings, flour the birds,

[1] " It was the custom of a hospitable friend of mine in Scotland, who was equally good with rod and gun, to keep a supply of grouse hanging till he could accompany them with salmon caught in a river which was by no means a very early opening one, and I never found birds taste better."—Professor Saintsbury.

and brown. Or the bacon and greaseproof paper may be omitted, and the birds basted frequently and freely with butter. The time allotted is twenty to thirty minutes, according to the size and age of the birds. (Pheasant and partridge must be well done, wild duck, solan geese, &c., underdone, but grouse must be removed in the nick of time—neither over nor actually under-done.)

Boil the livers for ten minutes and pound them in a mortar with a little butter, salt, and cayenne, and spread this on pieces of toast large enough to hold a bird. Place this toast under each bird during the last few minutes of roasting, but do not put it into the fat in the pan to get sodden. Serve with fried bread-crumbs, but without gravy in the dish.

The usual accompaniments are chip potatoes, watercress, French beans, mushrooms, and clear gravy. Bread, nut or fruit sauce, and melted butter[1] are also occasionally served. Cranberry or rowan jelly goes very well with grouse, and so do pickled peaches.

ROAST GROUSE À LA ROB ROY

Prepare as above, wrapping each bird in slices of fat bacon and sprigs of heather, to be removed before browning.

THE PROPER SAUCES FOR WILDFOWL

(Mrs. Cleland's Recipe)

Ducks and plover must be roasted very well; the sauce is gravy, crumbs of bread, shalots, and a little claret; season it with pepper and salt.

Partridges and moorfowl must be very well roasted. Their sauce is a little bread boiled in water, a blade of mace, an onion

---

[1] " It must be confessed that the thing is still done (the trimming being actually poured over the birds) in Scotland, where they certainly understand cookery, and where they ought to understand that of grouse in particular. But it seems to me an abomination, and it must be remembered that if Scottish cookery, admirable as it is, has a tendency to sin, that tendency is in the direction of what is delicately called ' richness ', and that this may be an instance. No doubt the counter tendency of the grouse to the original sin of dryness has also to be considered."

—Professor Saintsbury.

stuffed with cloves, a good piece of butter, and a little salt; you may put a little white wine and ketchup in it.

Woodcocks and snipes are roasted well with their guts in them; put toasted bread and beat butter in them; under other fowls put gravy, and about any small birds fried crumbs only.

The proper sauce for venison is claret boiled very thick, with sugar or currant jelly.

MEG MERRILIES STEW

(From " Guy Mannering ")

" Meg, in the meanwhile, went to a great black caldron that was boiling on a fire on the floor, and, lifting the lid, an odour was diffused through the vault which, if the vapours of a witch's caldron could in aught be trusted, promised better things than the hell-broth which such vessels are usually supposed to contain.[1] It was, in fact, the savour of a goodly stew, composed of fowls, hares, partridges, and moor-game, boiled in a large mess with potatoes, onions, and leeks, and from the size of the caldron, appeared to be prepared for half a dozen people at least.

" ' So ye hae eat naethin' a' day?' said Meg, heaving a large portion of this mess into a brown dish, and strewing it savourily with salt and pepper.

" ' Nothing,' answered the dominie, ' scelestissima!—that is —gudewife!'

" ' Hae then,' said she, placing the dish before him; ' there's what will warm your heart. . . . There's been mony a moonlight watch to bring a' that trade thegither,' continued Meg; ' the folks that are to eat that dinner thought little o' your game-laws.' "—Sir Walter Scott.

" To the admirers of good eating, gypsy cookery seems to have little to recommend it. I can assure you, however, that the cook of a nobleman of high distinction, a person who never reads even a novel without an eye to the enlargement of the culinary science, has added to the Almanach des Gourmands a certain Potage à la Meg Merrilies de Derncleugh, consisting of game and poultry of all kinds, stewed with vegetables into a soup, which rivals in savour and richness the gallant messes

[1] In Macbeth, Act IV, Sc. 1, Shakespeare supplies us with a complete recipe for hell-broth in the best manner of the Scottish witches.

of Camacho's wedding, and which the Baron of Bradwardine would certainly have reckoned among the *Epulae lautiores*."—*Blackwood's Magazine*, April, 1817.

" The artist alluded to in this passage is Monsieur Florence, cook to Henry and Charles, late Dukes of Buccleugh, and of high distinction in his profession."
—(Note to *Guy Mannering* in the Border Edition of the Waverley Novels.)

KINGDOM OF FIFE PIE

(*Traditional Recipe*)

*Rabbit, pickled pork, nutmeg, pepper, salt, forcemeat, gravy,
white wine (optional), egg (optional).*

Skin a rabbit, cut it into joints, and let it lie for an hour in cold water. Make a gravy with the carcass and liver. Cut into slices a pound of pickled pork, season with grated nutmeg, pepper, and salt. Make forcemeat balls as below, pack rabbit, pork, and balls into a dish with a sliced hard-boiled egg, if liked, and a teacupful of good gravy. The old recipes advise the addition of three tablespoonfuls of white wine, but this is often omitted. Cover with a puff paste. It is advisable to make three holes in the paste, as a rabbit pie needs plenty of ventilation. Bake for an hour. It may be eaten hot or cold.

FORCEMEAT

*Rabbit liver, bread-crumbs, fat bacon, minced parsley, pepper
and salt, lemon, thyme and grated nutmeg, if liked, egg.*

Mince the liver, chop the bacon, and beat the egg. Mix the dry ingredients and bind with the egg. Form into small balls.

A STOVED HOWTOWDIE, WITH DRAPPIT EGGS

(*Meg Dods's Recipe*)

*Fowl, butter, button onions, spices, herbs (optional), water
or broth, eggs, spinach, gravy.*

Prepare and stuff with forcemeat a young plump fowl.[1] Put it into a yetling concave-bottomed small pot with a close-fitting

[1] " A common and an approved smuggling way of boiling a pullet or howtowdie in Scotland, was in a well-cleaned haggis bag, which must have preserved the juices

lid, with button onions, spices, and at least a quarter-pound of butter. Add herbs, if approved. When the fowl has hardened and been turned, add a half-pint or rather more of boiling water or broth. Fit on the lid very close and set the pot over embers. A cloth may be wrapped round the lid if it is not luted on. An hour will do a small fowl, and so in proportion. Have a little seasoned gravy, in which parboil the liver. Poach nicely in this gravy five or six small eggs. Dress them on flattened balls of spinage round the dish, and serve the fowl, rubbing down the liver to thicken the gravy and liquor in which the fowl was stewed, which pour over it for sauce, skimming it nicely, and serving all very hot.

"This is a very nice small Scotch dish. Mushrooms, oysters, forcemeat balls, &c., may be added to enrich it; and celery may be put to the sauce; the spinage may be and often is omitted. Slices of ham may be served round the fowl, or two young boiled or stewed fowls with a small salted tongue between them will make a nice family dinner dish."—M. D.

ON DRESSING POULTRY

" MEG'S sauce for fowls was either the national ' drappit egg ', egg-sauce, parsley and butter, or, if the fowls were of a dark complexion, liver-sauce, as a veil of their dinginess. TOUCH-WOOD chose celery-sauce for fowls, and oyster-sauce for turkey; JEKYL preferred lemon-sauce, but often enjoined the Nabob. The best sort of stuffing or forcemeat for poultry was the cause of many disputes. MEG long stood out for sweet stuffing for her turkeys, orthodox apple-sauce for her goose, and a sweet pudding in the belly of her sucking pig. After a feud which lasted three days, the belligerents came to a treaty on the old

much better than a cloth. In the days of Popery and good cheer—and they were certainly synonymous, though we do not quite subscribe to the opinion of Dr. Red-gill, that no Presbyterian country can ever attain eminence in Gastronomy—in those days of paternosters and venison pasties, stoups of untaxed clarets and oral con-fession, a pullet so treated was, according to waggish legends, the secret regale provided for Mess John by his fair penitents. *Vide* Allan Ramsay's *Monk and Miller's Wife*, or *Friars of Berwick*; also *Traditions of the Cleikum*, and *Bughtrigg's Wife's Receipt for ' Ane capon stewed in brews '*. Butter, shred onions, and spice were put in the bag along with the fowl, and formed the sauce, or else oysters with their liquor strained."—*Annals of the Cleikum Club.*

(D 994)

basis of the *uti possidetis*, though the best stuffing for boiled or roasted poultry or veal was agreed to be—' Crumbs of stale bread, two parts; suet, marrow, or fresh butter, one part; a little parsley, boiled for a minute, and very finely shred; the quarter of a nutmeg grated, a teaspoonful of lemon-peel, grated, allspice and salt—the whole to be worked up to a proper consistence, with two or three yolks of eggs well beat.' If for roasted or boiled turkey, pickled oysters chopped, ham or tongue grated, and eschalot to taste may be added. MEG's sweet stuffing was made by discarding the parsley, ham, oysters, and tongue, and substituting a large handful of currants, picked, rubbed, and dried, as for puddings."—*Annals of the Gleikum Club.*

SCOTS RABBIT CURRY

(*Meg Dods's Recipe*)

Rabbit, streaky bacon, onions, butter, flour, curry-powder, mushroom-powder, celery (optional), coco-nut (optional), salt and cayenne, stock.

Choose a fat, fresh rabbit. (To test it, examine the kidney.) Cut it into at least twelve pieces; brown these in butter, with onions. When browned, if you wish delicate cookery, pour off the butter and add three-quarters of a pint of well-seasoned stock, one large spoonful of curry-powder and one of flour, six ounces of streaky bacon cut into half-inch cubes, and also half a dozen button onions. Season with a teaspoonful of mushroom-powder. Simmer this slowly for half an hour at least, stirring it. Add what more seasoning you think required, as cayenne, a little tumeric, or some acid. Pile up the pieces of rabbit and pour the sauce, which should be thickish as in all curry dishes, over them. Serve with plain boiled rice in a separate dish.

Fresh coco-nut is an excellent ingredient in mild curries. Rasp and stew it the whole time: we do not like *green* vegetables in curries though they are sometimes used. Mushrooms are an enrichment, celery is good, and onion indispensable

DISHES OF MEAT

HAGGIS

Fair fa' [1] your honest, sonsie [2] face,
Great chieftain o' the pudden race!
Aboon them a' ye tak your place,
    Painch,[3] tripe, or thairm.[4]
Weel are ye wordy o' a grace
    As lang's my airm.
        —Burns: *Ode to a Haggis.*

" In the peasant's home it was set in the centre of the table, all gathering round
with their horn spoons, and it was ' deil tak' the hindmost '."
        —T. F. Henderson: *Old-World Scotland.*

(*Traditional Cottage Recipe*)

*The large stomach bag, the smaller or knight's-hood bag,
the pluck (including lights, liver, and heart), beef suet, oatmeal,
onions, black pepper, salt, water.*

Brown and birstle (dry or toast) a breakfast-cupful of oatmeal
in front of the fire. Clean the great bag thoroughly and soak
it overnight in cold salted water. In the morning put it aside
with the rough side turned out. Wash the small bag and the
pluck and put them on to boil covered with cold water, leaving
the windpipe hanging out over the pot to let out any impurities.
Let them boil for an hour and a half, then take them out and
cut away the pipes and any superfluities of gristle. Mince the
heart and lights, and grate half the liver. (The rest of the
liver is not required.) Put them into a basin with half a pound
of minced suet, one or two finely chopped onions, and the
oatmeal, and season highly with black pepper and salt. Over

---

[1] Good befall.   [2] Comely, pleasant-looking.   [3] Paunch: a variety of tripe.
[4] Intestines: ditto.

the whole pour as much of the liquid in which the pluck was boiled as will make the composition sappy. Fill the great bag rather more than half full, say five-eighths, as it requires plenty of room to swell. Sew it securely and put it into a large pot of hot water (to which half a pint of milk is often added). As soon as it begins to swell, prick it all over with a large needle to prevent its bursting. Boil steadily, without the lid, for three hours. Serve very hot without any garnish.

Should the haggis be made some time before it is wanted, it should be re-heated by being put into a pot of boiling water and allowed to boil, without the lid, for an hour and a half.

The small bag may be omitted.

Haggis in a jar. The haggis may be put into a buttered jar or basin instead of the bag, and steamed for four hours. It should not be too moist.

Haggis-in-the-pan. Both bag and jar may be dispensed with, and the haggis may be cooked like a stew in a saucepan. It has to be stirred occasionally, and kept sufficiently moist to prevent its sticking to the bottom of the pan.

Two or three small haggises may be made in place of one large one by cutting up the great bag, wrapping some of the mixture in each piece and sewing it up. Always allow room to swell.

A little nutmeg or dried herbs may be added if desired, and a pinch of cayenne is to be recommended.

The name haggis is commonly thought to be derived from the French *hachis*, which is the form used by King Jamie's Scottish cook in *The Fortunes of Nigel*. Jamieson, however, derives the word from *hag* (S.), to chop (cf. E. *hack*); and it is very possible that the name was converted into French in the same way that Ayrshire embroidery became *broderie anglaise*.

The theory that the haggis is one of the nobler legacies of France may in any case be dismissed. The composition of the dish alone disproves the assumption, and the French themselves allude to the haggis, which appears to have been commonly sent to Scots in exile as long ago as the days of the Auld Alliance, as " le pain bénit d'Écosse ".

The choice of the haggis as the supreme national dish of Scotland is very fitting. It is a testimony to the national gift of making the most of small means; for in the haggis we have concocted from humble, even despised ingredients, a veritable *plat de gourmets*. It contains a proportion of oatmeal, for centuries the national staple, whilst the savoury and wholesome blending of the cereal with onion and suet (met with in its simplicity in such dishes as Mealie Puddings, The Fitless Cock, and Skirl-in-the-Pan) is typically Scottish. Further, it is a thoroughly democratic dish, equally available and equally honoured in castle, farm, and croft. Finally, the use of the paunch of the animal as the receptacle of the ingredients gives that touch of romantic barbarism so dear to the Scottish heart.

To such as still " look down wi' sneerin', scornfu' view on sic a denner ", we would point out that the most aesthetic of nations, the ancient Greeks, had a haggis of their own, which was immortalized by Aristophanes in *The Clouds*. Strepsiades entertains Socrates with a personal experience

> Why, now the murder 's out!
> So was I served with a stuffed paunch I broiled
> On Jove's day last, just such a scurvy trick;
> Because, forsooth, not dreaming of your thunder,
> I never thought to give the rascal vent,
> Bounce, goes the bag, and covers me all over
> With its rich contents of such varied sorts.

A similar incident is recounted with much gusto by Christopher North in the *Noctes Ambrosianae*. The uninitiated are advised to note the danger of a too sudden assault on the " chieftain o' the pudden race ".—F. M. McN.

MEG DODS'S HAGGIS

" The exact formula by which the Prize Haggis was prepared at the famous Competition of Haggises held in Edinburgh, when the Cleikum Haggis carried the stakes, and that of Christopher North came in second."—Meg Dods.[1]

Sheep's pluck and paunch, beef-suet, onions, oatmeal, pepper, salt, cayenne, lemon or vinegar.

Clean a sheep's pluck thoroughly. Make incisions in the heart and liver to allow the blood to flow out, and parboil the whole, letting the windpipe lie over the side of the pot to permit the discharge of impurities; the water may be changed after a few minutes' boiling for fresh water. A half-hour's boiling will be sufficient; but throw back the half of the liver to boil till it will grate easily; take the heart, the half of the liver, and part of the lights, trimming away all skins and black-looking parts, and mince them together. Mince also a pound of good beef-suet and four or more onions. Grate the other half of the liver. Have a dozen of small onions peeled and scalded in two waters to mix with this mince. Have ready some finely-ground oatmeal, toasted slowly before the fire for hours, till it is of a light brown colour and perfectly dry. Less than two teacupfuls of meal will do for this quantity of meat. Spread the mince on a board and strew the meal lightly over it, with

[1] " *Shepherd:* Tell me about the Haggis-Feast.

" *Tickler:* A dozen of us entered our haggises for a sweep-stakes—and the match was decided at worthy Mrs. Ferguson's, High Street. My haggis (they were all made either by our wives or cooks at our respective places of abode) ran second to Meg Dods's. The Director General's (which was what sporting men would have called a roarer) came in third—none of the others was placed."
—Christopher North: *Noctes Ambrosianae.*

a high seasoning of pepper, salt, and a little cayenne, first well mixed. Have a haggis bag (i.e. a sheep's paunch) perfectly clean, and see that there be no thin part in it, else your whole labour will be lost by its bursting.

Some cooks use two bags, one as an outer case. Put in the meat with a half-pint of good beef gravy, or as much strong broth as will make it a very thick stew. Be careful not to fill the bag too full, but allow the meat room to swell; add the juice of a lemon or a little good vinegar; press out the air and sew up the bag, prick it with a large needle when it first swells in the pot to prevent bursting; let it boil slowly for three hours if large.

"This is a genuine Scotch Haggis; the lemon and cayenne may be omitted, and instead of beef-gravy, a little of the broth in which the pluck is parboiled may be taken. A finer haggis may be made by parboiling and skinning sheeps' tongues and kidneys, and substituting these minced for the most of the lights, and soaked bread or crisped crumbs for the toasted meal. There are, moreover, sundry modern refinements on the above recipe—such as eggs, milk, pounded biscuit, &c.—but these, by good judges, are not deemed improvements. Some cooks use the small fat tripes, as in making lamb's haggis."—M. D.

HAGGIS ROYAL

"We find the following directions for Haggis Royal in the Minutes of Sederunt of the Cleikum Club."—Meg Dods.

Mutton, suet, beef-marrow, bread-crumbs or oatmeal, anchovies, parsley, lemon, pepper, cayenne, eggs, red wine.

Three pounds of leg of mutton chopped, a pound of suet chopped, a little, or rather as much beef-marrow as you can spare, the crumb of a penny loaf (our own nutty-flavoured browned oatmeal, by the way, far better), the beat yolks of four eggs, a half-pint of red wine, three mellow fresh anchovies boned, minced parsley, lemon grate, white pepper, crystals of cayenne to taste—crystals alone ensure a perfect diffusion of the flavour—blend the ingredients well, truss them neatly in a veal caul, bake in a deep dish, in a quick oven, and turn out. Serve hot as fire, with brown gravy, and venison sauce.

"Mr. Allan Cunningham, in some of his Tales, orders the parboiled minced meat of sheep's head for haggis. We have no experience of this receipt, but it promises well."—*Annals of the Cleikum Club.*

COLLOPS-IN-THE-PAN

(Meg Dods's Recipe)

Rump beef (sliced), butter, onions, salt, pepper, oyster-pickle or walnut catsup.

Cut the meat rather thinner than for broiling; make the butter hot and place the collops in the pan, with about the proportion of a couple of middle-sized onions sliced to each half-pound. If the butter be salt, pepper is used, but no additional salt. Cover the pan with a close lid or plate reversed. When done, the collops may be drawn aside, and a little oyster-pickle or walnut catsup and boiling water added to the onion-gravy sauce in the pan. Dish and serve hot. Ten minutes will dress them.

" This national dish possessed rather too much gusto for Jekyl; but the Doctor admired it exceedingly, and even suggested that, independently of the collops, this was an excellent method of preparing onion gravy, which only required the addition of a little red wine and lemon-juice, to those who like an acid relish, to be a complete sauce."—*Annals of the Cleikum Club.*

MINCED COLLOPS

(An everyday Scottish dish)

Minced steak, bread-crumbs or oatmeal or barley, dripping, onion, mushroom ketchup, stock, a pinch of nutmeg (optional), pepper and salt.

Take a pound of steak, which should be carefully minced with a small proportion of fat. Melt a tablespoonful of dripping in a stew-pan, and when it is smoking hot put in a finely chopped onion. Let it cook for a few seconds and add the minced steak. Brown it carefully, beating it well with a wooden spoon to keep it free from lumps. Add a teacupful of stock and a teaspoonful of salt, and let it simmer very gently for at least an hour. Then add a handful or more of bread-crumbs (which will absorb any liquid fat), or a dessertspoonful of oatmeal (which gives a very agreeable flavour) or of barley, with a seasoning of pepper. A tablespoonful of mushroom ketchup is an improvement. Cook a few minutes longer and serve on a hot ashet garnished with sippets of toast or fried bread and slices of hard-boiled egg, or with a border of mashed potatoes.

Minced collops may be baked in the oven, or first stewed and then baked. They will keep for some time, if packed in a jar and covered like potted meats.

Hare, venison, and veal collops are made as above, with the seasonings appropriate to each.

SCOTS WHITE COLLOPS

(*Meg Dods's Recipe*)

Veal, butter, broth or water, lemon, catsup or lemon-pickle, mace, pepper, salt, egg, bread-crumbs.

Cut small slices of equal thickness out of veal, and flour and brown them over a brisk fire in fresh butter. When enough are browned for your dish, put a little weak veal-broth or boiling water to them in a small close stew-pan, adding, when they are nearly ready, the juice of a lemon, a spoonful of catsup, or the same of lemon-pickle with mace, pepper, and salt to taste. Thicken and strain the sauce and pour it over the collops. They may be egged and dipped in crumbs. Serve curled slices of toasted bacon, or mushrooms if in season.

Mrs. Cleland's more elaborate eighteenth-century recipe:

" Cut the veal into thin slices, beat them with the rolling-pin; you may lard them if you please; season them with pepper, salt, cloves, mace, lemon peel, and grated bread, dipping them first into eggs; stew the knuckle well with a bunch of sweet herbs, two anchovies, cloves, mace, pepper and salt; strain it, and when you are going to send it up, thicken it with a bit of butter worked in flour, give it two or three boils, then put in the yolks of three eggs well beaten, a glass of white wine, the juice of a lemon, and give it a good heat on the fire, but don't let it boil, stirring all the while. Your collops being fried, but not brown, lay them in the dish and pour your sauce over them. Garnish it with mushrooms and oysters; don't make it too sour."

VEAL FLORY

(FLORENTINE PIE)[1]

(*Meg Dods's Recipe*)

Veal, bacon, spices, herbs, gravy, forcemeat, eggs or sweet-bread, truffles, morells or mushrooms; paste.

[1] This ancient and once honoured dish (mentioned by Scott in *The Bride of Lammermoor*) is a legacy of the Auld Alliance and may conceivably have come to us viâ Paris from Florence, as the name suggests. Certainly two French queens, Catherine and Marie, both of the famous Florentine family of Medici, exercised much influence on the French cuisine of their day.—F. M. McN.

Cut chops from the back-ribs or breast of veal. Trim off the bones and season the chops highly with mixed spices and such minced herbs as you choose. Add a few slices of lean bacon, forcemeat balls, and boiled yolks of eggs; or a scalded sweetbread cut into bits, and truffles, morells, or mushrooms as is convenient or approved. Add a little gravy drawn from the trimmings, and cover the pie.

Mrs. Cleland's recipe, being much older, is much more elaborate: " Cut your veal in small pieces; season with pepper, salt, cloves, and mace; put them in your dish with currants and raisins and a little bit of butter, the squeeze of a lemon and a gill of water. Cover your dish with a puff paste, and when it comes out of the oven, have a caudle of a gill of gravy, a gill of white wine, a little nutmeg, thickened with the yolks of two eggs, put a little sugar in it, and pour it in your pie. This caudle will serve for a sweet pie. Shake the dish after it is in."

Mrs. McIver writes: " Some people do not like sweet seasonings in their meat pies. In that case you may put in oysters, yolks of hard eggs, and artichoke bottoms."

HIGHLAND BEEF BALLS

(*From the Highland Feill Cookery-book*)

Beefsteak, suet, salt, saltpetre, black pepper, Jamaica pepper, sugar, ginger, cloves.

Mince finely two pounds of lean beefsteak and one pound of suet. Add to these a dessertspoonful of black pepper, the same of Jamaica pepper, one and a half dessertspoonfuls of salt, a teaspoonful apiece of saltpetre, sugar, and ginger, and half a teaspoonful of ground cloves. Mix well, roll into balls, and cover these with melted suet. When well covered with fresh suet they will keep for a week or ten days. When they are required for table, fry them a rich brown in deep fat.

This preparation can be put into ox-skins and tied into links.

This is an excellent breakfast or supper dish.

SMOKED SCOTS SAUSAGES

(To Keep and Eat Cold)

(*Meg Dods's Recipe*)

Beef, suet, pepper, salt, onion, ox-gut.

Salt a piece of beef for two days and mince it with suet Season it highly with pepper, salt, onion, or eschalot. Fill a large well-cleaned ox-gut, plait it in links, and hang the sausage in the chimney to dry.[1] Boil it as wanted, either a single link or altogether.

FORFAR BRIDIES [2]

(As originally made by Mr. Jolly, a baker in the Back Wynd [now Queen Street], Forfar, over fifty years ago)

Steak, pepper, salt, onions (optional), flour, water.

Take a pound of the best steak. Beat it with the paste roller, then cut it into narrow strips, and again cut these into inch lengths and season with salt and pepper. Divide into three portions. Mince finely three ounces of suet. Make a stiff dough with flour, water, and a seasoning of salt, and roll out thin into three ovals. Cover the half of each oval with the meat; sprinkle with the suet and a little minced onion if desired; wet the edges, fold over, and crimp with finger and thumb; nip a small hole on the top of each. Bake for about half an hour in a quick oven, and they will come out golden-brown dappled beauties, fit for a king's supper.

INKY-PINKY

(Meg Dods's Recipe)

Cold roast beef, carrots, onion, vinegar, flour, pepper, salt.

Slice boiled carrots; slice also cold roast beef, trimming away outside and skins. Put an onion to a good gravy (drawn from the roast beef-bones, if you like), and let the carrots and beef slowly simmer in this; add vinegar, pepper and salt. Thicken the gravy—take out the onion and serve hot, with sippets, as any other hash.

---

[1] " Some of these sausages used to be made when a Mart was killed; they formed an excellent article of supply for the hill, or moor, or the boat; and in the Hebrides and remote parts of the Highlands they still hold a favourite place in the wide open chimney."—M. D.

[2] These are mentioned by Barrie in *Sentimental Tommie*. Sir James is, of course native of Kirriemuir (Thrums), a village in Angus (Forfarshire).

POTTED HEAD
(OR SCOTS BRAWN)

(Old Family Recipe)

Ox head, ox foot, salt, pepper, cayenne, mustard, bay leaf, mace, cloves or allspice or nutmeg, water.

Soak half an ox head and a foot for a few hours. Break them up into several pieces. Remove from the foot as much of the fat and marrow as possible. Scald head and foot with boiling water and, when cool enough, scrape and clean them thoroughly. Put them into a large saucepan, plentifully covered with cold water, and add two tablespoonfuls of salt. Bring this very slowly to the boil, skim carefully, and let it simmer for three hours. Take out the head and foot and remove all the best meat from them. Return the bones to the pan, adding more water if there is not enough to cover them. Add a bay leaf, a blade of mace, and a very few cloves, if liked. Let this simmer for two or three hours longer. Strain into a basin and put aside till it gets cold. There should be at least eight breakfast-cupfuls of liquid. Next day (or sooner) remove all the fat from the top of the stock, which should now be a jelly. Trim and chop the meat and put it into a clean saucepan with the stock. Let this simmer for fifteen or twenty minutes. Add half a teaspoonful of mustard, the same of allspice or nutmeg if cloves have not been used, and season rather highly with pepper and cayenne. Pour into wetted moulds and set in a cool place to set. Turn out, and serve with salad.

POTTED HOUGH

(Old Cottage Recipe)

Hough, water, pepper, salt.

Take the nap end of hough, about three pounds or so, make the butcher break it through, put it into a saucepan and nearly cover it with water. Put it on the fire at night, bring it almost to boiling-point, then place it on the hob and let it simmer gently all night; don't let it boil. In the morning the meat will fall from the bones. Mince the meat as small as you can, put it in the saucepan again, add a little boiling water if required, and pepper and salt to taste, and let it boil for ten minutes, no longer. Put it into bowls or moulds and set aside to cool. It will have a rich taste, far before the common way of cooking it.

SCOTS KIDNEY COLLOPS

(*Meg Dods's Recipe*)

Kidney, flour, butter, eschalot or young onions, salt, pepper, parsley, vinegar or mushroom catsup.

Cut a fresh kidney in slices of the size of very small steaks, or into mouthfuls. Soak the slices in water and dry them well. Dust them with flour and brown them in the stew-pan with fresh butter. When the collops are browned, pour some hot water into the pan, a minced eschalot, or the white of four young onions minced, with salt, pepper, shred parsley, and a spoonful of plain or eschalot vinegar, or of onion-pickle liquor. Cover the stew-pan close and let the collops simmer slowly till done. If flavoured vinegar is not used, a spoonful of mushroom catsup put in before the collops are dished will be a great improvement. Thicken the gravy. Garnish this dish like liver with fried parsley.

" Some good cooks season this dish with an anchovy and lemon-pickle; others add made mustard."—M. D.

TO BOIL A GIGOT WITH TURNIP
(A SCOTTISH NATIONAL DISH)

(*Meg Dods's Recipe*)

A leg of mutton—the gigot of the French and Scottish kitchen—may be kept from two days to a week before boiling. The pipe, as it is technically called, must be cut out, and the mustiness which gathers on the surface and in the folds and soft places rubbed off occasionally. It is whitest when quite fresh, but most delicate when hung a few days in the larder, though not so long as to allow the juices to thicken and the flavour to deteriorate. Mountain wether mutton, from four to seven years old, is far the best, whether for boiling or roasting. Choose it short in the shank, thick in the thigh, and of a pure, healthy, brownish red. Chop but a very small bit off the shank; if too much is taken off the juices will be drained by this conduit in the boiling. If you wish to whiten the meat, blanch it for ten minutes in warm water or put it in a floured cloth if you like. Boil in an oval-shaped or roomy kettle, letting the water come very slowly to boil. Skim carefully. Boil carrots and turnips with the mutton, and the younger and more juicy they are the better they suit this joint. Be sure never to run a fork or anything sharp into the meat, which would drain its juices. *All meat ought to be well done*, but a leg of mutton rather under than over, to look plump and retain its juices. About two hours of slow boiling will dress it. Garnish with slices of carrot. Pour caper sauce over the meat and serve mashed turnip or cauliflower in a separate dish.

" This joint, above all others, should be boiled slowly to eat well. . . . The best balmy, mellow barley or rice broth may be made of what remains."—M. D.

" There is an adaptation, a *natural affinity*, to borrow a learned phrase, between certain vegetables and roots, and certain pieces and kinds of meat. A cook who would excel in her profession, ought, day and night, to study this doctrine of co-herence and natural affinity. Who but a fool would dissever from the round of salted beef the greens or cabbage which become part and parcel of it as soon as it reaches the pot?"—*Id.*

" *To grow a shoulder or leg of mutton.*—This art is well-known to the London bakers. Have a very small leg or shoulder; change it upon a customer for one a little larger, and that upon another for one better still, till by the dinner-hour you have a heavy excellent joint grown out of your original very small one."—P. Touch-wood in the *Annals of the Cleikum Club.*

POOR MAN OF MUTTON

This Scottish dish is the blade-bone grilled or cooked before the fire.

" There is a traditional story of Lord ——, after a long and severe fit of illness with which he was seized in London, horrifying his landlord by whining forth from behind his bed-curtains when urged to choose and eat, ' I think I could tak' a snap o' a Puir Man ' ".—*Annals of the Cleikum Club.*

SCOTS MUTTON PIES [1]

Maimed Hepburn from the croft gate cries,
" Come buy my hot and tottling pies!
Fine mutton pies, fat piping hot,
One for a penny, four for a groat!" [2]
　　　　　—Charles Spence: *Errol Winter Market.*

(*Traditional Recipe*)

Mutton, gravy, pepper, salt, mace or nutmeg, crust, flour, salt, dripping, milk or water.

Remove the skin, bone, and gristle from three-quarters of a pound of lean mutton. Cut the meat into small pieces, and season with salt, pepper, and, if liked, a little mace or nutmeg.

For six pies make a crust as follows: Put four ounces of fresh beef dripping into a saucepan with half a pint of water. Bring them to the boil, but do not let them reduce in quantity. Sieve a pound of flour into a bowl and add to it half a teaspoonful of salt. Make a well in the centre and pour in the hot liquid. Mix at first with a spoon or knife, but when cool enough use the hands and mix quickly into one lump. Turn out on a floured board and knead lightly till free from cracks. Put aside nearly a third of the paste to keep warm and divide the rest into six pieces. With these line six small ring tins or form them with the hand into small cases. (This may be done round a tumbler.) Fill the cases with meat, just moisten with water or gravy. Cut rounds from the remainder of the paste, wet the edges, and lay over the pies with the wetted side down, and press the two edges of paste firmly together. Trim round with a pair of scissors, make a small hole in the centre of each pie, and brush them with a little milk or beaten egg. Bake for from thirty to

[1] These were praised by Dr. Johnson. In his *Reminiscences*, Professor James Stuart pays tribute to Mrs. Gillespie, the pie-wife of his St. Andrews schooldays. Delightful as were her pigeon- and apple-pies, " her chef-d'œuvre . . . was a certain kind of mutton-pie. The mutton was minced to the smallest consistency, and was made up in a standing crust, which was strong enough to contain the most delicious gravy. . . . There were no lumps of fat or grease in them at all. . . . They always arrived piping hot. . . . It makes my mouth water still when I think of those pies."

[2] In *Guy Mannering*, Scott refers to the bells of the Edinburgh pie-men.

forty minutes in a moderate oven. Remove the pies from the tins, fill them up with a little hot gravy, and serve very hot.

" A little py of cocks' combs " figures in one of Lady Grisell Baillie's menus.

" The Pious Club was composed of decent, orderly citizens who met every night, Sundays not excepted, in a pye-house. . . . The agreeable uncertainty as to whether their name arose from their *piety*, or the circumstance of their eating *pies*, kept the Club hearty for many years."—R. Chambers: *Traditions of Edinburgh*.

" Soutar's clods, and other forms of bread fascinating to youngsters, as well as penny pies of high reputation, were to be had at a shop which all Edinburgh people speak of with extreme regard and affection—the Baijen Hole—situated immediately to the east of Forrester's Wynd, and opposite to the old Tolbooth. The name—a mystery to later generations—seems to have reference to the Baijens or Baijen * Class, a term bestowed in former days upon the junior students in the college."—*Id*.

* " Fr. *béjaune*, a novice, from *bec jaune*, ' yellow beak ', a term used for a fledgling or unfledged bird."—Jamieson.

First year students in the University of Aberdeen are still commonly designated " bejants ".—F. M. McN.

SHEEP'S HEAD BRAWN

(*Traditional Recipe*)

A sheep's head, bacon, pepper and salt.

Boil a sheep's head for three hours with half a pound of bacon. When cooked, remove the flesh, skin the tongue, and mince both finely together with the bacon. Season with pepper and salt and press into a basin. Put a plate over it and put a weight on the plate. Turn out when cold.

GLASGOW TRIPE

(*Meg Dods's Recipe*)

Tripe, knuckle of veal, pepper, salt, water.

When well cleaned and blanched, cut the tripe into pieces; roll them up neatly, fasten with a thread, and, with a marrow bone, or knuckle, or trimmings of veal, place them in a stoneware jar with pepper and salt. Place the closed jar in a pot of water, which keep full as it boils away. It will take eight hours at least. Keep the tripe in its own jelly in the jar, and dress it as it is wanted.

MUTTON-HAM [1]

(*Traditional Recipe*)

Mutton, coarse salt, brown sugar, saltpetre, Jamaica and black pepper, coriander seeds.

Cut a hind-quarter of good mutton into the shape of a ham. Pound an ounce of saltpetre with a pound of coarse salt and four ounces of brown sugar.[2] Add two ounces of Jamaica and black pepper and half an ounce of coriander seeds. Rub the ham well with this mixture, taking care to stuff some into the hole in the shank. Lay the hams in the trough, keep them carefully covered, and baste them with the brine every other day or even every day. Let it lie for a fortnight. Then take it out and press it with a weight for one day. Smoke it with sawdust[3] for ten or fifteen days or hang it to dry in the kitchen. In the Highlands, dried junipers are used in curing mutton-hams. " No sort of meat," says Meg Dods, " is more improved by smoking with aromatic woods than mutton."

If the ham is to be boiled soon after it is smoked, soak it for one hour, and if it has been smoked any length of time it will require to be soaked for several hours. Put it on in cold water, and boil it gently for two hours. It is eaten cold at breakfast, luncheon, or supper.

---

[1] Mentioned by Scott and other writers.

[2] " A mutton ham is sometimes cured with the above quantity of salt and sugar, with the addition of half an ounce of white pepper, a quarter of an ounce of cloves, and one nutmeg."—Mrs. Dalgairns.

[3] " Drive the end out of an old puncheon or cask. Invert it over birch or juniper branches, or a heap of sawdust of green hardwood (oak is best), in which sawdust a bar of red-hot iron is buried. Hang the tongues, hams, fish, &c.,[*] on sticks across the cask, and cover it to confine the smoke, giving a very little air below, that the material may smoke and smoulder slowly, but not burn."—Meg Dods.

[*] " In Caithness and elsewhere geese are still cured and smoked and are highly relishing."—*Id.*

BEEF-HAM

(*Traditional Recipe*)

Beef, salt, saltpetre, raw sugar, cloves, Jamaica and black pepper.

For a rump of about twenty pounds take a quarter-pound of saltpetre, two pounds of salt, a quarter-pound of coarse raw sugar, half an ounce of cloves, an ounce of Jamaica and one of black pepper, ground. Mix all thoroughly, rub the beef all over, and stuff as much as possible into the bone. Let it lie for two or three days. Then add another pound of salt, rub it well, and turn it every other day. It will be ready in three weeks. Drain it from the brine and hang it up. If you want it smoked, hang it over a barrel in which you burn peat or turf. The smoke will soon taste it, if you turn it well on every part. Then hang it up to dry. Or it may be boiled when taken out of the pickle, and allowed to stand till cold in the water in which it was boiled, or it may be baked in a deep dish, covered with a coarse paste.

TO SALT A YULE MART OR WHOLE BULLOCK

(*Meg Dods's Recipe*)

The following approved receipt has been communicated to us for salting meat for family use, in those families far from markets, where a winter-store, or *mart*, is still annually cured: Take as much spring water as you think will cover the pieces of meat, and, with Liverpool salt,[1] or bay salt, make of this a pickle so strong as to float a potato. Stir till the ingredients are dissolved, and afterwards boil the pickle till all the scum is thrown off. When quite cold, pour it over the meat in the

[1] "Rock salt, called Liverpool salt in the north-west of Scotland and in Ireland because it comes from that port. The best of all salt for preserving meat or fish is what is called bay or Lisbon salt. To it anchovies partly owe their rich mellowness."—M. D.

salting-tub or *beef-stand*. The meat must be wholly and constantly covered with the pickle, by occasionally adding fresh supplies as it wastes, and using a sinking-board. If the pickle becomes turbid, and a scum gather on it, either pour it off and boil and skim it well before returning it, when cold, to the meat; or use a fresh pickle, which may now be afforded cheaply. Meat preserved in this way is never disagreeably salt, and will keep for a long time. A little saltpetre boiled with the salt will tinge the meat, and if it is rubbed with salt and suffered to drain from the blood for a day and night, it will keep the better. If meat is not liked so salt, substitute sugar for one-third of the salt.

" The Natives are accustomed to salt their Beef* in a Cow's Hide, which keeps it close from Air, and preserves it as well, if not better than Barrels, and tastes they say best when this way used. This Beef is transported to Glasgow, a city in the West of Scotland, and from thence, being put into Barrels there, exported to the Indies in good Condition."—Martin: *Description of the Western Islands* (1703).

*" Their Beef is sweet and tender as any can be; they (the cows) live upon Seaware in Winter and Spring, and are fatned by it, nor are they slaughtered before they eat plentifully of it in December."—*Id.*

DISHES OF VEGETABLES

Amongst the rural population in Scotland vegetables (except potatoes) were and still are consumed almost entirely in the form of broth—though the old rhyme tells us that

> The buttered peas o' Lauderdale
> Are better than the best of kail—
> When Tammie's pith begins to fail.

Among the better-to-do, they are served also in stews, which are much more popular in Scotland than in England. There are, however, a few popular vegetable dishes, which are given here.

COLCANNON

(A Highland Dish)

Cabbages, carrots, potatoes, turnips, salt, pepper, mignonette, brown sauce, butter.

Take two cabbages, two or three good red carrots, eight or ten potatoes, and two turnips, all well boiled. Chop the cabbages finely, mash the other vegetables. Melt a good piece of butter in a stew-pan, put in all the vegetables, and mix thoroughly. Season with salt, pepper, and mignonette, and add a spoonful of good brown sauce. Serve piping hot.

KAILKENNY [1]

(Aberdeenshire and N.E.)

> There's cauld kail in Aberdeen
> And custocks [2] in Strathbogie,
> Where ilka lad maun ha'e his lass,
> But I maun ha'e my cogie.
> —Old Song.

Cabbage, potatoes, pepper, salt, cream.

Mash equal quantities of boiled cabbage and potatoes. Stir in a cupful of cream, season with pepper and salt, mix thoroughly, and serve very hot.

---

[1] Probably a corruption of *colcannon*.—F. M. McN.   [2] Stems of colewort.

CLAPSHOT
(ORKNEY)

Potatoes, turnips, chives, dripping, pepper, salt.

Mash together equal quantities of boiled potatoes and boiled turnips. Add some chopped chives, a good piece of dripping, and pepper and salt to taste. Mix thoroughly, and serve very hot.

RUMBLEDETHUMPS
(BORDERS)

Potatoes, cabbage, butter, pepper, salt.

" *North:* May I ask, with all due solemnity, what *are* rumbledethumps?

" *Shepherd:* Something like Mr. Hazlitt's character of Shakespere. Take a peck of purtatoes, and put them into a boyne [1]—at them with a beetle—a dab of butter—the beetle again—another dab—then cabbage—purtato—beetle and dab —saut [2] meanwhile—and a shake o' common black pepper— feenally, cabbage and purtato throughither—pree,[3] and you'll fin' them decent rumbledethumps."

—Christopher North: *Noctes Ambrosianae.*

Use boiled potatoes and cabbage in approximately equal quantities. Chopped chives or cooked onion are often added. The mixture may be put into a pudding-dish, covered with grated cheese, and browned in the oven.—F. M. McN.

STOVIES
(STOVED [4] POTATOES)

(Lady Clark of Tillypronie's Recipe)

Potatoes, butter, water, salt.

Choose potatoes of a good quality, and put them into a pot with a very little water—just enough to cover the bottom and prevent burning. Sprinkle with salt, and add tiny bits of butter here and there. Cover closely, and simmer very gently till soft and melted.

[1] Large pot. [2] Salt. [3] Taste. [4] Fr. *étuvé.*

Dripping may be used in place of butter, and onions (first tossed in the dripping) and pepper may be added, but the dish is best prepared as above.

" A cheap and delicious mess is furnished in summer to those healthy and happy children educated in what are called the *Maiden Hospitals* of Edinburgh. Good potatoes, boiled, peeled, and roughly broken, are boiled up with sweet milk, and a small proportion of butter."—Meg Dods.

SCOTS POTATO PIES

Potatoes, cooked scraps of meat, onion, pepper, salt, gravy, dripping.

Pare very finely some large potatoes, choosing those of nearly equal size. Cut off the tops about half an inch thick and hollow out the centre, leaving the potato at least half an inch thick all over. Mince some cooked scraps of meat, mix with it some chopped parboiled onion, season with pepper and salt, and moisten with a little gravy. A few drops of ketchup may be added. Stuff the potatoes with this mixture, put on the tops, place in a greased baking-tin, and bake for at least an hour, basting occasionally with melted dripping. Serve with a good gravy or hot tomato sauce poured round.

BANFFSHIRE POTATOES

Potatoes, dried sweet herbs, parsley, pepper, salt, bread-crumbs, butter, egg, milk.

Beat an ounce of butter to a cream; add the yolk of an egg (or half of a whole one), beat a little longer; then mix in three ounces of bread-crumbs, a pinch of sweet herbs powdered, a little minced parsley, pepper and salt to taste, and three-quarters of a gill of milk. Have seven good-sized potatoes well washed and brushed; flatten them by cutting at one end, cut a slice from the top to form a lid, and scoop out the hearts. Fill them with the mixture, put on the lids, bake in a quick oven for an hour, and serve hot in a napkin.

SCOTS POTATO FRITTERS

(Lady Harriet St. Clair's Recipe)

Potatoes, bread-crumbs, eggs, ham, olive oil.

Parboil half a dozen, or more if required, large kidney potatoes; cut them in slices about the thickness of a crown piece; beat up a couple of eggs with a tablespoonful of finely grated bread-crumbs, and an equal quantity of lean ham grated. Dip each slice of potato in this mixture, and fry in plenty of good olive oil.[1]

TO STEW AND ROAST ONIONS

(Meg Dods's Recipe)

Onions, stock, white pepper, salt, butter, flour, mushroom catsup

Scald and peel a dozen middle-sized, or two or three Spanish onions. If old and acrid, parboil them, and stew very slowly for nearly an hour in good veal or beef broth, with white pepper and salt; thicken the sauce with a little butter kneaded in flour, and, dishing the onions in a small hash-dish, pour it over them. A little mushroom catsup may be added, and they may be browned.

Onions are roasted before the fire in their skins, peeled, and served with cold butter and salt. They are eaten either alone or with roasted potatoes, or with red or pickled herrings. In the latter case we would recommend mustard as well as butter.

Stewed and roasted onions used to be a favourite supper-dish in Scotland, and were reckoned medicinal. The onions were stewed (after parboiling) in a butter-sauce, to which cream was put. . . . Onions used to form the favourite *bon-bons* of the Highlander, " who with a few of these and an oat-cake," says Sir John Sinclair, " would travel an incredible distance, and live for days without other food." . . . The Scotch peasants season their *chappit tatties* (mashed potatoes) and sometimes their brose with shred onion. " There is an admirable receipt for *gusty* chappit potatoes in an early volume of *Blackwood's Magazine*, the work which, in the mysteries of Comus, is wont to take the lead of all the periodicals of the day. The receipt to which we allude is after the practice of the pastoral inhabitants of Ettrick, Yarrow, and Teviotdale. Before calling the potato-beetle into operation, salt, pepper, and *an onion* finely shred are sprinkled over the potatoes, with a dash of sweet milk. The *onion* is the *bonne bouche*."—Meg Dods.

[1] Meg Dods says: " Fry in plenty of dripping, and serve with any sort of steak and chops, or alone as a supper dish. They may be dipped in small-beer fritter-batter."

TURNIP PURRY
(STEWED TURNIPS)

(Meg Dods's Recipe)

Turnips, fresh butter, white pepper, salt, ginger.

Pare off all that would be hard, woody, and stringy when boiled. Boil them in plenty of water for from three-quarters of an hour to nearly two hours, according to the age and size. Drain them and mash them with a wooden spoon through a colander. Return them into a stew-pan to warm, with a piece of fresh butter, white pepper, and salt. When mixed well with the butter place them neatly in the dish and mark in diamonds or sippets.

"The Cleikum Club put a little powdered ginger to their mashed turnips, which were studiously chosen of the yellow, sweet, juicy sort, for which Scotland is celebrated—that kind which, in the days of semi-barbarism, were served raw, as a delicate whet before dinner, as turnips are in Russia at the present day. Mashed turnips to be eaten with boiled fowl or veal, or the more insipid meats, are considerably improved by the Cleikum seasoning of ginger, which, besides, corrects the flatulent properties of this esculent."—M. D.

PUDDINGS AND PIES

Whilst sweets, pies, and tarts are common to many countries, the true home of the pudding is England. (Sweet puddings, that is, for savoury puddings have been eaten in Scotland from time immemorial.)

The French traveller, St. Fond, tells us that in 1784, at the house of Maclean of Torloisk, the dinner was concluded with " cucumbers and ginger pickled with vinegar, milk prepared in a variety of ways, and a pudding of barley-meal, currants, and cream done up with suet;" but until recently (and to a large extent still) puddings appeared only on middle and upper-class tables, the generality being too poor and too hardy for such " soft " feeding.

Most puddings are variations on two or three themes — the cabinet, the suet, and the milk.

Here are a few typical recipes, chiefly eighteenth and early nineteenth century.

AUNT MARY'S PUDDING

(Mrs. Dalgairns' Recipe)

Bread-crumbs, brown sugar, suet, raisins, currants, apples, ginger, nutmeg, brandy, eggs.

Of bloom raisins stoned, currants nicely cleaned, suet finely minced, bread grated, apples minced, and brown sugar, a quarter of a pound of each; four well-beaten eggs, a teaspoonful of pounded ginger, half a teaspoonful of salt, half a nutmeg grated, and one glass of brandy. Mix the ingredients well and boil in a cloth for two hours. Serve with a sauce of melted butter, a glass of wine, and some sugar.

CITRON PUDDING

(Mrs. McIver's Recipe)

Citron, sugar, sugar biscuit, eggs, spinach, wine or spirits, butter.

Slice half a pound of citron thin and shred it very small with a knife; beat and sift half a pound of sugar; beat sugar and citron very well together in a marble mortar; have the yolks of ten or a dozen eggs cast till they are like a cream. Then mix them by degrees into the beat sugar and citron and cast them very well with a spoon or knife. You may mix in a very little sugar biscuit. Put in as much of the juice of spinach as make it of a fine green; mix all well together. When you are just about putting it in the oven put in a dram and oiled butter and mix it very well. In all fine baked puddings let the oiled butter be the last thing you put in. Let it not be too hot.

SCOTS MARMALADE PUDDING

(*Old Family Recipe*)

Bread, raw sugar, raisins, marmalade, eggs, milk.

Grate six ounces of stale bread, pour over it three teacupfuls of boiling milk, and set it aside till nearly cold. While it is cooling, separate the yolks and whites of three eggs. Beat up the yolks with three ounces of sugar, add a good tablespoonful of marmalade, and stir into the bread and milk. Switch the whites to a stiff froth and stir lightly into the pudding. Butter a mould and ornament it with big raisins, stoned. Pour in the pudding mixture and put the mould immediately into a pan with boiling water that will just come up to the level of the pudding inside the mould. Draw the pan aside so that it may remain just under boiling-point, and let it cook thus for an hour and three-quarters. When ready, take it out of the water, lift off the lid, let it stand for five minutes or more, then turn out and serve with hot custard sauce.

HOLYROOD PUDDING

(*Mrs. Williamson's Recipe*) [1]

Semolina, butter, sugar, salt, ratafia biscuits, marmalade, eggs, milk.

Bring a pint of milk to the boil and stir in two ounces of semolina, with three ounces of castor sugar, two of ratafia

[1] Mrs. Williamson's cookery-book was a standard work in Scotland in the later nineteenth century.

biscuits, and one of butter. Let it boil for about five minutes, stirring all the time. Pour it into a basin and allow it to cool. Meanwhile switch the whites of three eggs to a froth and butter a pudding mould. Beat into the mixture the yolks of three eggs, one at a time; flavour with a dessertspoonful of orange marmalade, and, lastly, add the whites of the eggs, beaten to a stiff froth Mix gently, pour into the buttered mould, and steam for an hour and a quarter. Turn out and serve with almond sauce.

ALMOND SAUCE

Egg, sugar, milk, ground almonds, orange-flower water.

Mix together in a small sauce-pan one egg with one ounce of sugar, one gill of milk, one ounce of ground sweet almonds, and one tablespoonful of orange-flower water. Put it on over a slow fire and stir with a switch till it becomes like thick cream, but do not let it boil.

PLUM PORRIDGE[1]

> There the huge sirloin reeked; hard by
> Plum-porridge stood, and Christmas pie;
> Nor failed old Scotland to produce,
> At such high tide, her savoury goose.
> —Scott: *Marmion.*

(*Meg Dods's Recipe*)

Shin of beef, veal (optional), raisins, currants, prunes, pepper, mace, nutmeg.

Boil ten pounds of a shin for five hours in a gallon, or rather more, of water. Skim carefully. Strain off the liquor and put to it a piece of veal cut from the fillet. Soften the crumb of a penny loaf in the soup and beat it smoothly. Thicken the soup

[1] Plum porridge, though "nearly obsolete" a century ago, and now, we believe, quite obsolete, was in feudal times a popular Yuletide dish among the wealthier classes in Scotland, but appears to have been superseded by the plum pudding in the eighteenth century. In *The Household Book of Lady Grisell Baillie*, the menu for "Sunday, Christenmas, 1715," includes both "plumb patage" and "plumb puden".—F. M. McN.

with this and put to it half a pound of cleansed stoned raisins and half a pound of stoned prunes, a pound of currants well cleaned, and some pepper, mace, and grated nutmeg. When the fruit is soft the dish is ready. A little more bread may be used if greater consistence is wanted, and the veal may be omitted. Nearly obsolete.

" Plum-pottage can readily enough be identified as a very ancient British dish of Celtic origin associated with the festival of Yuletide.

" The Celtic god Dagda, or Dagodevos, was the deity of plenty, of the fruits of the earth, and lord of a capacious cauldron resembling the cornucopia, which contained all manner of delicious things. In this cauldron, which was called Undry, he cooked his porridge, a mess composed of corn-meal, meat, and fruit, the exact replica indeed of the ' plum-porridge ' of our ancestors.

" There is evidence that the pottage of the God of Plenty was in pagan Britain a dish associated with the Yuletide festival, when the sun was at its farthest distance from the equator, and when it was therefore on the point of returning on its genial course to fructify the earth, of whose future abundance the varied and luscious pottage of the Dagda was the symbol and portent."—Lewis Spence.

MEG DODS'S PLUM PUDDING

Biscuit, flour, raisins, currants, suet, sugar, nutmeg, cinnamon, mace, salt, lemon and orange and citron peel, blanched almonds, eggs, milk, wine or brandy.

Take four ounces of pounded pudding biscuit, or of good common biscuit, and two ounces of the best flour, a half-pound of bloom or muscatel raisins stoned, the same quantity of fresh Zante currants picked and plumped, and a half-pound of suet stripped of skins and filaments, and shred; a small teaspoonful of nutmeg grated, a quarter-pound of fine beat sugar, a drachm of pounded cinnamon, two blades of mace, and a saltspoonful of salt; three ounces of candied lemon, orange, and citron peel sliced, and two ounces of blanched almonds roughly chopped. Beat four eggs well, and put to them a little sweet milk, a glass of white wine or brandy, and then mix in the flour and all the ingredien ts minced. Tie up the pudding firm and boil it for three hours, keeping up the boil and turning the cloth. Serve with caudle sauce.

" Plum pudding will keep long, and re-warm when wanted, in slices, in the Dutch oven or frying-pan."—M. D.

" Instead of one huge plum pudding, we prepare at The Cleikum a hen and chickens, putting the hen, of ten or twelve pounds, to boil a couple of hours before her chickens. We have the hen for Christmas or company, and a plum-chicken can be heated up any day."—Meg Dods.

The plum pudding is pre-eminently an English national dish, but it has appeared on Scottish middle- and upper-class tables for over two centuries.

CAUDLE SAUCE
(For a Plum Pudding)

(Meg Dods's Recipe)

Melted butter, wine, rum, sugar, lemon, cinnamon.

A glass of white wine, a half-glass of brandy or old rum or rum-shrub, pounded sugar to taste, the grate of a lemon, and a little cinnamon, stirred into a little thickened melted butter; sprinkle a little cinnamon on the top.

PUFF PASTE
(Scots Fashion)

Flour, butter, salt, lemon.

Puff paste should always be made in a cool place.

Take a pound of flour, a pound of butter, a pinch of salt, and the juice of half a lemon. Sift the flour on to the board, add the salt, and make a well in the centre. Pour in, along with the lemon juice, just enough cold water to make a nice pliable dough. Cover with a cloth and let it stand for fifteen minutes. Sprinkle the board with flour and roll out with a rolling-pin square till about half an inch thick. Chop the butter into cubes, dot it over the paste, and fold the paste over in such a manner that the butter is entirely wrapped up, keeping the paste always in a square. Roll out, keeping it an equal thickness all over. This is called the first turn. The paste should then stand for ten minutes, covered with a cloth. It requires two other turns, with an interval of ten minutes between each. It is then ready for use.

For half-puff paste proceed as above, using only half a pound of butter to the pound of flour.

MRS. DALGAIRNS' SCOTS PUDDING

Eggs, loaf sugar, butter, lemon, puff paste.

Take eight well-beaten yolks and three whites of eggs, half
a pound of pounded loaf sugar, a quarter-pound of melted
butter, the grated peel and juice of a lemon. Mix all together
and bake it in a dish lined with puff paste. Turn it out to
serve and strew over the top grated loaf sugar.

A BRIDE'S PIE

(A Scots Pie)

(*Meg Dods's Recipe*)

*Calves' feet, mutton suet, apples, currants, raisins, candied
lemon and citron peel, cinnamon, nutmeg, mace, brandy,
Madeira, puff paste.*

This is just a very nice mince pie. Chop the meat of two
calves' feet, previously boiled, a pound of mutton suet, and a
pound of pared apples, all separately, till they are fine. Mix
them and add to them a half-pound of picked and rubbed
currants and the same quantity of raisins stoned and chopped.
Season with a quarter-ounce of cinnamon in powder, two
drachms of grated nutmeg and pounded mace, an ounce of
candied citron and double the quantity of lemon peel, both
sliced thin, a glass of brandy, and another of Madeira. Line
a thin pan which has a slip-bottom with puff paste, and put the
minced meat, &c., into it. Roll out a cover for the pie, which
usually has a glass or gold ring concealed somewhere in the
crust, and should be embellished with appropriate ornaments
and devices, as Cupids, turtles, torches, flames, darts, and other
emblematic devices of this kind.

ALMOND FLORY
(FLORENTINE TART)
(*Mrs. Cleland's Recipe*)

Almonds, currants, butter, sugar, cinnamon, nutmeg, candied lemon and citron peel (optional), eggs, cream, brandy, puff paste.

Blanch and beat very fine a pound of almonds with orange-flower water; beat eight eggs, but half of the whites; mix them with two gills of cream and half a gill of brandy, half a pound of clarified butter, a pound of currants well washed and picked; season it with sugar, cinnamon, and nutmeg, all pounded fine; mix them all very well; put them in a dish with puff paste under and over them. You may put candied lemon and citron in thin slices in it if you please. A little while bakes it.

APPLE FLORY

Apples, orange marmalade, cinnamon, lemon, sugar, water, puff paste.

Slice some pippins and simmer for a little in a syrup of sugar and water. Flavour with cinnamon and grated lemon rind. Line a meat-plate with puff paste, spread with apples and oranges or quince marmalade, cover with puff paste (moistening the edges to make them adhere). Pinch all round the edge and ornament.

PRUNE FLORY

Prunes, lemon, port wine, sugar, water, puff paste.

Stone the prunes and cook gently in a syrup of sugar and water. Add a squeeze of lemon and a spoonful or so of port wine. Prepare as above.

CRANBERRY TART
(*Meg Dods's Recipe*)

Cranberries, sugar, cloves, cinnamon, puff paste.

This may be made of either fresh or preserved cranberries. Season with beat cloves and cinnamon. Put in a sufficient quantity of sugar. Cover a flat dish with paste and put a rim of puff paste round the edges. Bake the paste and put in the jam, either when it is ready or a few minutes before. Paste stars, flowers, &c., may be cut out and baked on tins to ornament the top; or, if the fruit is put in at first, covered with a paste trellis-work. Serve with cream, which to this dry fruit is indispensable.

SCOTS APPLE PUDDING

(Meg Dods's Recipe)

Apples, biscuits, butter, sugar, lemon, orange-flower water, brandy, lemon or orange peel, eggs, puff paste.

Pare and grate three-quarters of a pound of juicy apples Put to them six ounces of butter beat cold to a cream, four beat eggs, two pudding biscuits, pounded, the rind of a lemon grated, sugar to taste, a spoonful of brandy and another of orange-flower water. Bake in a puff paste marked in leaves round the border, and when done, strew candied lemon or orange peel sliced over the top.

"A little lemon-juice or cider may be added if the apples are too mellow."—M. D.

APPLE PUDDINGS IN SKINS

(Meg Dods's Recipe)

Apples, biscuit, sugar, suet, cinnamon, nutmeg, wine or other liquor.

Mince apples and grate biscuit; take an equal weight to these of minced suet. Sweeten this with sugar, and season with cinnamon and grated nutmeg. Moisten the whole with wine or any well-flavoured liquor, and mix, and fill the skins, but not too full, as the bread swells. Boil, and serve hot.

"These will keep for a week or ten days and re-warm by boiling; they may be browned in the Dutch oven. Another kind of fine pudding is made of rice boiled in milk, with suet, currants, sugar, and seasonings. The suet in these puddings should not be shred too small, which makes it thaw and disappear, nor yet left in lumps."—M. D.

SCOTS PANCAKES

(Mrs. Dalgairns' Recipe)

Flour, cream, eggs, lemon, sugar, ratafia, butter or lard.

Mix with three tablespoonfuls of flour a little cream, add the beaten yolks of three eggs, then mix in half a pint of cream the grated peel of half a small lemon, a dessertspoonful of pounded sugar, and a little ratafia. When the batter is very well beaten, and just before using, mix in the whites of the eggs beaten with a knife into a stiff froth. Put a little butter or lard into a frying-pan and when hot pour in a teacupful of the batter; shake it, and when firm prick it a little with a fork, but do not turn it; hold it before the fire for a minute to brown. Serve them with pounded loaf sugar strewed over them.

" In the Cleikum, and probably in some other old-fashioned inns and Scottish families, pancakes were wont to be served with a layer of currant jelly between the folds—a practice for which much might be said by those familiar with it. Is not this the *omelette à la Celestine*, or *aux confitures*, of our old allies, still lingering in remote places of the country? Pancakes are still better with apricot marmalade."—P. Touchwood in the *Annals of the Cleikum Club.*

OATMEAL PANCAKES [1]

(Mrs. Cleland's Recipe)

Oatmeal, sugar, nutmeg, salt, lemon, eggs, milk.

Boil a chopin (quart) of milk and blend it in a mutchkin (pint) of the flour of oatmeal thus: keep a little milk and mix the meal by degrees in it, then stir in the boiling milk; when it is pretty thick put it to cool, then beat up six eggs with sugar, nutmeg, the grate of a lemon, and a little salt. Stir all together and fry them in butter, putting in a spoonful of the batter at a time. Serve them up hot, with beat butter, orange, and sugar.

[1] *Sauty* • or *Sooty Bannocks.* These were a variety of oatmeal pancake formerly made on Fastern's E'en (Shrove Tuesday). A thick batter was prepared, consisting of oatmeal, beaten eggs, beef bree or milk, and salt, and was poured, a ladleful at a time, on to a hot girdle previously rubbed with fat. The making of the bannocks was a great ploy, in which all present participated.—F. M. McN.

• Fr. *sauter*, to toss.

SWEETS

"As we are disposed to give the Monks full credit for many of the best French dishes, and for our own antiquated preparations, so are the fair recluses of France and Italy entitled to the merit of much that is elegant in confectionery, of which they long had, and still have, tasteful exhibitions on festivals. To their leisure and taste we owe caramelled and candied fruits, fruits *en chemise*, Chantilly, and caramel baskets, &c., &c., as really as we do the most delicate lace, needlework, and cut paper."—Meg Dods.

Some of the dishes in this section—Whipt Sillabubs, A Hedgehog, A Floating Island, for example, are Scottish variations of dishes to be found in other countries. —F. M. McN.

A CROKAIN [1]

(Mrs. Cleland's Recipe)

Sugar, water, lemon.

Take three-quarters of a pound of fine sugar, put it in a clear copper pan with two gills of water, put it on the fire, let it boil slow, skim it, but don't stir it; put in the juice of half a lemon, then let it boil brown; then take a spoon and try if it ropes; oil your mould and spin it on as neatly as you can and let it be pretty thick at the bottom; when it is done take it off as gently as you can. You may put any creams or any red or green preserved apples or oranges under it.

SCOTS FLUMMERY

(Mrs. Cleland's Recipe)

Milk, cream, eggs, rose-water, sugar, nutmeg, sack.

Take a mutchkin of milk and one of cream; beat the yolks of nine eggs with a little rose-water, sugar, and nutmeg; put it in a dish, and the dish over a pan of boiling water covered

---

[1] From *Croqu'en bouche.*

close; when it begins to grow thick have ready some currants plumped in sack and strew over it. It must not be stirred while it is over the fire, and when it is pretty stiff send it up hot.

WHIPT SILLABUBS
(Scots Fashion)
(Mrs. Cleland's Recipe)
Cream, white wine, lemon, sugar.

Take a mutchkin (pint) of thick cream, put to it half a mutchkin of white wine, the juice of a lemon, and grate the rind in it; sweeten it to your taste, whisk it up well, skim off the top as you are whisking it, and put it on a sieve; then put wine in the glass, either white or red, and a little sugar; then send it to table with teaspoons about it.

In one of the menus in *The Household Book of Lady Grisell Baillie*, there appears " a salver w^t jellies and sillie bubess "; in another (supper at Mr. Cockburn's), " In the middle of the table a pirimide sillibubs and orang cream in the past, above it sweet meets dry and wet."

A HEN'S NEST
(Mrs. Cleland's Recipe)
Calves-foot jelly, blancmange, lemon peel, egg-shells.

Take calves-foot jelly that is very strong and put it in a white bowl or a Turk's-cap, fill it near half-full of the jelly, let it be cold; take five eggs, make a hole in the narrow end of them that the yolks and whites may come out; then fill them with blamong; let them stand till they are cold, then take off the shells by pieces and take care not to break the blamong; then lay them in the middle of the jelly so that they don't touch one another; then pour more jelly on them when it is almost cold. Cut some lemon peel as straws and, when the jelly is stiff, strew it over it; then pour a little more jelly over it. When all is cold and very stiff, dip the bowl in hot water. Have an ashet ready and put it on the top of the bowl and turn it out quick. Don't let the bowl be a moment in the water.

A FLOATING ISLAND

(Scots Fashion)

" And for a Floating Island, or a Hedgehog, we could never pretend to ony sic grandery at the Cleikum."—Meg Dods, in the *Annals of the Cleikum Club.*

Eggs, quince, raspberry or red currant jelly, cream, wine, sugar, lemon peel.

Three spoonfuls of guava quince, or raspberry or red currant jelly and the whites of as many eggs; beat them together one way till the spoon will stand erect; pile it upon cream beaten up with wine and sugar and a little grated lemon peel.

A HEDGEHOG

(Scots Fashion)

(*Mrs. Cleland's Recipe*)

Almonds, sack or orange-flower water, eggs, cream, butter, currants.

Blanch and beat a pound of almonds very fine with a spoonful of sack or orange-flower water to keep them from oiling; make it into a stiff paste, then beat up six eggs and put two whites; sweeten it with fine sugar, then put in half a mutchkin of cream and a quarter of a pound of beat butter; set it on your stove and keep it stirring till it is so stiff that you can make it into the shape of a hedgehog, then stick it full of blanched almonds cut in straws; set them on like the bristles with two currants plumped for eyes, then place it in the middle of the dish and boil some cream; put in it the yolks of two eggs and sweeten it to your taste; put it on a slow fire and when it is scalding hot take it off; you must keep it stirring all the while; when it is cold put it about the hedgehog

CALEDONIAN CREAM

(Mrs. Dalgairns' Recipe)

Orange marmalade, brandy, loaf sugar, lemon, cream.

Mince a tablespoonful of orange marmalade; add it, with a glass of brandy, some pounded loaf sugar, and the juice of a lemon, to a quart of cream; whisk it for half an hour and pour it into a shape with holes in it, or put it into a small hair sieve with a bit of thin muslin laid into it.

WHIM-WHAM [1]

(Mrs. Dalgairns' Recipe)

Cream, white wine, lemon, Naples biscuit, red currant jelly, candied citron and orange peel.

Sweeten a quart of cream and mix with it a teacupful of white wine and the grated peel of a lemon; whisk to a froth, which drain upon the back of a sieve and put part into a deep glass dish; cut some Naples biscuit [2] as thin as possible and put a layer lightly over the froth and one of red currant jelly, then a layer of the froth and one of biscuit and jelly; finish with the froth and pour the remainder of the cream into the dish and garnish with citron and candied orange peel cut into straws.

[1] " Whim-whams " are mentioned by Scott in *The Bride of Lammermoor.*

[2] *(Mrs. Cleland's Recipe for Naples Biscuit)*

Take a pound of fine sugar pounded and sifted, a pound of fine flour; beat eight eggs with two spoonfuls of rose-water; mix flour and sugar, then wet it with the eggs and as much cold water as will make a light paste; beat the paste very well then put them (the biscuits) in papered tin pans.[*] Bake in a gentle oven.

[*] The correct Naples biscuit-tin is eight inches long, three wide, and one deep.— F. M. McN.

FAIRY BUTTER

(*Mrs. Dalgairns' Recipe*)

Butter, orange-flower water, eggs, sweet almonds, lemon peel,
loaf sugar, Naples biscuits, white wine.

Wash a quarter of a pound of fresh butter in orange-flower water and beat it with the pounded yolks of five or six hard-boiled eggs; blanch and pound to a paste with a little orange-flower water two ounces of sweet almonds; add a little grated lemon peel and pounded and sifted loaf sugar; mix all together and, with a wooden spoon, work it through a stone cullender. Soak some Naples biscuit in white wine and put over them the fairy butter in heaps as high as it can be raised.

A BURNT CREAM

(*Mrs. Cleland's Recipe*)

Cream, eggs, flour, sugar, cinnamon, orange.

Boil a mutchkin (pint) of cream and thicken it with the yolks of eight eggs and a spoonful of flour; boil cinnamon and the rind of an orange in the cream; take care it is not curdled, sweeten it to your taste; take a quarter-pound of loaf sugar in a stew-pan and pour over it a gill of water; let it boil till it ropes and don't stir it till you take it off; then by degrees strew it over your ashet of cream; brown it with a salamander or in the oven.

CUSTARD FOR A CENTRE DISH
(OLD SCOTS STYLE)

Make a strong whip of sweetened cream. Heap it over a rich custard, and garnish with bright green and scarlet preserved fruits.

CALEDONIAN ICE
(ICED STAPAG)

Cream, vanilla, sugar, oatmeal.

Whip some cream stiffly; sweeten it and flavour with vanilla; set it to freeze. When nearly frozen stir in coarse toasted oatmeal, well dried in the oven without being browned. Serve in a glass dish or in individual glasses.

EDINBURGH FOG
(MODERN)

Cream, sugar, vanilla, ratafia biscuits, almonds.

Beat half a pint of cream to a stiff froth with a little pounded sugar and vanilla flavouring. Mix thoroughly with a good handful of ratafia biscuits and some blanched and chopped almonds. Serve in a glass bowl or dish.

SAVOURIES

A SCOTS RABBIT

(*Meg Dods's Recipe*)

Cheese, porter, mustard, pepper, buttered toast.

Pare the crust off a slice of bread cut smooth and of about a half-inch in thickness. Toast it, but do not let it wither or harden in the toasting. Butter it. Grate down mellow Stilton, Gouda, Cheshire, or good Dunlop cheese; and, if not fat, put to it some bits of fresh butter. Put this into a cheese-toaster which has a hot-water reservoir and add to it a glassful of well-flavoured brown-stout porter, a large teaspoonful of made mustard, and pepper (very finely ground) to taste. Stir the mixture till it is completely dissolved, brown it, and then, filling the reservoir with boiling water, serve the cheese with hot dry or buttered toasts on a separate dish.

" This is one of the best plain preparations of the kind that we are acquainted with. Some gourmands use red wine instead of porter, but the latter liquor is much better adapted to the flavour of cheese. Others use a proportion of soft putrid cheese, or the whole of it in that state. This is of course a matter of taste beyond the jurisdiction of any culinary dictator. To dip the toasts in hot porter makes another variety in this preparation."—M. D.

SCOTS WOODCOCK

(*Old Family Recipe*)

Anchovy paste, eggs, cream, parsley, butter, cayenne, hot buttered toast.

Take six small rounds of buttered toast, spread them with anchovy paste, arrange on a hot dish, and keep hot. Melt two tablespoonfuls of butter in a sauce-pan, put in three tablespoonfuls of cream and the raw yolks of three eggs, and stir over the fire until the mixture is a creamy mass. Add a little finely chopped parsley and a dash of cayenne. Heap on the rounds of toast and serve very hot.

SCOTS TOASTS

Of these there are many varieties: flaked Finnan haddock done up with a little Béchamel, flaked kippered herring or salmon, minced cold game, &c., moistened and seasoned and heaped in pyramids on buttered rounds of toast. Recipes will be found in many contemporary cookery-books.

SCOTS EGGS

(Meg Dods's Recipe)

Eggs, forcemeat, ham, anchovy, bread, spices, &c.

Five eggs make a dish. Boil them hard as for salad. Peel and dip them in beat egg and cover them with a forcemeat made of grated ham, chopped anchovy, crumbs, mixed spices, &c.[1] Fry them nicely in good clarified dripping [2] and serve them with a gravy-sauce separately.

NUN'S BEADS

(Mrs. Dalgairns' Recipe)

Cheese, eggs, bread-crumbs, salt, puff paste, butter.

Pound in a mortar four ounces of good cheese with a little salt, the beaten yolk of three eggs, and some crumbs of bread; roll them as large as walnuts, cover them with puff paste, and fry them in butter a light brown colour. Serve them in a napkin.

[1] Pork sausage-meat is often used nowadays in place of forcemeat. Scots eggs may be served cold, with salad.—F. M. McN.

[2] They are usually first egged and bread-crumbed.

BANNOCKS, SCONES, AND
TEA-BREAD

In Scotland, amongst the rural population generally, the girdle takes the place of the oven, the bannock of the loaf.—F. M. McN.

BANNOCKS AND SCONES
GENERAL DIRECTIONS

The girdle should be put on to heat before the dough is mixed. To test the heat, sprinkle a little flour over it. If it browns at once the girdle is too hot; if it takes a few seconds to brown it will do. For scones and bannocks, sprinkle the girdle with flour, unless they are themselves sufficiently floury to prevent sticking; but for Scots crumpets and drop scones grease the girdle very slightly—just enough to prevent sticking —with a piece of suet wrapped in a clean rag. In a word, the girdle is floured for dough and greased for batter.

The girdle should never be washed, but should be cleaned when hot by being rubbed with coarse salt and a piece of paper, and then dusted with a clean cloth.

Use only the best materials. The best baking-soda is to be had from the chemist. Use the finest flour and see that it is dry. Sift it at least once, allowing the air to get into it as much as possible, into a basin, or, better, straight on to the baking-board or marble slab. Mix the dry ingredients thoroughly and gather them into a heap in the centre of the board. Make a hole in the centre into which pour the milk. Then go round the edge of the pool of milk with a wooden spoon and toss the flour lightly in. Never stir in the centre.

The dough should be as soft as is compatible with its being lightly handled, and should be handled as little as possible. Roll out lightly, and fire slowly for about ten minutes on the one side, then turn and fire for about five on the other. Turn only once.

Buttermilk, with bicarbonate of soda, is always used for bannocks and girdle scones. It produces a much better scone—bulkier, softer, and moister-eating—than does sweet or sour milk. This is due to the softening or maturing or ripening action of the lactic acid it contains on the gluten of the flour, an action somewhat akin to that which takes place during fermentation.

A very fine scone can be obtained thus: Drop a spoonful of the dough on a heap of flour; flour the hands, lift the dough lightly with one hand and transfer it to the other, shaking off the loose flour in the transference. Pass the dough lightly from hand to hand, and then drop it on the hot girdle.

The names scone and bannock are applied rather loosely. In modern usage the bannock is the large round scone, about the circumference of a meat-plate, which is baked on the girdle. When the bannock is cut into sections before being fired, or when the dough is cut into small rounds, you have scones.

The etymology of scone (pronounced *skonn*, which is Sir John Sinclair's spelling (1772)) is uncertain. Chambers suggests the Gaelic *sgonn*, a shapeless mass. Bannock is from the Gaelic *bonnach*, a cake or bannock.

In Gavin Douglas's translation of the seventh *Æneid*, we read that at a feast at the mouth of the Tiber

" The flour sconnis weir set in by and by
With other mesis ".—F. M. McN.

BERE OR BARLEY BANNOCKS

Leeze me on thee,[1] John Barleycorn,
    Thou king o' grain!
On thee auld Scotland chaws her cood
In souple scones, the wale [2] o' food.
       —Burns: *Scotch Drink.*

Fair fa' [3] the gudewife and send her gude sale,
She gies us gude bannocks to drink her ale.
      —Old Song: *Todlen But and Todlen Ben.*

At the sight of Dumbarton once again,
I 'll cock up my bonnet and march amain,
With a gude claymore hanging down at my heel,
To whang at the bannocks o' barley-meal.
      —John, Duke of Argyll.

Wha in a brulyie [4]
    Will first cry a parley? [5]
Never the lads wi'
    The bannocks o' barley!
      Bannocks o' bere meal,
      Bannocks o' barley,
      Here 's to the Hielandman's
      Bannocks o' barley!
      —Old Song.

" Did our swank country lads know how appetisingly sustaining a barley scone can be made—especially did our comely country lasses . . . realize the virtues, of beauty to the skin and sweetness to the temper, which reside in bannocks of bear-

[1] Dear thou to me (Lief is me).   [2] Choicest.   [3] Good befall.   [4] Broil.   [5] Truce.

meal—there would be, I am firmly convinced, such a revival of this well-approved ancient feeding-stuff as would send down the price of wheat and drive tapioca and similar foreign stinking ware that jaups in luggies clean out of caup and market."
—Hugh Haliburton: *Furth in the Field.*

(Old Method)
Barley-meal, butter, salt, sweet milk.

Put half a pint of milk into a pan with a pinch of salt and an ounce or more of butter. Bring to the boil and stir in quickly enough barley-meal to make a pliable dough. Turn out on a floured board, roll out thinly, cut into rounds the size of a meat-plate. Bake on a hot girdle, turning them once, on a rather sharp fire. They should be eaten hot.

(Modern Method)
Barley-meal, flour, bicarbonate of soda, salt, buttermilk.

Put into a bowl a pound of barley-meal, four ounces of flour, and half a teaspoonful of salt. Mix well. Put three teacupfuls of buttermilk into a jug and into it stir two small teaspoonfuls of carbonate of soda. Stir briskly, and, as it fizzes up, pour it into the flour mixture. Make into a soft dough, turn out on a floured board, handle as little as possible, but roll out lightly to about half an inch in thickness; cut into rounds the size of a meat-plate, place on a hot girdle, and bake (not too quickly) until the under side is brown; turn the bannock and brown the other side.

A survival of an old Druidical belief, mentioned by Sir James Frazer in *The Golden Bough*, and still prevalent in some parts of the Highlands, is that in kneading bannocks, stirring porridge or kail, sending a glass round the company, &c., the movement must be " deiseal ", sunwise—i.e. the right-hand turn. This is the lucky way. Widdershins—i.e. the left-hand turn—is unlucky.

PEASE BANNOCKS

Sae brawly [1] did a pease-scon toast
Biz i' the queff [2] and flie the frost,
There we got fu' wi' little cost,
    And muckle [3] speed.
        —Allan Ramsay.

Make as barley-bannocks, substituting pease-meal for barley-meal.

[1] Finely. [2] Quaigh, drinking-cup. [3] Much.

MASHLUM BANNOCKS

" Twa mashlum bannocks."—Burns: Cry and Prayer.

Bannocks made of any mixture of flours are known as mashlum or meslin bannocks, and in some parts as brash-bread. They are prepared like barley bannocks.

In the Hebrides there is a traditional cake called the *Struan Micheil* (St. Michael's Cake) made of a mixture of oats, barley, and rye (representing the fruits of the field) which is baked on September 29th in honour of St. Michael. As the bannock gains consistency in the firing, it is covered on both sides with three successive layers of a batter of cream, eggs, and butter, in the manner of the Beltane bannock. Various ingredients are introduced into the small struans, as cranberries, blaeberries, brambles, caraways, and wild honey. The elaborate ritual used in the preparation of this cake is described by Alexander Carmichael in the introduction to his collection, *Carmina Gadelica*.

Aran Isenach (Indian Bread) is a bannock made in the Outer Isles of a mixture of flour and fine Indian meal, shortened with butter.

OATCAKES

O whar did ye get that hauvermeal [1] bannock?
O silly blind body, O dinna ye see?
I got it frae a brisk young sodger laddie
Between St. Johnston [2] and bonnie Dundee.
—Old Song.

The carline [3] brought her kebbuck [4] ben
Wi' girdle-cakes weel toasted broon.
Weel does the canny kimmer [5] ken [6]
They gar [7] the scuds [9] gae glither [9] doon.
—*Andro and his Cutty Gun.*

O gie me the time when auld ploys were in vogue,
An' the cake an' the kebbuck gaed doon wi' the cog. [10]
—Hew Ainslie.

Oatmeal, fat or dripping, baking-soda, salt, hot water.

Four special implements are used for baking oatcakes—the *spurtle*, or porridge-stick, for stirring the mixture; a notched *bannock-stick*, or rolling-pin, which leaves a criss-cross pattern on the upper side; the *spathe*, a heart-shaped implement with a long handle, made of iron, used for transferring the cakes from board to girdle; and the *banna-rack*, or toaster.

If a quantity is to be made, the dough should be rather soft,

[1] Oatmeal.   [2] Perth.   [3] Old Woman.   [4] Cheese.   [5] Gossip.   [6] Know.
[9] Make.   [8] Liquor.   [9] Easier   [10] Wooden vessel to contain liquor

as it stiffens whilst lying about to be made up. The best results
are obtained by mixing enough for one bannock, or round, at
a time (using the quantities given below), the next bannock
being prepared whilst the last is on the girdle.

Put into a bowl four ounces of oatmeal, a pinch of baking-
soda, and a pinch of salt. Melt a teaspoonful of fat. (Bacon
or poultry fat or butter or dripping. Goose fat is excellent.)
Make a well in the centre of the oatmeal and add the melted fat
with just enough hot water to make a stiff dough. Rub plenty
of meal on to the baking-board; turn out the mixture and
form into a smooth ball; knead with gradually spreading
knuckles, working as quickly as possible, and roll out as thinly
as possible—say an eighth of an inch. The process is not quite
easy to one unfamiliar with the work, owing to the stickiness
of the dough and the tendency of the edges to break. The
dough must be kept from sticking by constant rubbing over on
both sides with dry meal, and the edges must be kept as even
as possible by pinching with the thumb and forefinger. Give
a final rub with meal to make the cakes white. They may be
left whole (bannocks) or cut into quarters (farles)[1]. Place on a
moderately hot girdle over a clear fire, smooth side uppermost,
and bake steadily till the cakes curl up at the edge. Remove
them carefully, rub a little oatmeal over them, and toast the
smooth side slightly before a bright smokeless fire. (Toasting-
stones with an incised pattern to permit the sweating of the
cakes were formerly used on the open hearth. An attachable
iron toaster is used on the ordinary coal-range.) Place for a
few minutes in a warm place, e.g. a moderate oven. Keep buried
in oatmeal in the girnel or meal-chest; or, failing these, in a
tin. They are improved by being heated shortly before they
are served, unless they are freshly baked.

[1] A.S. *feorth-dael*. Also called *corter* (quarter), Aberdeenshire.

> Wi' sweet-milk cheese i' mony a whang,
> An farlies baked wi' butter.
> —Burns: *The Holy Fair*.

Some bakers nowadays use the term *farle* for the thin quarters and *bannock* for
the thick ones of the same dimension.

An excellent oatcake is baked with whey, in place of fat and water. Buttermilk and cream, fresh or sour, may be used, but milk renders them flinty.

Oatcakes were at one time the gala-bread of the cottager; barley-bread was the ordinary fare.

" Oatcakes are a delicate relish when eaten warm with ale."—Burns.

" Oatcakes should always be sent to table with fresh herrings garnished with raw onions and cold butter."—Mrs. McEwen: *Elements of Cookery*, 1835.

Oatcakes are especially good with herrings, sardines, cheese, curds, buttermilk, broth, and kail; or spread with butter and marmalade to complete the breakfast.—F. M. McN.

SOME VARIETIES OF OATCAKES

Branderbannock. A thick bannock cooked on a brander.

Een-cake or *Oon-cake.* Thick cake made of yeast and oatmeal and baked in the oven.

Clauti-scone. A coarse scone of oatmeal and yeast made in Kinross.

Mill-bannock. " A circular cake of oatmeal, with a hole in the centre, generally a foot in diameter and an inch in thickness. It is baked at milnes and *haurned* or toasted on the burning seeds of shelled oats, which makes it as brittle as if it had been baked with butter."—*Gall. Ency.*

Caper. A piece of oatcake and butter with a slice of cheese on it. Gael. *ceapaire*.

Beltane Bannocks. Oatcakes, prepared in a special way, were used from time immemorial in the rites of Beltane (May 1st, O.S.). Pennant (1769) writes: " Everyone takes a cake of oatmeal, upon which are raised nine square knobs, each dedicated to some particular being, the supposed preserver of their flocks and herds, or to some particular animal, the real destroyer of them. Each person turns his face to the fire, breaks off a knob, and, flinging it over his shoulder, says: ' This I give to thee, preserve thou my horses; this to thee, preserve thou my sheep,' and so on. After that, they use the same ceremony to the noxious animals: ' This I give to thee, O Fox, spare thou my lambs; this to thee, O Hooded Crow, this to thee, O Eagle!' "

" The Beltane cakes with the nine knobs on them," writes the Rev. Walter Gregor in *Folklore*, " remind us of the cakes with twelve knobs which the Athenians offered to Cronus and other deities."

In Badenoch, until recently, oatcakes marked on one side with a cross and on the other with a circle were rolled down the hillside on Beltane morning.

According to Sir James Frazer, Beltane bannocks were oatcakes baked in the usual way, but washed over with a thin batter composed of whipped egg, milk, and cream, and a little oatmeal. (See *The Golden Bough*.) This batter is called the Beltane caudle. Pennant (1774) describes how in every village the herdsmen light the Beltane fire and on it " dress a large caudle of eggs, butter, oatmeal, and milk ", some of which they spill on the ground " by way of libation ".

John Ramsay, the Laird of Ochiltree and a contemporary of Burns, mentions " a large cake baked with eggs and scalloped round the edge, called *an bonnach beal-tine*, the Beltane bannock ".

" It is no longer made in Uist," writes Miss Goodrich-Freer in *More Folklore from the Hebrides* (1902), " but Father Allan [1] remembers seeing his grandmother make one about twenty-five years ago."

The Beltane bannock appears to be the last survivor of the old Highland Quarter Cakes; the *bonnach Bride*, St. Bride's bannock, baked for the first day of spring; the

[1] The late Father Allan Macdonald of Eriskay, a distinguished folk-lorist and much-loved priest.

Bannocks, Scones, Tea-bread

bonnach Bealltain, Beltane bannock, baked for the first day of summer; the *bonnach Lunastain,* Lammas bannock, baked for the first day of autumn; and the *bonnach Samhthain,* Hallowmas bannock, baked for the first day of winter.

Bonnach Salainn (salt bannock). An oatcake, baked in the ordinary way save for the addition of a great deal of salt, which used to be eaten in the Highlands at Hallowe'en to induce dreams that would foretell the future. No water might be drunk, nor any word spoken, after it was eaten, or the charm would not work.

Cryin'-bannock. When a child was born, in some districts a bannock, called a cryin'-bannock, made of oatmeal, cream, and sugar, and cooked in a frying-pan, was served up to the " kimmers " (gossips) present.

Teethin'-bannock. When a child first showed symptoms of cutting teeth, a bannock of oatmeal and butter or cream, sometimes with a ring in it, was made and given to the child to play with till broken. The child got a small bit and so did each one present. See *Notes on the Folklore of the North-east of Scotland,* by the Rev. W. Gregor.

St. Columba's Cake. A bere, rye, or oaten cake, baked on the eve of St Columba's Day (June 9th). A small silver coin was put into the dough, and the cake was toasted before a fire of rowan, yew, oak, or other sacred wood. The child who got the coin got the crop of lambs for the year.

The original oatcake was made of oatmeal and cold water. In the Hebrides, this is called a *potag* or *ollag.* Until quite recent times, the Skye fishermen used to dip a handful of oatmeal over the side of the boat into the sea, and when it was thoroughly moistened, kneaded into a bannock. On this frugal fare they could subsist, if need were, for days.

According to Froissart, the accoutrements of the Scottish soldier in the fourteenth century included a flat plate at his saddle and a wallet of meal at his back, " the purpose whereof is this: Whereas a Scottish soldier hath eaten of flesh so long that he beginneth to loathe the same, he casteth this plate into the fire, he moisteneth a little of his meal in water, and when the plate is heated, he layeth his paste thereon and maketh a little cake, the which he eateth to comfort his stomach. Hence it is no marvel that the Scots should be able to make longer marches than other men."

While staying some time ago in the Mackintosh country, the writer was told of an old woman who lived in a cottage between Culloden and Moy during the Forty-five. On the day of the battle, word having reached her of the Prince's defeat, the old soul carried her table, her girdle, and a quantity of oatmeal down to the roadside, lit a gipsy fire, and baked for all she was worth; and when presently Charlie's men came by, speeding to the hills for safety, each seized an oatcake from the pile.

In old Scotland, preparations for " the daft days ", between Yule and Hogmanay (Christmas and New Year), included the baking of a quantity of ceremonial fare and the brewing of festive ale.

> Atween Yule and Yearsmas,
> Auld wives shouldna spin;
> An' nae hoose should be waterless
> Whare maidens lie within.
> —Old Rhyme.

The *Yule bread* proper was a thin bannock of oatmeal cut into quarters, to symbolize the cross, before being placed on the girdle. There was also a sour cake, known in Moray and Banffshire as *Soor Poos,* made of oatmeal moistened with the water poured off sowens. These cakes were baked before daybreak on Christmas morning, when each member of the family received one, which he endeavoured to keep intact until the time of the evening feast. If it remained whole, the owner might expect unbroken prosperity throughout the year; if it were broken, shattered likewise were his hopes of good fortune.—F. M. McN.

SOUR-SKONS

(*Orkney*)

Oatmeal, flour, baking-soda, sugar, caraway seeds, butter-milk.

Soak some oatmeal in buttermilk for a few days, then take it and beat it up with flour into which you have stirred a little baking-soda (allow roughly a teaspoonful to each pound of oatmeal and flour), sugar to taste (don't over-sweeten), and a few caraway seeds. Make into a soft dough, roll out, and bake on the girdle.

RUTHERGLEN SOUR CAKES

(A SPECIAL CAKE AT ST. LUKE'S FAIR)

(Traditional Recipe, abbreviated from the " New Statistical Account of Scotland ", 1845.)

Oatmeal, water, sugar, aniseed or cinnamon.

Eight or ten days before St. Luke's Fair, a certain quantity of oatmeal was made into a dough with warm water and laid up in a vessel to ferment. Being brought to a proper degree of fermentation and consistency, it was rolled up into balls pro-portionable to the intended size of the cakes. With the dough there was commonly mixed a small quantity of sugar and a little aniseed or cinnamon. The cakes were beaten out until as thin as a piece of paper, and were toasted on a girdle.

The elaborate ritual with which these cakes were prepared, and which clearly derives from a pagan origin, is fully described in the *New Statistical Account* (under *Rutherglen*).

SOWEN SCONES

(*Orkney*)

Flour, sugar, salt, bicarbonate of soda, the liquid poured off sowens,[1] caraways (optional).

Mix together a pound of flour, a pinch of salt, a teaspoonful of sugar, another of bicarbonate of soda, and a few caraways, if

[1] For sowens, see p. 202.

liked. Make this into a thinnish batter with the liquid poured off sowens, adding a little of the sediment. (The amount is a matter of taste: some like it strongly, some mildly flavoured.) Rub a hot girdle with a piece of suet and drop on the batter in spoonfuls, as for Scots crumpets. When ready on one side, turn quickly with a knife and brown the other. Serve hot with butter.

WHITE GIRDLE SCONES
(OR SODA SCONES)

Flour, bicarbonate of soda, cream of tartar, salt, buttermilk or sour milk.

Sieve into a basin a pound of flour, a teaspoonful of carbonate of soda, a teaspoonful of cream of tartar, and half a teaspoonful of salt. Add enough buttermilk or thick sour milk to make a very soft dough. Turn out on a floured board and divide into four. Flatten each piece into a round scone, about half an inch in thickness. Cut each in quarters, flour them, and place them on a hot girdle. Let them cook steadily till well risen and of a light brown underneath (about five minutes), then turn with a knife and cook on the other side about the same length of time. When the edges are dry they are ready. Serve fresh-baked with butter. They are especially popular on the breakfast-table.

These scones are often baked as bannocks, i.e. in one large round, the size of a meat-plate, and are cut up on the table. They may be made richer by having an ounce or two of butter rubbed into the flour.

MRS. MACNAB'S SCONES[1]

Flour, butter, salt, bicarbonate of soda, cream of tartar, egg, buttermilk.

[1] Mrs. Macnab was the wife of a farmer who lived near Ballater. Such was her reputation as a baker that King Frederick of Prussia and other distinguished guests at Balmoral used frequently to go over and have tea with her. It is not possible to impart Mrs. Macnab's lightness of touch, nor the wine-like air of these regions, which doubtless contributed to her visitors' enjoyment; but here, at least, is the recipe for her celebrated scones.

Mix thoroughly a pound of flour, a teaspoonful of salt, a small teaspoonful of carbonate of soda, and two small teaspoonfuls of cream of tartar. Rub in two ounces of butter. Stir in gradually a beaten egg and half a pint of buttermilk.[1] Turn out the dough on a floured board, flour the top, and knead with the hand as little as possible. Cut off pieces of dough and flatten them with the knuckles, but do not roll out at all. Prick with a fork and cut into quarters. Bake in a pretty quick oven for from ten to fifteen minutes.

The secret of success lies in not working the dough with the hands except just once kneading it.

POTATO SCONES

Cooked potatoes, flour, salt, sweet milk.

Mash half a pound of boiled potatoes and add, if necessary, a pinch of salt. Knead in as much flour as it will take up (about two ounces) and add about half a gill of sweet milk or enough to make a very stiff dough. Roll out very thinly on a floured board. Cut into rounds and prick with a fork. Bake on a hot girdle for about five minutes, turning when half cooked. When baked, butter the scones, roll up, and serve very hot.

CLAP SCONES

(Old Cottage Recipe)

Flour, salt, boiling water.

Put a quantity of fine flour into a basin, add salt to taste, and stir in enough boiling water to make a nice pliable dough. Form into rounds and pat them lightly out with the palm of the hand, sprinkling when necessary with flour. They should be as thin as it is possible to make them. Bake them on a pretty hot girdle. When nearly cold, pile them one over the other and

---

[1] Fresh milk may be substituted in the above recipe, but buttermilk is better. Scones in Scotland are served fresh-baked—warm from the oven, but not hot. Serve with butter, and jam if desired.

There are many varieties of scone—syrup, treacle, spice, raisin, and so on, the recipes for which are available in contemporary cookery-books.—F. M. McN.

roll them up tightly in a clean towel. They must not lie flat.
These scones are exceedingly sweet, but must be baked fresh
every day. Spread them with butter and syrup or honey, and
roll up each separately.

HIGHLAND SLIM CAKES

(*Meg Dods's Recipe*)

Flour, butter, eggs, hot milk.

Are often used in the Highlands, and in country situations,
for breakfast or tea. To a pound of flour allow from two to
four ounces of butter, as much hot milk as will make a dough
of the flour, and two beat eggs, if the cakes are wished to rise.
Handle quickly, and lightly roll out, and stamp of any size wanted
with a basin, a saucer, or tumbler. Bake on the girdle or in a
thick-bottomed frying-pan. They must be served hot, kept in
a heap, and used newly baked, as on keeping they become tough.

DROP SCONES

(*Family Recipe*)

Flour, sugar, baking-soda, cream of tartar, egg, buttermilk.

Mix in a basin a pound of flour, two tablespoonfuls of sugar,
a small teaspoonful of baking-soda, and another of cream of
tartar (or half that quantity of tartaric acid). Rub the lumps
well out of the soda before putting it in. Add gradually a beaten
egg and a scant pint of buttermilk, beating well with the back
of a spoon for a few minutes. Have ready a hot girdle, grease
it slightly with a piece of suet wrapped in a white rag, and drop
on the batter, a spoonful at a time until the girdle is full. Take
care that they are a neat round shape. (A greased tin ring
may be placed on the girdle and the batter poured through it,
the tin being removed in a minute or two.) When the scones
are covered with bubbles on the top, slip a broad knife under
them, and if they are of a golden brown colour, turn them and
brown the other side. They should be turned only once. Lay
them on a clean towel, and keep them covered with it till cool.

These scones may be made with sweet milk, but it is necessary to double the quantity of cream of tartar, and the quality is not quite the same. A small piece of butter may be rubbed into the flour. The egg may be omitted. Maize flour and ordinary flour may be used in the proportion of 3 to 1.

SCOTS CRUMPETS [1]

(*Traditional Recipe*)

Flour, sugar, eggs, milk.

Make the batter some hours before it is required.

Beat separately the yolks and whites of four eggs. Pour into a basin and add half a pint of milk and three tablespoonfuls of sugar. Mix well, and gradually add flour till you have a thickish batter. Beat till quite smooth and set aside. Put a girdle or frying-pan on a bright clear fire and rub with suet. To have light, pretty crumpets the fire must be brisk and the girdle hot, so that they will rise quickly. Drop with a spoon as many as the girdle will hold, and before they have time to form a skin and get dry on the top they should be ready to turn. Do this quickly, and a lovely golden-brown skin as smooth as velvet will be formed, and a delightfully light crumpet produced.

BUTTERMILK BREAD
(Or Soda Loaf)

(*Traditional Recipe*)

Flour, bicarbonate of soda, cream of tartar, salt, sugar, butter (optional), buttermilk or thick, sour milk.

Mix thoroughly in a basin four teacupfuls of flour, a teaspoonful of bicarbonate of soda (the lumps rubbed out), another of cream of tartar, a pinch of salt and a small tablespoonful of

---

[1] These resemble English crumpets only in name, and are much more closely akin to Shrove-Tuesday pancakes. It is extremely probable that they are identical with the old Scottish *car-cakes* (mentioned by Scott in *The Bride of Lammermoor*), which Jamieson defines as " a kind of thin cake, made of milk, meal or flour, eggs beaten up, and sugar, baked and eaten on Fastern's E'en ".

sugar. An ounce of butter is an improvement, but is not necessary. It should be lightly rubbed into the dry ingredients.
Make into a soft dough with about half a pint of buttermilk or
thick sour milk. Put into a floured tin and bake in a moderate
oven for three-quarters of an hour or till ready.

SELKIRK BANNOCK [1]

(*Traditional Border Recipe*)

*Baker's dough, butter, lard, sugar, sultanas, candied orange
peel.*

Get two pounds of dough from the baker. Into this rub
four ounces of butter and four ounces of lard until melted but
not oiled. Then work in half a pound of sugar, three-quarters
of a pound of sultanas (or half a pound of sultanas and a quarter-
pound of currants), and a quarter-pound of finely chopped orange
peel. Put the dough into a buttered tin, let it stand before the
fire for about thirty minutes to rise and then bake in a good
steady oven.

BAPS [2]

(*Traditional Recipe*)

Flour, salt, lard, yeast, sugar, milk, water.

Sift a pound of flour into a warm bowl and mix with it a small
teaspoonful of salt. Rub in, with the finger-tips, two ounces of
lard. In another bowl, cream an ounce of yeast and a teaspoonful
of sugar (that is, work them together with a wooden spoon till
liquid); add half a pint of tepid milk-and-water (half and half),
and strain into the flour. Make into a soft dough, cover, and
set to rise for an hour in a warm place. Knead lightly and divide
into pieces of equal size to form oval shapes about three inches

---

[1] Mentioned by Scott in *The Bride of Lammermoor*.

[2] The etymology of the word is unknown. We learn from a sixteenth-century document that they were sold at nine for twelve pence. In Allan Ramsay's *Tea-Table
Miscellany*, one line unites

Sowens, farles, and baps.

long and two wide. Brush with milk or water (to give a glaze), and, if " floury baps " are desired, dust them with flour just after brushing them, and again just before they go into the oven. Place the baps on a greased and floured tin and set again in a warm place, to prove, for fifteen minutes. To prevent blisters, press a finger into the centre of each before they are placed in the oven. Bake in a hot oven for from fifteen to twenty minutes. Baps appear exclusively on the breakfast-table, and should be eaten warm from the oven.

" The grandfather of a late Prime Minister of Great Britain [1] kept a small shop in Leith Walk, Edinburgh, where he sold ' baps ', flour, oatmeal, peas, &c., and where he was popularly known to the boys of the neighbourhood as ' Sma' Baps ', because his baps were reputed to be smaller than those of his brother tradesmen."— C. Mackay: *Dictionary of Lowland Scots*.

SOFT BISCUITS
(ABERDEEN AND N.E.)

Baker's dough, butter, sugar.

To every pound of baker's dough add three ounces of melted butter and a tablespoonful of sugar. Form into rounds shaped like flattened buns and about three or four inches in diameter Bake in a good oven.

COOKIES [2]

(*Traditional Recipe*)

Flour, sugar, butter, yeast, salt, eggs, milk.

Sieve one and a half pounds of flour into a warm basin and make a hole in the centre. Melt three ounces of butter in a sauce-pan, add three gills of milk and make lukewarm. Cream an ounce of yeast with a teaspoonful of salt, pour over this the warm milk and butter, and strain into the middle of the flour. Add two well-beaten eggs and beat the mixture till smooth

[1] W. E. Gladstone.
[2] The " cukie " is mentioned in *Foulis of Ravelstone's Account Book*, 1671–1707. Teut. *koeck*; Belg. *koekie*.

and light. Cover the basin and set it in a warm place till the dough has risen to about twice its original size. Then mix in six ounces of fine sugar. Stiffen the dough with flour so that it will not adhere to the baking-board. Divide into two-ounce pieces, and form into rounds. Place the cookies on greased and floured tins. Set them in a warm place till they begin to swell and puff out, then bake in a good oven. When almost ready, glaze them with a little sugar dissolved in hot milk. Split and spread with butter, jam, or whipped cream.

A richer cookie may be made as follows: Rub six ounces of butter into a pound and a half of flour; put it into a basin and break in four eggs; add one pint of lukewarm water with a small teacupful of yeast, mixing them together; cover it up, and let it sponge all night. Proceed as above, adding six ounces of sugar.

Note.—A *cooky-shine* is the Scottish equivalent of the English *bun-fight* (tea-party).

HOT CROSS BUNS

(Scots Fashion)

Flour, salt butter, yeast, eggs, water, sugar, cinnamon, ginger, nutmeg, cloves, scraps of paste.

Rub six ounces of salt butter into two pounds of flour and break three eggs among it, in a basin. Add a breakfast-cupful of yeast and mix all together with sufficient tepid water to make it into a thin batter. Cover it up and let it stand all night in a warm place. Mix it up next morning with half a pound of sugar, half an ounce of cinnamon, half an ounce of ginger, a little grated nutmeg, and a very little ground cloves. Mix all well together with as much flour as will keep the dough from sticking to the hands. Allow two ounces of dough to each bun and shape them into rounds. Prove them for an hour in a steam press or some other warm place. Cut some scraps of pastry into thin narrow strips and place these on the buns in the form of a cross. Bake in a quick oven for a few minutes and glaze with sugar and water.

ABERDEEN CRULLA [1]

(Mrs. Dalgairns' Recipe)

Flour, butter, sugar, eggs, lard or suet.

Beat to a cream a quarter-pound of fresh butter and mix with it the same quantity of pounded and sifted loaf sugar and four well-beaten eggs; add flour till thick enough to roll out; cut the paste into oblong pieces about four or five inches in length; with a paste cutter divide the centre into three or four strips; wet the edges and plait one bar over the other so as to meet in the centre; throw them into boiling lard or clarified suet; when fried of a light brown, drain them before the fire and serve them in a napkin, with or without grated loaf sugar served over them.

DEER HORNS

(Mrs. Dalgairns' Recipe)

Flour, sugar, almonds, lemon, eggs, cream.

Beat one white and six yolks of eggs; mix them with five tablespoonfuls of pounded and sifted loaf sugar, the same quantity of sweet (fresh) cream, ten sweet almonds, blanched and pounded, the grated peel of one lemon, and as much flour as will make the whole into a paste sufficiently thick to roll out. Then cut it with tins for this purpose into the forms of horns, branches, or any other shape, and throw them into boiling lard.

SOME VARIETIES OF BREAD

In sixteenth-century Scotland there were four kinds of wheaten bread, the finest called *Manche*, the second *Cheat*, or trencher bread, the third *Ravelled*, and the fourth *Mashloch*. The Ravelled was baked just as it came from the mill, flour, bran, and all. From the Mashloch the flour was almost entirely sifted; a portion of rye was mixed with the bran, and this composition was used by poor people and servants. (See Arnot's *History of Edinburgh.*)

Breid o' Mane. A very light and savoury white bread.

Breid o' Trayt. A superior kind of white bread.

Ankerstock. A large loaf of rye, oblong in shape.—Jamieson. " The anker-stock

---

[1] A crule is a small cake or bannock; N. of S. Isl. *kril*, anything very small.—Jamieson.

was a round loaf made of rye flour, and seasoned with spice and currants, and used as New Year gingerbread."—Hislop's *Scottish Anecdotes* (1875). "A Musselburgh ankerstoke" is mentioned by D. M. Moir in *Mansie Waugh*. Ankerstock gingerbread is still sold by Edinburgh bakers. Probably from Dutch *anker*, a measure (the fourth part of a boll).

Bake. A small cake, a biscuit.—Fergusson, Burns.

Bakin-Lotch. "A species of bread, perhaps of an enticing quality."—Jamieson.

Bawbee Raw. A ha'penny roll.—*St. Ronan's Well.*

Birlin. A small cake made of oatmeal or barley-meal. Gael. *builin*, a loaf.

Clod. A flat kind of loaf, made of coarse wheaten flour or peasemeal. *Clods.* Small raised loaves, baked of coarse flour, of which three were sold for five farthings. *Soutar's Clods.* A kind of coarse brown wheaten bread used in Selkirk, leavened and surrounded with a thick crust, like clods.—Jamieson.

"The Baijen Hole, a celebrated and very ancient baker's shop, . . . was famed for a species of rolls called Soutar's Clods, which were in great request among the boys of Edinburgh on account of their satisfactory dimensions."—R. Chambers: *Traditions of Edinburgh.*

Derrin. A broad thick cake or loaf of oat or barley meal or mixed pease and barley meal, which is fired in the oven or on the hearth covered with hot ashes; Roxburghshire. "This term is very ancient and is probably derived from the mode of preparation. Teut. *derren*, to dry or parch."—Jamieson.

Fadge, fage. A large flat cake or loaf. Fr. *fouace*, a thick cake.—Allan Ramsay.

Foal. A bannock or cake; any soft, thick bread (Orkney).

Meldar. A salted cake.—Douglas. Isl. *malldr*, from *mal-a*, to grind.—Jamieson.

Nacket (Roxburgh), *Nockit* (Galloway), *Nackie* (Ayrshire). A small cake or loaf; a piece of bread eaten at noon; something to eat with wine. Sueo-Goth. *kneck*, globulous.—Jamieson.

Snoddie. A thick cake or bannock baked among hot ashes (Orkney). Isl. *snad*, food.—Jamieson.

Sod. A species of bread (Ayrshire).

Tivlach. A thick cake of oatmeal (Shetland).

Tod, Toddie. A small round cake of any kind of bread, given to children to keep them in good humour (Roxburgh), *Todgie* (Berwickshire), *Toly, Toddle* (Upper Clydesdale). Isl. *taata, placenta infantum.*—Jamieson.

Wafrans. Wafers, thin cakes. *Wafroun* (Lanarkshire). *Treas. Acts.*

Whig. A fine wheaten tea-bread.—Sir John Sinclair.

CAKES AND SHORTBREADS

" In the beginning, the professional baker in the towns may possibly have borrowed his methods from the French. At any rate, being patronized chiefly by the nobles and the wealthier burghers, he was accustomed to use the very best materials, and he rejoiced in every encouragement to devote himself to the perfection of his methods. To beat the Edinburgh baker, you must go—not to London, but—to Paris or Vienna."—T. F. Henderson: *Old-World Scotland.*

DUNDEE CAKE

(*Old Family Recipe*)

Flour, butter, sugar, currants, raisins, sultanas, mixed candied peel, almonds, orange, eggs.

Prepare the fruit, a quarter-pound each of currants, raisins, and sultanas. Shred two ounces of candied peel. Sift half a pound of flour. Beat half a pound of butter and half a pound of sugar to a cream. Into this break six eggs, one at a time, beating well.[1] Beat in the flour very gradually. Add the fruit, with three ounces of ground almonds and the zest of an orange. Pour into a cake-tin lined with buttered paper, flatten the top, and strew with blanched and shredded almonds. Bake in a steady oven.

MONTROSE CAKES

(*Mrs. Dalgairns' Recipe*)

Flour, sugar, butter, currants (optional), brandy, rose-water, nutmeg, eggs.

Of dried and sifted flour, pounded and sifted loaf sugar, and of fresh butter, one pound each will be required; also twelve well-beaten eggs, three-quarters of a pound of cleaned

---

[1] Four eggs may be used, with half a teaspoonful of baking-powder. In other cake recipes the number of eggs may be similarly reduced. Many of them were written before the invention of baking-powder.—F. M. McN.

and dried currants; beat the butter to a cream with the sugar; add the eggs by degrees and then the flour and currants with two tablespoonfuls of brandy and one of rose-water and half a grated nutmeg; beat all well together for twenty to thirty minutes, when it is to be put into small buttered tins, half filling them and baking in a quick oven. The currants may be omitted.

SCOTS SEED CAKE

(Mrs. Dalgairns' Recipe)

Flour, butter, sugar, almonds, orange and citron peel, nutmeg, ground caraways, eggs, rose-water, brandy, caraway comfits.

Take a pound of dried and sifted flour, the same quantity of fresh butter washed in rose-water and of finely pounded loaf sugar, four ounces of blanched sweet almonds, half a pound of candied orange peel, five ounces of citron, all cut into thin narrow strips; a small nutmeg grated, a small teaspoonful of grated caraway seeds, ten eggs, the yolks and whites beaten separately; then with the hand beat the butter to a cream, add the sugar and then the eggs gradually; mix in the flour a little at a time, and then the sweetmeats, almonds, and spice, and, lastly, stir in a glass of brandy; butter the hoop or tin pan, and pour in the cake so as nearly to fill it; smooth it over the top, and strew over it caraway comfits. Bake it in a moderate oven; it must not be moved or turned till nearly done, as shaking it will occasion the sweetmeats sinking to the bottom

SCOTS SNOW CAKE [1]

(Old Family Recipe)

Arrowroot, butter, sugar, eggs, lemon, almond or vanilla flavouring.

Beat half a pound of butter to a cream. Mix a pound of arrowroot with half a pound of pounded white sugar, and roll them out till perfectly smooth and free from lumps. Stir them

[1] This is practically identical with Mrs. Beeton's " genuine Scotch recipe ".

gradually into the butter, beating well. Whisk the whites of six eggs to a stiff froth, add, and beat for twenty minutes. Add a few drops of essence of lemon, almonds, or vanilla. Pour into a buttered tin and bake in a moderate oven for an hour to an hour and a half.

SCOTS DIET LOAF [1]

(*Meg Dods's Recipe*)

Flour, sugar, eggs, lemon, cinnamon.

Take a pound of fine sugar sifted, the same weight of eggs very well whisked, and mix and beat these together for twenty minutes. Season with lemon grate and cinnamon. Stir in very smoothly three-quarters of a pound of sifted flour. This is a very light cake and will bake quickly. It may either be iced or have sifted sugar strewed over it before baking.

BLACK BUN [2]

(A Festive Cake at Hogmanay)

Thou tuck-shop king! Joy of our gourmand youth!
  What days thou mark'st, and what blood-curdling nights!
Nights full of shapeless things, hideous, uncouth;
  Imp follows ghoul, ghoul follows jinn, pell mell;
Fierce raisin-devils and gay currant-sprites
  Hold lightsome leap-frog in a pastry hell.
          —Augustus Bejant: " Invocation to Black Bun"
                    (*Glasgow University Magazine*).

(*Old Family Recipe*)

Big blue raisins, currants, sweet almonds; orange, lemon, and citron peel; flour, Demerara sugar, ground cloves or cinnamon, ground ginger, Jamaica pepper, black pepper, baking-soda, buttermilk or eggs, brandy; crust: flour, butter, water.

Wash and dry two pounds of currants. Stone two pounds of big blue raisins. Blanch and chop half a pound of almonds. Chop half a pound of mixed candied peel. Sift a pound of flour

---

[1] Mentioned by Scott in *St. Ronan's Well*.

[2] "Bun: An old word for plumcake or twelfthcake."
          —Sir John Sinclair, *Observations on the Scottish Dialect* (1782).

and mix with it four ounces of sugar, half an ounce of ground cloves or cinnamon, half an ounce of ground ginger, a teaspoonful of Jamaica pepper, half a teaspoonful of black pepper, a small teaspoonful of baking-soda. Add to these the prepared fruits. Add just enough buttermilk or beaten egg, with a tablespoonful of brandy, to moisten the mixture.

Make a paste by lightly rubbing half a pound of butter into a pound of flour and mixing in quickly enough water to make a stiff dough. Roll out thinly. Grease a large cake-tin and line it evenly with the paste, retaining enough to cover the top. Trim the edges, put the mixture in, and make the surface flat and smooth. Moisten the edges of the pastry with cold water and flatten on the round top. Make all secure and neat. With a skewer make four holes right down to the bottom of the cake. Prick all over with a fork, brush with beaten egg, and bake in a moderate oven for about four hours.

An eighteenth-century recipe: "Take half a peck of flour, keeping out a little to work it up with; make a hole in the middle of the flour, and break in sixteen ounces of butter; pour in a mutchkin (pint) of warm water, and three gills of yeast, and work it up into a smooth dough. If it is not wet enough, put in a little more warm water; then cut off one-third of the dough, and lay it aside for the cover. Take three pounds of stoned raisins, three pounds of cleaned currants, half a pound of blanched almonds cut longwise, candied orange and citron peel cut, of each eight ounces; half an ounce of cloves, an ounce of cinnamon, and two ounces of ginger, all beat and sifted. Mix the spices by themselves, then spread out the dough; lay the fruit upon it; strew the spices over the fruit, and mix all together. When it is well kneaded, roll out the cover, and lay the bun upon it; then cover it neatly, cut it round the sides, prickle it, and bind it with paper to keep it in shape; set it in a pretty quick oven, and, just before you take it out, glaze the top with a beat egg."
—Mrs. Frazer. *Practice of Cookery* (Edinburgh, 1791).

SCOTS CURRANT LOAF [1]

(*Old Family Recipe*)

Flour, sugar, currants, raisins, orange peel, mixed spice, black pepper, ginger, cream of tartar, bicarbonate of soda, buttermilk (or fresh milk); crust: flour, baking-powder, butter, water.

Rub half a pound of butter into a pound and a half of flour. Add half a teaspoonful of baking-powder and mix to a paste

[1] This is a poor relation of Black Bun, which it replaces at Hogmanay in all households where the richness or expense of Black Bun is an objection.

with water. Roll out rather thinly and line a large cake-tin with the paste, reserving enough to cover the top.

Now put into a basin a pound of flour, half a pound of sugar, a pound of currants, washed and dried, half a pound of raisins, cleaned and stoned, a quarter-pound of orange peel, a teaspoonful of mixed spice, half a teaspoonful of ginger and the same of black pepper, one teaspoonful of bicarbonate of soda and one of cream of tartar. Just moisten with buttermilk. About a breakfast-cupful will be required. Complete as for Black Bun.

HALLOWE'EN CAKE

Prepare a plain white or birthday cake, but just before you put the batter into the cake-tin, stir in a few silver or nickel charms [1], each wrapped in a morsel of grease-proof paper. The cake should be iced appropriately.[2]

SCOTS GINGERBREAD [3]

(Traditional Recipe)

Flour, oatmeal, butter, green ginger, lemon peel, treacle, cream.

Beat eight ounces of butter to a cream. Mix with it twelve ounces of flour, four ounces of oatmeal, and half a gill of cream. Stir in twelve ounces of treacle, one ounce of green ginger, and four ounces of lemon peel cut into fine shreds. Work the

---

[1] The charms most commonly used are the ring (foretelling marriage to the recipient), the button (bachelordom), the thimble (spinsterhood), the coin (wealth), the wish-bone (the heart's desire), the horse-shoe (good luck), and the swastika (happiness).

[2] Orange and black are the Hallowe'en colours, and in the principal bakers' windows one may see cakes coated with tangerine icing, on which are silhouetted, in chocolate icing, witches on broom-sticks, black cats, owls, bats, and such-like emblems of witchery. Other cakes are shaped like apples or pumpkins and covered with marzipan icing appropriately moulded and tinted.

[3] There are many varieties of gingerbread in Scotland We give only a selection See p. 184, note on Ankerstock.

whole into a light dough. Put in a well-greased tin and bake for forty-five minutes.

FOCHABERS GINGERBREAD

(*Moray*)

Flour, butter, castor sugar, treacle, sultanas, currants, ground almonds, mixed peel, mixed spices, ground ginger, ground cinnamon, ground cloves, bicarbonate of soda, eggs, beer.

Beat a pound of butter and half a pound of sugar to a cream. Warm a pound of treacle slightly and add. Then break in four eggs, one at a time, beating well. Mix together two pounds of flour, half a pound of sultanas, half a pound of currants, six ounces of ground almonds, six ounces of finely chopped candied peel, an ounce of mixed spices, an ounce of ground ginger, half an ounce of ground cinnamon, a quarter-ounce of ground cloves, and add these to the butter, &c. Dissolve two tea-spoonfuls of bicarbonate of soda in a pint of beer and add. Mix thoroughly. Put into buttered cake-tins and bake in a slow oven for two hours. These quantities make six pounds of cake.

BROONIE [1]

(ORKNEY OATMEAL GINGERBREAD)

Oatmeal, flour, brown sugar, butter, ground ginger, baking-soda, treacle, egg, buttermilk.

Mix in a basin six ounces of oatmeal and six of flour. Rub in two ounces of butter. Add a teaspoonful of ground ginger and barely three-quarters of a teaspoonful of baking-soda, free from lumps. Melt two tablespoonfuls of treacle, and add, together with a beaten egg and enough buttermilk to make the mixture sufficiently soft to drop from the spoon. Mix thoroughly. Turn into a buttered tin and bake for from one to one and a half hours in a moderate oven till well risen and firm in the centre.

[1] Correctly, *Brüni*, a thick bannock (Orkney and Shetland).

PARLIES (PARLIAMENT CAKES)

" A species of gingerbread supposed to have its name from being used by the members of the Scottish Parliament."—Jamieson.

(Mrs. Fletcher's [1] Recipe, from Meg Dods's " Manual ")

Flour, sugar, ginger, butter, treacle.

With two pounds of the best dried flour mix thoroughly one pound of the best brown sugar and a quarter-pound of ground ginger. Melt a pound of fresh butter, add to it one of treacle, boil this, and pour it on the flour. Work up the paste as hot as your hands will bear it and roll it out in very large cakes, a sixth of an inch thick or less. Mark it in squares with a knife or paper-cutter, and fire in a slow oven. Separate the squares when soft and they will soon get crisp.

SNAPS [2]

Flour, sugar, butter, ground ginger, syrup or treacle.

Beat to a cream twelve ounces of sugar and six of butter. Add eight ounces of flour and a quarter-ounce of ground ginger, and lastly eight ounces (four tablespoonfuls) of syrup or treacle. Mix well, and let the mixture stand in a hot place till it is of a thin, creamy consistency. Spread thinly with a knife over a buttered sheet tin, cut into rounds, and bake in a hot oven. When nearly ready, brush with a syrup of sugar and water to give a glaze. Store in air-tight tins.

[1] " This worthy lady was the universal favourite of the schoolboys of Edinburgh, the contemporaries of Sir Walter Scott. We regret not being able to recover her recipe for White Quality Cakes."—Note to Mistress Dods's *Manual.*

I am of the opinion that this Mrs. Fletcher, whom I have been unable to identify, is one and the same with the celebrated Mrs. Flockhart (see p. 67) who, Chambers tells us in his *Traditions of Edinburgh*, supplied her customers with gingerbread " either in thin, crisp cakes called *Parliament*—in round pieces, denominated *Snaps*—or in thick, soft cakes, chequered on the surface, and, according to the colour, called *White* or *Brown Quality Cakes*."—F. M. McN.

[2] Mentioned by Scott in *St. Ronan's Well.* They are also called brandy snaps, and probably were originally flavoured with brandy.

HONEY CAKES

(Mrs. Dalgairns' Recipe)

Flour, honey, sugar, citron and orange peel, ginger, cinnamon.

One pound and a half of dried and sifted flour, three-quarters of a pound of honey, half a pound of finely pounded loaf sugar, a quarter of a pound of citron, and half an ounce of orange peel cut small, of pounded ginger and cinnamon three-quarters of an ounce. Melt the sugar with the honey and mix in the other ingredients; roll out the paste and cut it into small cakes of any form.

The Fair Maid of Perth served at breakfast " thin soft cakes, made of flour and honey according to the family receipt", which were " not only commended, but done liberal justice to ". Unfortunately her receipt has not survived six centuries!

—F. M. McN.

SCOTS SHORTBREAD

(A Festive Cake at Hogmanay)

" The triumph of Scottish baking on the old national lines."
—T. F. Henderson.

(Compiled from Traditional Recipes)

Flour, rice flour, butter, castor sugar.

Only the best materials should be used. The flour should be dried and sieved. The butter, which is the only moistening and shortening agent, should be squeezed free of all water. The sugar should be fine castor. Two other things are essential for success—the careful blending of the ingredients and careful firing.

The butter and sugar should first be blended. Put eight ounces of butter and four ounces of castor sugar on a board, and work with the hand until thoroughly incorporated Mix eight ounces of flour with four ounces of rice flour, and work gradually into the butter and sugar, until the dough is of the consistency of short crust. Be careful that it does not become oily (a danger in hot weather) nor toughened with over-mixing.

(D 994)   14

The less kneading, the more short and crisp the shortbread. Do not roll it out, as rolling too has a tendency to toughen it, but press with the hand into two round cakes, either in oiled and floured shortbread moulds or on a sheet of baking-paper. The most satisfactory thickness is three-quarters of an inch for a cake eight inches in diameter, or in such proportion. If you make a large thick cake it is advisable to protect the edges with a paper band or hoop, and to have several layers of paper underneath and possibly one on the top. Pinch the edges neatly all round with the finger and thumb, and prick all over with a fork. Decorate with " sweetie " almonds (for small cakes, caraway comfits may be used) and strips of citron or orange peel. Put into a fairly hot oven, reduce the heat presently, and allow the shortbread to crisp off to a light golden brown.

The *Infar-Cake*, or *Dreaming-Bread*. A decorated cake of shortbread is still the national bride's-cake of rural Scotland, and was formerly used as infar-cake. The breaking of the infar-cake over the head of the bride, on the threshold of her new home, is a very ancient custom, having its origin in the Roman rite of *confarratio*, in which the eating of a consecrated cake by the contracting parties constituted marriage. (Scots law, unlike English, is based on the old Roman Law.) Portions were distributed to the young men and maidens " to dream on ".

Immense quantities of shortbread are dispatched from Scotland every year, for the festive season, to relatives and friends in every quarter of the globe.—F. M. McN.

AYRSHIRE SHORTBREAD

(*Traditional Recipe*)

Flour, rice flour, castor sugar, butter, egg, cream.

Sieve four ounces of flour and four ounces of rice flour into a basin and rub in four ounces of butter with the finger-tips. Add four ounces of castor sugar and bind the mixture to a stiff consistency with the beaten yolk of an egg and two tablespoonfuls of cream. Roll out thinly, prick with a fork, and cut into rounds or fingers. Place the cakes on a greased paper and bake in a steady oven for about fifteen minutes or until of a golden brown colour. Cool on a wire sieve.

PITCAITHLY BANNOCK

(*Traditional Recipe*)

Flour, rice flour, butter, sugar, sweet almonds, citron peel.

Blanch an ounce of sweet almonds and chop them very finely along with an ounce of candied citron peel. Mix them with six ounces of flour and an ounce of rice flour. With the hand work three ounces of sugar into four ounces of butter, and work in the dry ingredients, as for shortbread. Ornament, if desired, with large caraways and orange peel. Make into a round flat cake, pinch the edges with the finger and thumb, lay on a sheet of paper on a tin, and bake in a moderate oven from thirty to thirty-five minutes.

PETTICOAT TAILS [1]

(*Meg Dods's Recipe*)

Flour, butter, sugar, caraway seeds (optional), milk.

Mix half an ounce, or fewer or none, caraway seeds [2] with a pound and three-quarters of flour. Make a hole in the middle of the flour and pour in eight ounces of butter melted in a quarter-pint of milk, and three ounces of beat sugar. Knead, but not too much, or it will not be short. Divide it in two and roll it out rather thin. Cut out the cake by running a paste-cutter round a dinner plate or any large round dish inverted on the paste. Cut a cake from the centre of this one with a small saucer or large tumbler. Keep this inner circle whole, and cut the outer one into eight *petticoat-tails*. Bake all these on paper laid on tins, serve the round cake in the middle of the plate, and the petticoat-tails as *radii* round it.

[1] "An English traveller in Scotland and one very well acquainted with France states in his very pleasant book that our club have fallen into a mistake in the name of these cakes, and that petticoat tails is a corruption of the French *Petites Gatelles*. It may be so: in Scottish culinary terms there are many corruptions, though we rather think the name petticoat tails has its origin in the shape of the cakes, which is exactly that of the bell-hoop petticoats of our ancient Court ladies."
—*Annals of the Cleikum Club.*

[2] This cake is usually made without caraways.

THE QUEEN'S TEA CAKES

(Mrs. Dalgairns' Recipe)

Flour, sugar, salt, butter, lemon, rose-water, eggs.

Mix together half a pound of dried and sifted flour, the same quantity of pounded and sifted loaf sugar, the weight of two eggs in fresh butter, the grated peel of a lemon, and a little salt; beat the two eggs with a little rose-water, and with them make the ingredients into a paste; roll it out, cut into round cakes, and bake upon floured tins.

TANTALLON CAKES

(Old Edinburgh Recipe)

Flour, rice flour, butter, sugar, bicarbonate of soda, lemon, eggs.

Mix together four ounces of flour, four ounces of rice flour, and a pinch of bicarbonate of soda. Cream four ounces of butter with four ounces of sugar. Beat two eggs and add these alternately with the flour to the butter and cream. Flavour with lemon. Make into a stiff dough, roll out thinly, and cut with a small scalloped round into biscuits. Bake for half an hour in a fairly hot oven. When cool, dust them with fine white sugar.

ABERNETHY BISCUITS

Flour, butter, sugar, caraways (optional), baking-powder, egg, milk.

Rub three ounces of butter into eight ounces of flour; add three ounces of sugar, half a teaspoonful of baking-powder, and (if liked) a small teaspoonful of caraway seeds. Beat an egg well, and pour it amongst the dry ingredients with a tablespoonful of milk. Mix thoroughly, and turn the paste on to a floured board. Roll out thinly, cut into rounds, place on a greased baking-tin, and bake for ten minutes in a moderate oven.

MISCELLANEOUS

PREPARATIONS OF OATMEAL, OF BLOOD, OF MILK, OF SEAWEEDS, ETC.

1. Preparations of Oatmeal

PORRIDGE

" The halesome parritch, chief o' Scotia's food."—Burns.

(The One and Only Method)

Oatmeal, salt, water.

It is advisable to keep a goblet exclusively for porridge.

Allow for each person one breakfastcupful of water, a handful of oatmeal (about an ounce and a quarter), and a small salt-spoonful of salt. Use fresh spring water and be particular about the quality of the oatmeal. Midlothian oats are unsurpassed the world over.

Bring the water to the boil and as soon as it reaches boiling-point add the oatmeal, letting it fall in a steady rain from the left hand and stirring it briskly the while with the right, sun-wise, or the right-hand turn for luck—and convenience. A porridge-stick, called a spurtle,[1] and in some parts a theevil,[2] or, as in Shetland, a gruel-tree, is used for this purpose. Be careful to avoid lumps, unless the children clamour for them. When the porridge is boiling steadily, draw the mixture to the side and put on the lid. Let it cook for from twenty to thirty minutes according to the quality of the oatmeal, and do not add the salt, which has a tendency to harden the meal and prevent its swelling, until it has cooked for at least ten minutes. On the other hand, never cook porridge without salt. Ladle

---

[1] A.S. *sprytle*.   [2] A.S. *thyfel*.

straight into porringers or soup-plates and serve with small individual bowls of cream, or milk, or buttermilk. Each spoonful of porridge, which should be very hot, is dipped in the cream or milk, which should be quite cold, before it is conveyed to the mouth.

Children often like a layer of sugar, honey, syrup, or treacle, or of raw oatmeal on top. A morsel of butter in the centre of the plate agrees with some digestions better than milk.

Porter, skeachan, and brisk small beer used to be popular accompaniments to porridge. In his poem "Scotch Drink" (which in his day was ale) Burns writes:

> The poor man's wine,
> His wee drap parritch, or his breid,
> Thou kitchens [1] fine.

In Scots, porridge, like broth, is spoken of as "they". "'Why do ye no sup yer parritch?' 'I dinna like them; they're unco wersh [2]; gi'e me a wee pickle saut.'"—Jamieson.

The old custom is to stand whilst supping porridge. A friend of the writer's recollects being slapped by her Highland nurse for not standing up to "them". As to whether the custom has any mystical significance or is merely an application of the proverb that "a staunin' (standing) sack fills the fu'est", I profess no opinion.

—F. M. McN.

Brochan is the name commonly used for porridge or gruel in the Highlands (Gael. *brochan*).

Bleirie (Lanarkshire) and *Lewands* (Clydesdale) is "oatmeal and buttermilk boiled to a consistency somewhat thicker than gruel with a piece of butter put into the mess."—Jamieson.

Bluthrie is the name given in Ettrick and Forfarshire to thin porridge or gruel.

Gogar (Roxburghshire) and *Whillins* (Fife) is whey boiled with a little oatmeal.

Whey-whullions. "Formerly a common dish among the peasantry of Scotland; consisting of the porridge left at breakfast, which was beaten down among fresh whey, with an additional quantity of oatmeal."—Jamieson.

Meal-and-milk or *Milk-meat* is porridge made with milk in the ordinary way.

Bere-meal Porridge is a popular dish in Orkney and Shetland.

AIGAR (OATMEAL) BROSE

(Old Cottage Recipe)

Oatmeal, salt, butter, water.

Put into a bowl two handfuls of oatmeal. Add salt and a piece of butter. Pour in boiling water to cover the oatmeal and stir it up roughly with the shank of a horn spoon, allowing it to form knots. [3] Sup with soor dook or sweet milk, and you have a dish that has been the backbone of many a sturdy

[1] Give a relish to.   [2] Very insipid.

[3] The cant designation is *knotty tams*. The oatmeal should be raw inside the knots.

Scotsman. *Brose and Butter* is as favourite an old tune as this is a nourishing dish.

Blind Brose or *Water Brose* is brose without butter; " said to be so denominated from there being none of those small orifices in it called eyes, which appear when butter is used."—Jamieson.

Cadger's Brose is like aigar brose, only the meal is placed among boiling water in a little pan, and stirred till all the lumps are broken.

Knotty Tam (Caithness) is a brose made of beist milk and oatmeal.

Milk Brose, Madlocks, or *Milk-Madlocks* (Renfrewshire), is brose made with milk instead of water.

Pot-brose is a dish consisting of milk and oatmeal made by dashing compressed handfuls of meal into boiling milk and boiling the mixture for a few minutes (Banff-shire).

GRUEL

In the Best Manner, as made in Scotland.

(Meg Dods's Recipe)

Fine oatmeal, water, salt, sugar, wine or honey, &c., to taste.

Take very finely ground oatmeal of the best quality. Infuse as much as you wish in cold water for an hour or two. Stir it up, let it settle, and pour it from the grits (or strain it), and boil slowly for a long time, stirring it up.[1] Add a little salt and sugar, with any addition of wine, rum, fruit, jelly, honey, butter, &c., you choose. This gruel will be quite smooth; and when cold will form a jelly. With a toast it makes an excellent luncheon or supper dish for an invalid. It may be thinned at pleasure.

[1] " The English language is very deficient in terms descriptive of culinary processes. The Scotch retain the word ' to skink' in defining the process of continually lifting high a sauce or gruel by spoonfuls, and rapidly letting it fall back into the pan. The French language, which is peculiarly rich in culinary terms, calls what is signified above by stirring, to *vanner* a sauce or soup; and to see a French cook thus engaged at the stove with the *velouté*, or sauce *à la Lucullus*, an Englishman might well suppose that life and death were depending on a process for which *his* language has no name."—P. Touchwood, in the *Annals of the Cleikum Club.*

" For coughs and colds, Water-gruel with a little Butter is the ordinary cure. . . . Water-gruel is also found by experience to be good for Consumptions; it purifies the Blood and procures Appetite when drunk without Salt. The Natives (of St. Kilda) make a pudding of the Fat (of the Solan Goose) in the Stomack of it, and boyl it in their Water-gruel, which they call Brochan; they drink it likewise for removing the Cough: it is by daily experience found to be an excellent Vulnerary."
—Martin: *Description of the Western Islands,* 1703.

A bowl of gruel, "laced with usquebaugh," is given to a sick soldier in John Buchan's *Witchwood.*

In Dumfriesshire gruel is called water-berry (Fr. *purée*).

CROWDIE, or FUARAG

O that I had ne'er been married,
I wad never had nae care.
Now I 've gotten wife and weans,
And they cry crowdie evermair.
　　Ance crowdie, twice crowdie,
　　Three times crowdie in a day;
　　Gin ye crowdie ony mair,
　　Ye 'll crowdie a' my meal away.
　　　　　—Old Song, used by Burns.

My sister Kate cam up the gate
　Wi' crowdie unto me, man,
She swore she saw the rebels run
　Frae Perth unto Dundee, man.
　　　　　—*The Battle of Sheriffmuir.*

(*Traditional Method*)

Pour cold spring water or good fresh buttermilk into finely
ground oatmeal till as thin as pancake batter. Stir the mixture.

Crowdie was at one time a universal breakfast dish in Scotland. The name was
applied generally to all food of the porridge kind. Crowdie-time is an old name for
breakfast-time, used by Burns (" Then I gaed hame at crowdie-time."—The Holy
Fair) and by Scott.

Sour milk and meal stirred together in a raw state is known as *Cauld Steer*. *Meal-
and-ale* and the original *Athole Brose* (meal and whisky) are also forms of crowdie.

In the Highlands the name *crowdie* (Gael. *gruth*, curd) is given to a species of milk-
cheese, and the name *drammoch* (Gael. *dramaig*), or *fuarag* (Gael. *fuar*, cold), or
stapag, is applied to what in Lowland Scotland is called *crowdie* (possibly from
Gael. *cruaidh*, thick, firm).

CREAM-CROWDIE[1]

An indispensable dish at the Kirn, or Harvest Home.

Oatmeal, cream, sugar and flavouring to taste.

Toast some coarse oatmeal lightly before the fire or in the
oven. Beat some cream to a stiff froth and stir in the oatmeal. Do not make it too substantial. It may be sweetened and
flavoured to taste. The toasted oatmeal gives an agreeable,
somewhat nutty, flavour to the dish.

This is a very old dish, commonly served in farmhouses on festive occasions. In
the Scottish National Museum of Antiquities, there is to be seen, in the section of
domestic articles, one of the old fro'ing sticks, having a wooden cross surrounded
with a ring of cow's hair at one end, formerly used for beating cream and whey.

[1] Called *stapag* in the Highlands and *pram* in Shetland.

BUTTER-CROWDIE

Oatmeal, butter fresh from the churn, salt or sugar to taste.

Make as above, mixing the toasted oatmeal with soft butter fresh from the churn.

MEAL-AND-ALE

(A special dish at the Kirn, or Harvest Home)

> A cogie [1] o' yill [2],
> An' a pickle oatmeal,
> An' a dainty wee drappie o' whisky—
> An' hey for the cogie,
> An' hey for the yill—
> Gin ye steer a' thegither, they 'll do unco weel.
> —Andrew Shirrefs: *A Cogie o' Yill* (1787).

Ale, treacle, oatmeal, whisky.

This is a variety of crowdie.

A large earthenware pot or milk-bowl is filled with ale, and treacle is added to sweeten it. Then oatmeal is stirred in until the whole is of a sufficient consistency, and finally whisky in such quantity as is desired. The dish is prepared on the morning of the festival to allow the meal time to be completely absorbed. It is served up at the end of the feast. A ring is always put into the mixture, and whoever gets it will be the first to be married.

CROWDIE-MOWDIE

(A Cottage Recipe)

Oatmeal, salt, milk.

The night before it is wanted put into a jar oatmeal, salt, and milk, allowing a handful of oatmeal, a small teaspoonful of salt, and a breakfast-cupful of milk for each person. Stir, cover, and let it stand all night. In the morning set the jar in a goblet of water and let it steam for two hours or longer.[3]

---

[1] A wooden vessel.   [2] Ale.   [3] This dish goes well with stewed figs.

SOWANS [1]

Till buttered so'ns wi' fragrant lunt *
Set a' their gabs a-steerin',†
Syne wi' a social glass o' strunt ‡
They parted aff careerin'
    Fu' blythe that night.
                        —Burns: *Hallowe'en*.

    * Steam.   † Mouths watering.   ‡ Any spirituous liquor.

(Traditional Method)

Oatmeal sids, water, salt.

Put a quantity of sids (the inner husks of the oat grain) into a small wooden tub or jar,[2] and pour on to them twice their bulk of lukewarm water. The sids rise to the surface, and must be pressed down with a spatula or spoon till all are wet. Leave them for at least three or four days in a warm place until they are quite sour.[3] The preparation, before the acetous fermentation begins, is called the serf.[4] When ready turn out on a fine sieve placed over a wide-mouthed jar, and let all the liquor run through. Squeeze the seeds to get all the goodness out of them, adding a little more cold water in the process. Throw away the sids and let the liquor you have obtained stand for a day or more till the starchy matter it contains sinks to the bottom. The more solid part is *sowans*; the liquid part is *swats*. When required for use the clear liquor is poured off, and some of the sediment is put into a pan with as much water as will thin it. Add a little salt and boil it for ten minutes or more, stirring it briskly until it thickens. Pour into a bowl or deep plate and serve with milk separately.

In Skye, a mixture of *pron* (chaff) from the mill and coarse oatmeal, in the proportion of three to one, is used for sowans.

This dish, though on first acquaintance many find the sour flavour unpalatable,

---

[1] Spelt also *sowens*. From Gael. *sùghan*, pron. soo-an. (*Sowans-Nicht* was Christmas Eve (O.S.) when friends foregathered round a big bowl of sowans.) Sowans cooked with butter is a traditional Hallowe'en dish. A ring was put into the dish, and whoever got it would be, it was held, the first to be married.—F. M. McN.

[2] A special tub called a sowan-bowie, like a small barrel with an open end, was formerly used for this purpose.

[3] Another method is to pour cold water over the sids and leave them for a week in summer, and a few days longer in winter.   [4] Gael. *searbh*

Is exceedingly wholesome. I have been told—I do not vouch for the truth of the tale—that a certain wealthy Scottish peer who was for years a martyr to dyspepsia and had been treated with no effect by several London specialists, was recently cured by an obscure Highland doctor, who prescribed a diet of sowans.—F. M. McN.

" It could be cooked like porridge, and this was *brownplate sowans*. Or the sowans was simply heated: this was *gaun-'e-gither sowans*. If something lighter was desired, *duochrea* was produced by pouring a quantity of the raw stuff into boiling water and adding a touch of fresh butter. . . . From the creamy deposit pancakes were made, and these were sowan scones."—J. Horne: *The County of Caithness.*

BURSTON[1]

In Caithness, " it was got by drying quickly and thoroughly over the fire a quantity of oats and bere, and then grinding it on a quern, or a ' knocking-stone '. . . . After being winnowed in a sieve called a ' wecht ' and rubbed in a coarse cloth, this rude meal was served with cream or thick-milk; but it could also be mixed with cabbage or made into brose."—J. Horne: *The County of Caithness.*

(*An Orkney Dish*)

Make the girdle hot. Spread a handful or two of oatmeal on one half and the same quantity of bere meal on the other, and when thoroughly toasted mix them together in a bowl and serve with buttermilk separately.

WHITE OR MEALIE PUDDINGS

(*Traditional Method*)

Oatmeal, suet, salt, Jamaica pepper, onions, tripe skins.

Toast two pounds of oatmeal in the oven, mix with it from a pound to a pound and a half of suet and two or three fair-sized onions, all finely chopped. Add about a tablespoonful of salt and half that quantity of Jamaica pepper. Prepare your tripe skins as for Black Puddings (p. 205) and fill, not too full, with the oatmeal mixture in the manner there indicated. Boil for an hour, pricking them occasionally with a fork to prevent them from bursting. These puddings will keep good for months if hung up and kept dry, or better, if kept buried in oatmeal in the girnel, or meal-chest. When required, warm them through

---

[1] Jamieson defines Burston as: " A dish composed of corn, roasted by rolling hot stones among it till it be made quite brown, then half ground, and mixed with sour milk ".

in hot water and brown them in the frying-pan. They make a savoury addition to a stew.

The same mixture makes an excellent stuffing for a fowl, boiled or roasted, and for a stag's heart.

Mrs. M'Ewen (1835) recommends plenty of onions, which should be first stewed in a little suet. Don't put in too much salt, she adds, and don't *boil* the puddings, but *stew* them.

DEER'S PUDDINGS

(Recipe from the Kitchen of a Highland Chief)

Deer tripe skins, venison suet, coarse oatmeal, onion, salt, pepper.

Take some deer tripe skins, wash in water and a very little salt, turning the skins out to be thoroughly cleansed, but leaving the fat that adheres to the inside of the skins. Take a large cupful of finely chopped venison or beef suet, a handful of coarse oatmeal, some finely chopped onion, and salt and pepper to season. Fill the skins loosely and prick with a needle to prevent their bursting. Boil for forty-five minutes. When required, brown them in a sauté pan with some hot fat, or grill them for fifteen minutes and serve very hot.

A FITLESS COCK [1]

(Meg Dods's Recipe)

Oatmeal, suet, pepper, salt, onion, egg.

This antique Scotch dish, which is now seldom seen at any table, is made of suet and oatmeal, with a seasoning of pepper, salt, and onions, as for white puddings, the mixture bound together with an egg and moulded somewhat in the form of a fowl. It must be boiled in a cloth like a dumpling.

[1] The *Fitless* or *Festy* (Fastyn) *Cock* was formerly eaten on Fastern's E'en, the evening which precedes the first day of the Fast of Lent. In the eighteenth century, cock-fights were commonly held in the parish schools to celebrate the festival.

The original *Festy Cock* (called *Dry Goose* in the south of Scotland) was composed of a handful of the finest meal pressed very close together, dipped in water, and then roasted among the ashes of a kiln. (See Jamieson.)—F. M. McN

SKIRLIE

(SKIRL-IN-THE-PAN)[1]

(Recipe obtained in Morayshire)

Oatmeal, suet, onion.

Chop two ounces of suet finely. Have a pan very hot and put in the suet. When it is melted, add one or two finely chopped onions and brown them well. Now add enough oatmeal to absorb the fat—a fairly thick mixture. Stir well till thoroughly cooked (a few minutes). Serve with potatoes.

" Skirl-in-the-Pan. 1. The noise made by a frying-pan when the butter is put in which prepares it for receiving the meat. 2. The dish prepared in this manner. 3. A sort of drink, also called Blythe-meat or Merry-meat, made of oatmeal, whisky, and ale, mixed and heated in a pan, and given to the gossips at *inlyings*, Mearns."
—Jamieson.

In the south of Scotland, at the Lammas feast the shepherds are provided with a dish called *Butter Brughtins*, which consist of oatcakes toasted before the fire, crumbled down and put into a pot with butter and made into a sort of pottage. *Brughtin* is allied to Gael. *brochan*, gruel or porridge. See Jamieson.

OATMEAL HODGILS

(Borders)

Oatmeal, pepper, salt, fat, chives (optional).

Put some oatmeal into a bowl, season it with pepper and salt and a few chopped chives (if liked). Mix with fat from the top of the beef broth. Form into balls and pop into the boiling broth. Cook for twenty minutes. Serve with the meat.

Other preparations of oatmeal will be found under Bannocks, Beverages, &c.—F. M. McN.

2. Preparations of Blood

BLACK PUDDINGS

> Puddens a' hot,' a' hot,
> Pipin' hot, pipin' hot!
> Hot or cold, they must be sold.
> Puddens a' hot, a' hot!
> —*Old Edinburgh Street Cry.*[2]

[1] Mentioned by Scott in *Old Mortality.*

[2] In 1581, the Town Council of Edinburgh ordained " the pudden mercat to be removit of the calsay and placeit in the flesche mercat ".

It fell about the Martinmas time
And a gay time it was then, O;
That our gudewife had puddins to mak'
And she boiled them in the pan, O.
—*The Barrin' o' the Door.*

Pig's or ox blood,[1] *milk, suet, oatmeal, onions, pepper, salt.*

Let the blood run into a deep pan; stir it all the time, and when it is nearly cold, throw in a little salt, allowing a large teaspoonful to every quart. Rub it through a hair sieve. To each quart of blood allow half a pint of milk; stir them together and add, again to each quart, a pound of shred suet or of the inward fat of the pig, a large handful of oatmeal, and plenty of minced onions, pepper, and salt.

To clean the pudding-skins, wash them thoroughly, and let them lie a night in salt and water. When they are to be filled, tie one end and turn inside out. Half fill them and tie them in rings or in equal lengths. When the water boils throw in a little cold to put it off the boil and put in the puddings. In five minutes prick them over with a large needle, removing them if necessary for the purpose. Return them to the pot and boil them for half an hour. Hang them up in a dry cool place to keep them. When they are to be used, put them in hot water for ten or fifteen minutes and then broil them.[2]

LAMB'S BLOOD PUDDING

(*Mrs. McIver's Recipe*)

Blood, cream, salt, spice, mint, chives or young onions, fat.

Take as much blood as with half a mutchkin (half a pint) of cream will fill an ashet; mix the blood and cream together and

---

[1] "Of all blood, that of the hog is thought the richest, and this is always employed in France in their boudins of this kind, which are excellent. The blood of the hare has the most delicate flavour of any, but is not to be got in sufficient quantity for puddings."—Meg Dods.

[2] In *My Schools and School-masters,* Hugh Miller, describing the " genuine Highland breakfasts " he enjoyed on his visits to an aunt in Sutherland, writes: " On

run through a search. Season with salt and spices, a sprig of mint and chives or young onions, minced small; mince the fat of the near or kidney small; mix all together and fire in the oven or in a frying-pan.

Lamb's blood is the sweetest of all blood.

GOOSE-BLOOD PUDDING

(Mrs. Glasse's Recipe)

Goose blood, grits, spice, salt, sweet herbs, suet.

In Scotland they make a pudding with the blood of a goose Chop off the head and save the blood, stir it till it is cold, then mix it with grits, spice, salt, and sweet herbs, according to fancy, and some beef suet chopped. Take the skin off the neck, then pull out the wind-pipe and fat, fill the skin, tie it at both ends, so make a pie of the giblets and lay the pudding in the middle.

This pudding is still made in rural districts. It is usually thickened with barley-meal and cooked in the broth.

more than one occasion I shared in a not unpalatable sort of blood-pudding, enriched with butter, and well seasoned with pepper and salt, the main ingredient of which was derived, through a judicious use of the lancet, from the *yeld* cattle of the farm. The practice was an ancient, and a by no means unphilosophic one. In summer and early autumn there is plenty of grass in the Highlands; but of old, at least, there used to be very little grain in it before the beginning of October; and as the cattle could, in consequence, provide themselves with a competent supply of blood from the grass when their masters, who could not eat grass, and had very little else that they could eat, were able to acquire very little, it was opportunely discovered that, by making a division in this way of the all-essential fluid, accumulated as a common stock, the circumstances of the cattle and their owners could be in some degree equalized."

Neil Munro, too, in his short story, *War*, describes a woman making a *marag* (pudding) with blood drawn from a living cow.

At " the Duck of Montrose's super " in 1715, one of the dishes was " Scots collips w^t marow and black pudins about them " (see *The Household Book of Lady Grisell Baillie*); Faujas de St. Fond describes among the dishes served to him in the Highlands in 1784, a " pudding of bullock's blood and barley-meal, seasoned with plenty of peppea and ginger "; and Hogg (the Ettrick Shepherd) mentions a " blood ker-cake " of blood and oatmeal prepared in a frying pan and eaten on Fastern's E'en.

3. Preparations of Milk

"A dinner in the Western Isles differs very little from a dinner in England, except that in the place of tarts there are always set different preparations of milk."
—Dr. Johnson: *Journey to the Western Isles of Scotland*, 1775.

CORSTORPHINE OR RU'GLEN CREAM

(Meg Dods's Recipe)

Milk, moist sugar.

Pour a quart of new milk into a jar. On this, next morning, pour another, and mix well; at night do the same; and next day beat up the thickened milk with moist sugar.

"This cooling preparation was patronized by Sir John Sinclair. It may be made like hatted kit, of mixed buttermilk and sweet milk. Indeed, there is a learned controversy on the genuine preparation; and another as to whether its invention really belongs to Corstorphine near Edinburgh, or to the village of Rutherglen in the neighbourhood of the western metropolis."—*Annals of the Cleikum Club.*

"Rutherglen is famous for making sour cream of an excellent quality. It is made in the following manner. A certain quantity of sweet (i.e. new) milk is put into a wooden vessel or vat, which is placed in a proper degree of heat, and covered with a linen cloth. In due time, the serous or watery part of the milk begins to separate from the rest, and is called *whig*. When the separation is complete, which, according to circumstances, requires more or less time, the whig is drawn off from near the bottom of the vessel. The substance that remains is then beat with a large wooden spoon or ladle, till the particles of which it is composed are properly mixed. A small quantity of sweet milk is sometimes added to correct the acidity if it is in excess. The cream thus prepared is agreeable to the taste and nourishing to the constitution."—*New Statistical Account of Scotland, 1845.*

HATTED KIT

"Their efter I suld meet your lo: in Leith or quietlie in Restal, quhair we sould have preparit ane fyne haitit kit, with suckar and confeittie and wyne, and therefter confer on materis."—Logan of Restalrig: *Letters*, 1609.
"He has spilled the hatted kit that was for the master's dinner."
—Scott: *Bride of Lammermoor.*

(Meg Dods's Recipe)

Buttermilk, new milk, sugar, nutmeg or cinnamon.

Where this cooling and healthy article of diet is in constant use for children or delicate persons, a kit with a double bottom, the upper one perforated with holes and furnished with a fosset and a cover, should be got. Into this vessel put in the proportion of two quarts fresh good buttermilk and a pint of milk hot from the cow. Mix well by jumbling; and next milking add another pint of milk, mixing all well. It will now firm and gather a hat. Drain off the whey whenever it runs clear, by the spigot; remove what of the top or hat is necessary to take up the quantity wanted. This dish if to present at table may be moulded for an hour in a perforated mould, and strewed over with a little pounded sugar and then nutmeg or cinnamon. The kit must be well sweetened with lime-water or charcoal every time it is used; and too much should not be made at once, it gets so quickly very acid. A slight degree of coagulation assists digestion, but milk highly acidulated is not wished for in this dish.

Mrs. Dalgairns' recipe: Make two quarts of new milk scalding hot and pour it quickly upon four quarts of fresh made buttermilk, after which it must not be stirred. Let it remain till cold and firm; then take off the top part,[1] drain it in a hair sieve, and put it into a shape for half an hour. It is eaten with cream, served in a separate dish.

Lady Colebrooke (1877) writes: " Serve the curds in a glass dish at luncheon, as you would clotted cream. To eat with stewed fruit or with brown bread and salt, adding plain cream. Do not butter the brown bread. This kit is instead."

SACK OR WINE WHEY

(*Mrs. McEwen's Recipe*)

Milk, wine.

Put a pint of new milk in a saucepan on the fire; when it boils take it from the fire, put a breakfast-cupful of wine to it— sherry, Madeira, or mountain; stir it, cover it up; in a little the curd will fall to the bottom; strain it off; it is now ready.

GREEN WHEY

[In the Highlands] " Mrs. Macfarlane told me she should send the servant up with a basin of whey, saying, ' We make very good whey in this country '; indeed, I thought it the best I had ever tasted."

—Dorothy Wordsworth: *Recollections of a Tour made in Scotland*.

[1] This was called the *hat*.—F. M. McN.

(Mrs. McEwen's Recipe)

Have a stew-pan on the fire half full of boiling water; have a quart of new milk in a jug that has a stroup, set it in the stew-pan on the fire, put a tablespoonful of rennet or yearning to it, take it from the fire and let it stand in hot water; if the yearning is good it will be curds in a few minutes; this you will know by leaving a spoon in the jug. If you find that it does not fasten in five minutes put a little more to it; take care that you do not make it too salt; when it is fastened draw the spoon through it two or three times; let it stand; the whey will rise to the top, the curd fall to the bottom. It is now fit for use.

Whey was formerly a common summer drink in Scotland. ".Curds and green whey!" is an old Edinburgh street-cry.—F. M. McN.

Whig (O. Scots *quhig*) is the acetous liquor that subsides from sour cream. This is the origin of the political term, which was first applied by Scottish Episcopalians (who were almost invariably Tories) to Presbyterians, and by Presbyterians of the Established Church to those of the dissenting bodies.

"Whey in which Violets have been boyl'd is used as a cooling and refreshing Drink for such as are ill of Fevers."—Martin: *Description of the Western Islands* (1703).

OON[1], OR FROTHED WHEY

(Recipe from Martin's " Description of the Western Islands " (1703))

" Oon, which in English signifies Froath, is a Dish used by several of the Islanders, and some of the opposite mainland, in the time of scarcity, when they want bread. It is made in the following manner. A quantity of Milk or Whey is boiled in a Pot, and then it is wrought up to the mouth of the Pot with a long Stick of Wood, having a Cross at the lower-end. It is turned about like the Stick for making Chocolat, and being thus made it is supped with Spoons; it is made up five or six times, in the same manner, and the last is always reckoned best, and the first two or three froathings the worst; the Milk or Whey that is in the bottom of the Pot is reckoned much better in all respects than simple Milk."

" It may be thought that such as feed after this rate are not fit for action of any kind, but I have seen several that lived upon this sort of Food, made of Whey only, for some Months together, and yet they were able to undergo the ordinary Fatigue

[1] Gael. *omhan*, froth of milk or whey. Called also *onaich*, from *omhanach*, frothy.

of their Imployments, whether by Sea or Land, and I have seen them travel to the tops of high Mountains, as briskly as any I ever saw."—M. Martin.

" Some who live plentifully, make this dish as above said of Goat's Milk, which is said to be nourishing; the Milk is thickened and tastes much better after so much working; some add a little Butter and Nutmeg to it.

" I was treated with this Dish in several Places, and being asked whether this said Dish or Chocolat was best, I told them that if one judge by the Effects, this Dish was preferable to Chocolat, for such as drink often of the former, enjoy a better state of health than those who use the latter."—*Id.*

OTHER PREPARATIONS OF MILK

Beist-cheese. The first milk after a calving, boiled or baked to a thick consistency, somewhat resembling new-made cheese. Teut. *biest melck.*—Jamieson.

Brughtin Cake. Green cheese parings, or wrought curd, kneaded with butter and broiled in the frying-pan. It is eaten with bread by way of kitchen; Roxburghshire. Apparently allied to Welsh *brwchan,* Gael. *brochan.*—Jamieson.

Flot-whey (Clydesdale), *Fleetings* (Angus), *Scadded Whey* (Roxburghshire). A dish used in farmhouses, made by boiling whey on a slow fire, by which a great part of it coagulates into a curdy substance.

Lappered Milk. Coagulated milk. Excellent with blaeberries and sugar.

Sour Kit. A dish of coagulated cream.

Usted. The curd of buttermilk heated with sweet milk till the curd separates from the whey; Shetland. Sueo-Goth. and Isl. *ysta* (pron. usta), coagulate.—Jamieson.

Ustin. Curds made without rennet; Shetland.

Yerned Milk. Curds made with rennet in the ordinary way.

See also *Beverages.*

Slightly turned milk is called *bleezed* or *blaized* (Angus), *blinked* or *winkit* (Lothians). In Aberdeenshire, skim milk that is slightly turned is called *blenched* (analogous to *blinket*). In Tweeddale the name *whittens* is given to the last part of what is called a " male of milk ", which is considered the richest, and is usually milked by the thrifty housewife into a vessel by itself, and put among the cream reserved for the churn.—See Jamieson's *Dictionary of the Scottish Language.*

BUTTERMILK

This was formerly an extremely popular beverage with all classes in Scotland.

In old Edinburgh, throughout the summer months, one might witness daily the picturesque sight of milkmaids on horseback riding into town with soor-dook barrels strapped across the saddle behind them. About the middle of the last century, the soor-dook stances extended from the Tron Church to St. Mary's Wynd. It has been estimated that at the end of the eighteenth century a thousand pounds a year was paid in Edinburgh during the months of June, July, August, and September for this very inexpensive beverage, which was sold at a penny the Scots pint (i.e. two Imperial quarts). See " Street Cries of Edinburgh " by J. Jamieson, in the *Book of the Old Edinburgh Club.*

Bland is an agreeable very acid beverage made by blending buttermilk with boiling water, and formerly much drunk in the Shetlands.

Bradwardine's Drink. " A silver jug, which held an equal mixture of cream and buttermilk, was placed for the Baron's share of this repast (breakfast)."
—Scott: *Waverley.*

Gudeman's Milk is the name given to the milk first skimmed from a sour cog, after the cream has been taken off for the churn. The first milk usually contained a little cream and was apportioned to the gudeman, or head of the family.

Kirn Milk an' Sourocks. Buttermilk boiled with sorrel.

" Drink off this wersh (insipid) brew, sir. It was my mither's way to caller (cool) the blood—just kirn milk boiled wi' sourocks."—John Buchan: *Witchwood.*

Other names for buttermilk are *kirn milk, sour milk, soor dook, bladoch* or *blada* (Gael. *blathach*), N. of Scotland, and *bleddoch*, Roxburghshire; and *fochtin milk* (Buchan), possibly from its being produced by fighting at the churn. In Aberdeenshire a cant name is *soutar's brandy*. In Shetland, thin, ill-curdled milk is called *giola*, and in Ettrick Forest, buttermilk very much soured is called *pell*.

CROWDIE[1], OR CRUDDY BUTTER

(HIGHLANDS)

(Recipe supplied to the Cleikum Club by P. Touchwood, Esq.)

Sweet milk curd, fresh butter.

In Inverness and the Ross shires there is a rural breakfast article called crowdie, not the common composition, oatmeal and water or milk, but made thus: Take two parts fresh sweet-milk curd and one of fresh butter. Work them well together and press them in a basin or small shape and turn it out, when it will slice nicely. When whey is much used for drink in hot weather the curd may be usefully thus disposed of. It is eaten with bread and butter and keeps a long time, if gout is liked. This preparation, when the curd is well broken and blended with the butter, is sometimes made up in deep narrow cogs, or wooden moulds, and kept for months, when it becomes very high flavoured though mellow. The celebrated Arabian cheese is made in the same way in vats, and both are uncommonly fine. These preparations deserve trial. In the Lowlands this is sometimes seen but is not kept, and is, for this reason, called a one-day's cheese.

A Cottage Recipe: Place some thick scur milk in a pan and heat over a slow fire until the curd is cooked. Put the curd into a colander and strain for two hours till quite dry, then mix with cream and salt to taste.

[1] Gael. *gruth*, curd.

DUNLOP CHEESE[1]

(*Meg Dods's Recipe*)

As soon as the milk is taken from the cows it is poured into a large pail, or pails, and before it is quite cold the substance called the steep, i.e. rennet, is mixed with it. When it is sufficiently coagulated it is cut transversely with a broad knife made for the purpose, or a broad three-toed instrument, in order to let the curd subside and to procure the separation of the whey from it. When this separation is observed to have taken place the curd is lifted with a ladle, or something similar, into the chessel (for it is to be observed, that where a proper attention is paid to the making of these cheeses, no woman's hand ought ever to touch the curd, from the milking of the cow to the finishing of the whole), where it remains a few hours, till it has acquired something of a hardness or consistency. It is then taken out of the cheese press and cut into small pieces with the instrument above mentioned, of the size of one or two cubic inches, after which it receives the due proportion of salt, and is again replaced in the chessel and put into the press, where it remains a few hours again. Then it is taken out a second time, cut as before, and mixed thoroughly, so as every part may receive the benefit of the salt; and for the last time it is put into the cheese press where it remains until replaced by its successor. After this is done it must be laid in a clean and cool place till sufficiently dried and fit to be carried to market; great care is to be used in frequent turning and rubbing, both to keep the cheese dry and clean and to preserve it from swelling and bursting with the heat, vulgarly " fire-fanging ". When these cheeses are properly made and dried as they ought to be, they have a rich and delicious flavour.

" This and all sorts of cheese, may be pricked, with a bodkin, to allow the escape of air, which, if left, forms what are called *eyes* in the cheese."—M. D.

" The cheese made here, as well as in other parts of the country, was made of skimmed milk, till about the end of the seventeenth century, when one Barbara

[1] Dunlop is a village in Ayrshire.

Gilmour introduced the practice of using the whole milk."—*New Statistical Account of Scotland*.

Dunlop has always been regarded as the national cheese of Scotland. It is, or used to be, manufactured principally in Ayrshire, Lanarkshire, and Renfrewshire. The cheddars of Somerset and the west of Scotland are said to be unrivalled. The standard in Ayrshire used to be very unequal, and in 1855 the Ayrshire Agricultural Association brought in a Somerset farmer and his wife to teach the cheddar method. Since then the average quality in Ayrshire has been higher than in Somerset, though Somerset at its best cannot be surpassed. (See *Enc. Brit.* " Ayrshire ".)   Liberton used also to produce cheeses of repute, and the hilly pastures of Buckholmside were famous for the best ewe-milk cheese in the south of Scotland. A cheese known as the Crying Kebbuck used to be part of the kimmers' feast at a lying-in.

ORKNEY CHEESE

Take two pailfuls (eight Scots pints) of whole milk and heat to 85° F. Add a teaspoonful of rennet mixed with a little cold water and stir with a wooden spoon for five minutes. Let it stand for half an hour, when it will be a smooth firm curd. With a bread-knife, or any knife with a long blade, cut the curd across in several directions. Let it stand again for a short time. Stir up and strain through a cheese cloth. Break up the curd gently with the hand, add a little salt,[1] and mix well. Place the cheese in a cheese cog or chessit with the cloth underneath. Cover the top smoothly with the cloth, then put on the lid and place on it a seven-pound weight. Take out the cheese every day, put on a clean cloth, replace in the chessit, always turning it the other way. After a day or two add more weight to press out the whey. After eight days remove from the chessit and dry at an open window or shelf.

This cheese is a staple article of diet in Orkney. On the smaller crofts it is usually made with skim milk. Keep buried in oatmeal until required.

4. Dishes of Seaweed

Seaweeds are rich in potassium iodide.

The edible seaweeds found on our coasts include Carrageen or Sea-moss; Tangle or Redware (Eng. Sea-girdle); Henware or Honeyware (Eng. Bladderlock); Sloke (Eng. Laver); Green Laver; and Dulse (*Fucus palmatus*, Linn.).

[1] In the Hebrides, " burnt Ashes of Sea-ware preserves Cheese instead of Salt ".—Martin (1703).

Miscellaneous 215

SEA-TANGLE

In Orkney, children eat the stems of the sea-tangle raw, as they would stalks of rhubarb.

In the Hebrides, Martin tells us, " the blade is eat by the Vulgar Natives ".[1] In Barra, the blade is cut away from the fronds and stalk and roasted on both sides over the embers. It is then placed on a buttered barley bannock. Children eat it with avidity.

A DULSE DISH
(Isle of Barra)

Dulse, water, butter, pepper, salt.

Wash the dulse carefully and let it simmer in water till very tender. Strain, cut small, and put into a pan with a little butter, and make thoroughly hot. Add salt and pepper to taste.

Dulse is also eaten raw, or boiled, or cooked over the peat embers on a brander, or rolled about on a stone with a red-hot poker till it turns green. It is often dried and eaten as a savoury or as a relish with potatoes. Pepper dulse is an aromatic variety which is used as a spice. A jelly may be made by letting the dulse simmer in milk until dissolved and set aside to cool, as for Carrageen Jelly (q.v.).

" It is eat raw, and then reckoned to be loosning, and very good for the sight; but if boiled it proves more loosning, if the juice be drank with it. . . . The Natives eat it boil'd with butter, and reckon it very wholesome."—Martin: *Description of the Western Islands* (1703).

SEAWEED SOUP
(Hebrides)

Gather sloke on the rocks and wash in cold water till the salt and sand are removed. If the seaweed is allowed to steep for a few hours in cold water to which a little bicarbonate of soda

[1] " I had an account of a young man who lost his Appetite, and taken Pills to no purpose, and being advised to boil the Blade of the Alga, and drink the infusion boil'd with a little butter, was restored to his former state of health "—Martin: *Description of the Western Islands* (1703).

has been added it will lose some of the bitterness. Stew it in milk, rubbing it hard now and then with a wooden spoon or potato-beater, until it becomes tender and mucilaginous. Strain if desired, or serve the weed in the bree. Pepper, vinegar or lemon juice, and butter may be added according to taste.

Sloke, when thoroughly boiled, becomes a dark green. When cold it can be stored in earthenware jars. It will keep good for two or three weeks. In fashionable circles sloke used to be highly esteemed as " marine sauce ".

" The Natives eat it [sloke] boil'd and it dissolves into Oil; they say that if a little butter be added to it, one might live many years on this alone, without Bread, or any other Food, and at the same time, undergo any laborious exercise."—Martin: *Description of the Western Islands* (1703).

" In Caithness, sloke was a tasty addition to bread: it was sea-weed washed, boiled, and cooled, and then used as a jelly."—J. Horne: *County of Caithness.*

SLOKAN

(ISLE OF BARRA) [1]

Sloke, water, butter, pepper, salt.

Prepare the sloke as above. Put it in a pan with a very little sea-water. Make it hot, withdraw it, and beat well; heat it up, withdraw it. and beat again; and continue this process until it is reduced to a pulp. Do not let it cook. Add salt, pepper, and a little butter. Serve hot, with mashed potatoes round it.

CARRAGEEN OR SEA-MOSS JELLY

(*As prepared in the Hebrides*)

Gather the weed on the rocks, wash the salt and sand well out of it, and spread it on the rocks, or on the window-sill, or on a white cloth on the grass, and leave it there for several days to bleach and dry. When thoroughly dry put it into bags and hang these up in a dry place, preferably the kitchen. When required, allow a heaped tablespoonful to each quart of milk,

---

[1] The *cailleach* from whom this recipe was obtained used to make it for the Big House on the island, and prided herself on being the last of her generation to make the dish properly.—F. M. McN.

and put both into a saucepan. Let it simmer till the milk begins to thicken, strain, and pour it into a bowl and allow it to cool and set.

Another method is to pour the boiling milk over the carrageen, and let it stand for two hours where it will keep hot without coming to the boil. An egg beaten to a froth is often added, but must not be allowed to reach boiling-point. Carrageen thus made, and served with cream, makes a delicate and wholesome sweet.

The strained juice of two Seville oranges may be used to flavour this jelly. An old Manse recipe gives a stick of cinnamon, a bit of lemon peel, and lump sugar to taste.

The jelly may be made with fresh carrageen in season.

Carrageen contains iodine and sulphur and used to be recommended for chest troubles.

CARRAGEEN DRINK

Proceed as for Carrageen Jelly, using double the quantity of milk or water. Let it simmer for four or five hours. Flavour and sweeten to taste.

5. Miscellaneous

LIVER KETCHUP

(*A Highland Recipe*)

Ox liver, salt herrings, celery, whole black pepper, whole Jamaica pepper, cloves, salt, cayenne, eggs, water.

Take an ox liver, as dark as possible, and cut it into pieces about an inch square. Cut up also three salt herrings and a large bunch of celery, and put all into a large pot with water to cover it and a choppin (quart) over and above. Bring it to the boil and let it simmer for sixteen hours, taking care that it does not go off the boil. Strain it. Cast the whites of three eggs very well, and put them, with the shells, into the ketchup. Put it on the fire and boil for five minutes. Strain it through a jelly-bag. Now add to it two ounces of whole black pepper, two of whole Jamaica pepper, an ounce of cloves, a little cayenne, and half a pound of salt. Put it on the fire once more and boil for twenty minutes. If not dark enough, burn a small quantity of refined sugar and mix it with the ketchup before taking it off the fire. Bottle it with the peppers and let it stand for twenty-four hours before corking it. Seal carefully.

A HIGHLAND FISH-SAUCE [1]
(For the Store-room)

Red wine, vinegar, anchovies, horse-radish, onions, parsley, lemon-thyme, bay-leaves, nutmeg, mace, cloves, black pepper, cochineal.

To an English pint of red port (Burgundy or claret is better) add fifteen anchovies, chopped and prepared by steeping in vinegar in a close-covered vessel for a week; add to this a stick of horse-radish scraped, two onions, and a handful of parsley chopped, a dessertspoonful of lemon thyme stripped of the stalks, two bay-leaves, nutmeg, and six blades of mace roughly pounded, nine cloves, and a small dessertspoonful of black pepper bruised. Pour over these ingredients a large half-pint of port-wine vinegar, and simmer slowly in a silver or new block-tin saucepan, or earthen pipkin, till the bones of the anchovies are dissolved. Add a few grains of cochineal if the colour is not good. Strain the liquor through a hair sieve and, when cold, bottle it for use, securing the vials well with corks and leather. When to be used shake the vials before pouring out the sauce; two tablespoonfuls will impart a high flavour to four ounces of beat butter, in which it must be simmered for a minute before it is served.

DEER-HORN JELLY

A personal friend of the writer, whilst travelling recently in the Rannoch district, fell in with a young girl of the locality

[1] The Cleikum Club were favoured with this original recipe from an intelligent Highland lady, who has contributed several valuable original recipes to this volume.* This sauce boasts neither the name of Burgesse nor Harvey, but we would advise those who wish to combine economy with what is healthful and elegant, to make a fair trial of it.

* Meg Dods's *Manual.*

who was carrying a small deer horn. On inquiry, the girl explained that she was taking it home, and that when boiled for several hours the horn would make "a delicious jelly". Only the horn of a *young* deer is used.

This information having been received just as the book was going to press, it has been impossible to obtain details of the mode of preparation.

Another correspondent, a native of Ballindalloch, recollects that her mother made some sort of oil from a deer's foot.—F. M. McN.

MARMALADE AND JAMS

There are almost as many ways of making marmalade as there are varieties of jam. As these may be readily obtained elsewhere, I give only Meg Dods's marmalade recipe with a very few of the less-known jams.—F. M. McN.

Although, generally speaking, the Scottish climate is unfavourable to fruit, an exception must be made in favour of berries. It is to the native sweetness of the strawberries and raspberries that the excellence of Scottish jams is mainly due; whilst " the Highlands," remarks Mrs. C. W. Earle, in *Pot-pourri from a Surrey Garden*, " seem to be the home of the gooseberry—such old and hoary bushes, more or less covered by grey lichens, but laden none the less with little hairy gooseberries. both red and green, and full of flavour."

SCOTS ORANGE-CHIP MARMALADE

" [At breakfast] there is always, besides butter and toasted bread, honey and jelly of currants and preserved orange peel."—Bishop Pococke: *Tours in Scotland* (1760).

(*Meg Dods's Recipe*)

Seville oranges, lemons, loaf sugar, water, white of egg (to clarify sugar).

Take equal weight of fine loaf sugar and Seville oranges. Wipe and grate the oranges, but not too much. (The outer grate boiled up with sugar will make an excellent conserve for rice, custard, or batter puddings.) Cut the oranges the cross way and squeeze out the juice through a small sieve. Scrape off the pulp from the inner skins and remove the seeds. Boil the skins till perfectly tender, changing the water to take off part of the bitter. When cool scrape the coarse, white, thready part from the skins, and, trussing three or four skins together for dispatch, cut them into narrow chips. Clarify the sugar,[1] and put the chips, pulp, and juice to it. Add, when boiled for ten minutes, the juice and grate of two lemons to every dozen of oranges. Skim and boil for twenty minutes; pot and cover when cold.

The name marmalade (Pg. *marmelo*, quince) was originally applied to a conserve of quince, as porridge (Lat. *porrum*, a leek) was originally applied to pottage or broth. These two dishes are Scotland's chief culinary gifts to the world. The great Dundee manufacturers spread the popularity of marmalade in the south. Its first stronghold was Oxford, where it figured at undergraduate breakfasts as *squish*. It now appears, with its compatriot, on the breakfast table of every cosmopolitan hotel.

Marmalade may be served with roast pork, duck, or goose, and with hot boiled ham. Eaten with buttered oatcake, brown bread, or wheaten meal scone, it is an excellent last mouthful at breakfast.

ROWAN JELLY

(*Old Family Recipe*)

Rowan berries, apples, water, sugar.

Gather your rowan berries when almost ripe. Remove the stalks and wash and drain the berries. Put them in a preserving-pan with enough cold water to float them well. Let them simmer for about forty minutes or until the water is red and the berries are quite soft. Strain off the juice, being careful not to press the fruit in the least. Measure the juice and return it to the pan. Add sugar in the proportion of a pound to each pint of juice. Boil rapidly for half an hour or until some of it sets quickly on a plate when cold. Skim it well, pour it into small pots, and tie down quickly.

If you allow pound for pound of apple juice to rowan juice you will get a delightful jelly. Allow a pound of sugar to each pint of apple juice.

Rowan jelly is an excellent accompaniment to grouse, venison, and saddle of mutton.

[1] To clarify sugar: To every pound of broken sugar of the best quality take a quarter-pint of water, and the half of the white of an egg beat up, or less egg will do. Stir this up till the sugar dissolves, and when it boils, and the scum rises strong and thick, pour in another quarter-pint of cold water to each pound. Let it boil, edging the pan forward from the stove till all the scum is thrown up. Set it on the hearth and when it has settled take off the scum with a sugar-skimmer, and lay this on a reversed hair-sieve over a dish, that what syrup is in it may run clear from it. Return the drained syrup into the pan, and boil and skim the whole once more.

SLOE AND APPLE JELLY

(A Highland Recipe)

Sloes, apples, sugar, water.

Wash four apples and cut them up roughly. Put them in a jelly-pan with two pounds of sloes, cleared of stalks. Cover with water and boil to a pulp. Strain through a cheese-cloth, but do not squeeze. Measure the liquid and return to the pan, adding a pound of sugar for every pint of juice. Boil for fifteen minutes and fill into jars.

BLAEBERRY JAM [1]

(A Highland Recipe)

Blaeberries, rhubarb, sugar, water.

Allow a pound of sugar to every pound of blaeberries and a pound of thin red rhubarb to every seven pounds of fruit. Wipe the rhubarb and cut it into inch lengths. Put it into the preserving-pan with the sugar and boil for ten minutes. Add the blaeberries and boil again, skimming well. Test in the usual way by putting a little in a saucer to see if it firms when cool. Pour into pots

" Fluxes are Cured by taking now and then a Spoonful of the Syrup of blew Berries that grow on the Mertillus."—Martin: *Description of the Western Islands* (1703).

GEAN [2] JAM

(A Highland Recipe)

Geans (wild cherries), gooseberry or currant juice, sugar, water.

Weigh your wild cherries, stone them, and put them into a preserving-pan. Cover them with water and boil until nearly all the juice is dried up (about three-quarters of an hour). Add sugar, allowing a pound to every six pounds of fruit,

[1] Mentioned by St. Fond in his account of his travels in the Hebrides in 1784.
[2] The G is hard. From Fr. *guigne*.

and gooseberry or currant juice, allowing a pint to every six pounds. Boil all together until it jellies (twenty to thirty minutes), skimming it well and keeping it well stirred. Pour into pots.

RHUBARB AND GINGER JAM

(*A Family Recipe*)

Rhubarb, sugar, lemon, ginger.

Choose a good quality of rhubarb (which varies considerably): Victoria rhubarb, when tender and full grown, is excellent. Cut off both ends, do not peel the stalks but wipe them with a cloth and cut them into pieces about an inch long. To six pounds of rhubarb allow five pounds of sugar, and put them in a deep dish in alternate layers. Let this stand for twenty-four hours, by which time the sugar should be in a liquid state. Pour the liquid into a preserving-pan, add the grated rind of a lemon and three-quarters of a pound of preserved ginger cut small, and boil briskly for half an hour. Then add the rhubarb and boil half an hour longer. Take it off and let it stand near the fire for half an hour before you pot it.

CONFECTIONERY

" In rural districts in Scotland candy-making is a regular adjunct to courting. . . .
It draws together all the lads and lasses round about for miles, and the fun and the
daffing that go on during the boiling, pulling, clipping, cooling, are, both lads and
lasses declare, worth the money. . . . A few of the lasses club their sixpences together, a night is set, a house is named, and, of course, the young men who are
specially wanted are invited to lend a hand and a foot too, for dancing is not an
uncommon adjunct to such gatherings."—From an old book on cottage cookery.

SCOTS BARLEY SUGAR

(*Mrs. McIver's Recipe*)

Barley, liquorice, sugar, water, egg (to clarify), butter.

Wash a little barley and put it on with boiling water; let
it boil a little, then turn out that water and pour more boiling
water on it. Put in a pennyworth of liquorice stick, let it boil
till all the strength is out of it; then pour off the liquor and let
it stand to settle and pour all the clear from the grounds; then
take half a mutchkin (pint) of it to the pound of sugar; clarify
it with white of egg. It must be on a soft equal fire; you must
not stir it much on the fire; it must be boiled until it crackles.
Have a stone ready, rubbed with fresh butter or fine oil. Pour
the sugar on it. You must double it together and cut it as fast
as you can with big scissors. Give it a little twist as you cut it.

If you think the sugar boils too furiously, add a very little
bit of fresh butter amongst it.

Both barley water and barley sugar are included in Mrs. McIver's list of Scottish
national dishes. See her *Cookery and Pastry* (Edinburgh, 1773).

BUTTER SCOTCH

(An Edinburgh Recipe)

Brown sugar, butter, ground ginger or lemon.

Put a pound of brown sugar into an enamelled saucepan and let it dissolve on the range. Beat four ounces of butter to a cream, add it to the sugar when dissolved, and stir over the fire until it has boiled sufficiently to harden when dropped into cold water. Add a quarter-ounce of powdered ginger dissolved in a little water or a little essence of lemon. Beat with a fork quickly for a few minutes. Pour on to a buttered slab or dish and when sufficiently cool mark into squares. When cold, a slight tap will break them off.

BLACK MAN, or TREACLE CANDY
(An Old-fashioned Sweetmeat)

(A Cottage Recipe)

Treacle, vinegar, baking-soda.

Put into a saucepan four pounds of treacle and a dessert spoonful of vinegar. Bring it to the boil and let it boil very slowly, stirring it to prevent burning. When it has boiled for twenty minutes try it by dropping in cold water. If it snaps it is done. Add flavouring to taste—peppermint, almond, or lemon. Then put in half a teaspoonful of baking-soda and stir hard. Take it off the fire immediately and pour on to buttered dishes. As soon as it is possible to handle it, butter the hands, take it from the dish, and pull it rapidly with both hands as long as it is possible to do so. This makes it light coloured and tender. (Confectioners used to use an iron hook driven into the wall to assist them in pulling it. Two pairs of hands, their owners *vis-à-vis*, can do it even better.) When too hard to work longer, cut the sticks to the desired length (one inch or six or eight inches) with scissors.

Another Recipe

Put into a saucepan one pound of brown sugar, one teacupful of treacle, half a cup of water, a teaspoonful of cream of tartar. Prepare exactly as above.

MEALIE CANDY

(*Old Cottage Recipe*)

Sugar, treacle, oatmeal, ginger, water.

Put three and a half pounds of loaf sugar and a pound of treacle into a saucepan with one and a quarter pints of water, bring it to the boiling-point and let it boil for ten minutes. Remove it from the fire and, with the back of a wooden spoon, rub the syrup against the sides of the pan until it looks creamy. Then stir in gently half a pound of toasted oatmeal and two ounces of ground ginger. Pour into shallow tins lined with well-oiled paper. When it has cooled a little cut it into cubes, and when cold remove it from the tins and take off the paper. This is a very wholesome sweetmeat, as the oatmeal is soothing and the ginger stimulating.

GLESSIE

(An Old-fashioned Sweetmeat)

Soft sugar, syrup, butter, cream of tartar, water.

Put into an enamelled pan two tablespoonfuls of water, a teaspoonful of cream of tartar, half a pound of soft sugar, and a small piece of butter. Boil for five minutes. Add a pound and a half of syrup and boil briskly, without stirring, for half an hour. Try in cold water to see if it is crisp. Pour in thin sheets on buttered tins. When cold, chop it up, or pull out as for Black Man and cut into sticks.

GUNDY [1]
(An Old-fashioned Sweetmeat)

Brown sugar, syrup or treacle, butter, aniseed or cinnamon.

Put into a saucepan a pound of brown sugar, a teaspoonful of syrup or treacle, and two ounces of butter. Boil it to the crack, that is, till it becomes quite hard when a little is put into cold water. Flavour with aniseed or cinnamon. Pour out very thinly on a buttered tin or slab, and when it is cold and hard break up roughly with a small hammer; or when cool enough to handle form into thin round sticks.

ALMOND CAKE

Sugar, syrup, butter, almonds, lemon, water.

Put into a saucepan four teacupfuls of sugar, three table-spoonfuls of syrup, and one and a quarter cupfuls of water. Boil for twenty minutes. Add a piece of butter the size of an egg, and boil till the mixture hardens. Flavour with lemon. Blanch four ounces of almonds by throwing them into boiling water for two minutes and removing the skins. Halve them and strew them thickly on the bottom of a flat buttered tin. When fairly cool cut into bars, or break up with a small hammer when cold.

FIG CAKE

Make as above and pour over split figs.

HELENSBURGH TOFFEE

Loaf sugar, condensed milk, salt butter, water, vanilla.

Put into an iron or enamelled pan two pounds of loaf sugar, the contents of a tin of condensed milk (ordinary size), four ounces of salt butter, and a teacupful of water. Stir

---

[1] " Gundy was sold by Mrs. Flockhart in the Potter-row."—R. Chambers: *Traditions of Edinburgh.*

continuously over the fire for forty-five minutes. Add a teaspoonful of vanilla and stir off the fire for one minute. Pour
into a buttered tin and, when cool, cut into squares.

If desired the toffee may be dotted with halved walnuts
immediately after it has been poured out.

SCOTS TABLETS

" Taiblet's awfu' guid."
—*Wee Macgreegor.*

(*Traditional Recipe*)

Granulated sugar, thin cream or milk, flavouring.

Put into an enamelled saucepan two pounds of granulated
sugar and three teacupfuls of thin cream or milk. Bring it
gradually to the boiling-point, stirring all the time. Let it boil
a few minutes. Test as for toffee, but do not boil it so high.
When it has reached the consistency of soft putty when dropped
in cold water (about 245° F.), remove the pan from the fire.
Add flavouring as below. Now put the pan into a basin of
cold water and stir rapidly with a spoon. It soon begins to
solidify round the edge, and this must be scraped off repeatedly.
Keep stirring until the mass is sufficiently grained, and then
pour it immediately on to a buttered slab. If too highly
grained, it will not pour out flat; if too thin, it will be sticky.
Only practice makes perfection. When sufficiently firm, mark
into bars with a knife, or cut into rounds with the lid of a circular tin.

FLAVOURINGS

Cinnamon. Add a few drops of oil of cinnamon.

Coco-nut. Add four ounces of coco-nut and boil for two minutes, then add a pinch
of cream of tartar and remove from the fire. It should be vigorously stirred till
quite creamy.

Fig. Add a pinch of cream of tartar just before removing from the fire. Then
stir in four ounces of finely chopped figs, previously washed and dried.

Ginger. Add two teaspoonfuls of ground ginger, dissolved in a little cold water,
and (if liked) some chopped preserved ginger.

Lemon. Add a small teaspoonful of essence of lemon.

Orange. Add the grated rind and juice of an orange.

Peppermint. Add a few drops of oil of peppermint.

Vanilla. Add a small teaspoonful of essence of vanilla.

Walnut. Add half a teaspoonful of essence of vanilla, and four ounces of shelled
and chopped walnut.

Confectionery

GRANDMAMMA'S BON-BONS

(Meg Dods's Recipe)

Sugar, lemon grate, citron or orange-peel.

Cut candied citron or orange peel into strips an inch long, and then as small dice. String them apart on a fine wire skewer or knitting-needle, and dip them in boiling barley-sugar made as follows: Clarify and boil sugar to the fourth degree or crackling height, and when nearly boiled enough add lemon grate, a drop of citron oil, or a little beat spermaceti.

Have a baking-slab or large flat dish rubbed with oil that they may not stick, and lay them on it to dry. When crisp, pack them in paper bags.

EDINBURGH ROCK [1]

Crushed loaf sugar, cream of tartar, water, colour and flavouring as follows: white, lemon or vanilla; pink, raspberry or rose; fawn, ginger; yellow, orange or tangerine.

Put into a pan a pound of crushed loaf sugar and half a pint of cold water. Stir gently over the fire until the sugar is dissolved. When nearly boiling, add a good pinch of cream of tartar and boil without stirring until it reaches 258° F. in cold weather or 260° F. in hot—that is, until it forms a hard lump in cold water. Remove from the fire, add colouring and flavouring, and pour on a buttered marble slab, preferably through buttered candy bars. As it begins to cool, turn the ends and edges inwards with a buttered knife. When cool enough to handle, dust it with powdered sugar, take it up and pull gently (being careful not to twist it) until it is dull. Cut in pieces with a pair of scissors. Place the rock in a warm room and let it remain there for at least twenty-four hours, until the process of granulation is complete, and the rock is powdery and soft.

[1] The original Edinburgh Rock is made by the famous Edinburgh firm of Ferguson. Confectionery is an important industry in the capital, and the world-famous rock is one of the triumphs of the Scottish confectioner's art.

BEVERAGES

In olden times, the common beverage of Lowland Scotland was ale. There is evidence that it was in general use in the thirteenth century; in *The Friars of Berwick* (*c.* 1500) the " silly friars ", Robert and Allan, are regaled on " stoups of ale with bread and cheese "; and even in the eighteenth century we find that the subject of Burns's poem, *Scotch Drink*, is not whisky, but ale.[1]

In the days of the Auld Alliance, French wines were freely imported. They were drunk at the court of Alexander III (1241–1286), and successive travellers comment on their excellence, abundance, and cheapness.

The origin of whisky is wrapped in mystery. The Highlander was content in the ordinary way with water from the spring and milk from the byre and the churn. *Usquebaugh* was reserved for festive occasions, and even then it was used sparingly, for, unlike the Saxon, the Celt was temperate in both eating and drinking. There is good reason to believe that the distillation of whisky received its chief impetus from the acts of the Scottish Privy Council, which in the early seventeenth century forbade the importation of wines into the Isles. The heavy taxation subsequently imposed had the ultimate effect of banishing claret [2] from the Scottish dining-

---

[1] " To birl the brown bowl " is the old expression for " to drink ale ".

[2] The Tappit Hen, a measure containing three quarts of claret, was formerly a feature at Scottish country inns.

> Blythe, blythe, and merry was she,
> Blythe was she but and ben;
> Weel she loo'ed a Hawick gill,[*]
> And leugh to see a tappit-hen.
>
> *—Andro and his Cuttie Gun.*

[*] Half an Imperial pint.

" I have seen one of these formidable stoups at Provost Haswell's at Jedburgh in the days of yore. It was a pewter measure, the claret being in ancient days served from the tap, and had a figure of a crested hen upon the lid. In later times, the name was given to a glass bottle of the same dimensions. These are rare apparitions among the degenerate topers of modern days."—Scott: *Guy Mannering*, Note.

The following epigram was written by John Home, author of the tragedy of *Douglas*, when the Government at Westminster laid a tax upon port:

table and substituting the over-alcoholized beverage which
has become an evil and a reproach to the Scottish nation.[1]

The women of Lowland Scotland were great brewers in
their day.[2] Tibbie Shield's green grozet (gooseberry) wine,[3]
Mrs. Gentle's primrose wine,[4] the elder - flower wine that
Mistress Jean, the " penniless lass wi' a lang pedigree ", was
making when the Laird o' Cockpen came a-wooing [5]—there are
many references in reminiscence and fiction.

> Firm and erect the Caledonian stood,
> Old was his mutton, and his claret good;
> " Let him drink port," an English statesman cried—
> He drank the poison, and his spirit died.

The lines, Dean Ramsay tells us, were great favourites with Sir Walter Scott
who delighted in repeating them.

[1] See *Leaves from a Physician's Portfolio*, by James Crichton-Browne, M.D., LL.D.

[2] In Kinross, the browst which the guid-wife of Lochrin produced from a peck
of malt is thus commemorated:

> Twenty pints o' strong ale,
> Twenty pints o' sma',
> Twenty pints o' hinky-pinky,
> Twenty pints o' plooman's drinkie,
> Twenty pints o' splitter-splatter,
> An' twenty pints was waur nor water.

[3] " North: Now, sir, you have tasted Tibbie's Green Grozet. St. Mary, what
are the vine-covered hills and gay regions of France to the small yellow, hairy goose-
berry-gardens of your own forest!"—Christopher North: *Noctes Ambrosianae.*

[4] " Mrs. Gentle: Mr. Hogg, Mr. North requested me to take charge of the making
of his primrose wine this season, and I used the freedom of setting aside a dozen
bottles for your good lady at Altrive."—*Ibid.*

> [5] Mistress Jean, she was makin' the elder-flo'er wine:
> " And what brings the Laird at sic a like time?"
> She put off her apron and on her silk goon,
> Her mutch wi' red ribbons, and gaed awa' doon.
>   —Lady Nairne: *The Laird o' Cockpen.*

AN OLD HIGHLAND TOAST *

" Suas e, suas e, suas e!	" Up with it, up with it, up with it!
Sios e, sios e, sios e!	Down with it, down with it, down with it!
A null e, a null e, a null e!	Away from me, away from me, away from me!
A nall e, a nall e, a nall e!	Towards me, towards me, towards me!
Sguab as e!	Drink it off!
. . . .	. . . .
Agus cha' n'òl neach eile as	And no other shall ever drink from this glass
a ghloine so gu bràth!"	again!"

* The proposer stands on his chair with one foot on the table, holding the glass
in his right hand. He accompanies the toast with appropriate gestures, and at the
last words, flings the glass over his left shoulder on to the floor, where it is shattered
to atoms. I have seen it drunk thus in the Isle of Skye.—F. M. McN.

ATHOLE BROSE[1]

Aye since he wore the tartan trews
He dearly lo'ed the Athole Brose.
                                —Neil Gow.

(Very Old)

Heather honey, whisky, cold water.

Put a pound of dripped honey into a basin and add sufficient
cold water to dissolve it (about a teacupful). Stir with a *silver*
spoon, and when the water and the honey are well mixed, add
gradually one and a half pints of whisky, alias mountain dew.
Stir briskly till a froth begins to rise. Bottle and keep tightly
corked.

" It is sometimes used in the Highlands as a luxury, and sometimes as a specific
for a cold. Meal is occasionally substituted for honey."—Jamieson.
The original Athole brose consisted of oatmeal and whisky.—F. M. McN.
" The yolk of an egg is sometimes beat up with the brose."—Meg Dods.
On Hogmanay, the Athole Brose, carried by two subalterns and preceded by a
piper and all the officers, is carried to the sergeants' mess of the Argyll and Sutherland Highlanders, where a quaich is filled for each officer and sergeant.—F. M. McN

AULD MAN'S MILK

(Meg Dods's Recipe)

Cream, rum, whisky, or brandy, eggs, nutmeg or lemon zest.

Beat the yolks and whites of six eggs separately. Put to the
beat yolks sugar and a quart of new milk or thin sweet cream.
Add to this rum, whisky, or brandy to taste (about a half-
pint). Slip in the whipt whites, and give the whole a gentle
stir up in the china punch-bowl, in which it should be mixed.
It may be flavoured with nutmeg or lemon zest. This morning
dram is the same as the egg-nogg of America.

[1] Mentioned by Scott in *The Heart of Midlothian.*

HIGHLAND BITTERS

(*Very Old*)

Gentian root, coriander seed, bitter-orange peel, camomile flower, cinnamon stick, whole cloves, whisky.

Cut one ounce and three-quarters of gentian root and half an ounce of orange peel into small pieces. Put them in a mortar with one ounce of coriander seed, quarter of an ounce of camomile flower, quarter of an ounce of cinnamon stick, and half an ounce of cloves. Bruise all together. Put in an earthenware jar, empty two bottles of whisky over it, cover so that the jar is air-tight, and let it stand for about ten days. Strain and bottle. More whisky may be added to the flavouring materials, which remain good for a long time.

HIGHLAND CORDIAL

(*Traditional Recipe*)

White currants, lemon, ginger, sugar, whisky.

Take a pint of white currants stripped of their stalks, the thin peel of a lemon, a teaspoonful of essence of ginger, and a bottle of whisky. Mix and stand for forty-eight hours. Strain, add a pound of loaf sugar, and stand for a day to dissolve. Bottle and cork. It will be ready in three months, but will keep longer.

CALEDONIAN LIQUOR

(*Mrs. Dalgairns' Recipe*)

Whisky, sugar, cinnamon.

One ounce of oil of cinnamon is to be dropped on two and a half pounds of bruised loaf sugar; one gallon of whisky, the best, is to be added, and the sugar being dissolved, it is to be filtered and bottled.

HET PINT

(Meg Dods's Recipe)

Ale, sugar, eggs, whisky, nutmeg.

Grate a nutmeg into two quarts of mild ale, and bring it to the point of boiling. Mix a little cold ale with sugar necessary to sweeten this, and three eggs well beaten. Gradually mix the hot ale with the eggs, taking care that they do not curdle. Put in a half-pint of whisky, and bring it once more nearly to boil and then briskly pour it from one vessel into another till it becomes smooth and bright.[1]

TODDY

Sit roun' the table well content
An' steer aboot the toddy.

(Traditional Recipe)

Whisky, sugar, hot water.

Pour boiling water slowly into a tumbler till about half full. Let the water remain until the crystal is thoroughly heated, then pour it out. Put in loaf sugar to taste with a glassful of boiling water. When melted put in half a glass of whisky and stir with a silver teaspoon. Then add more boiling water, and finally another half glass of whisky. Stir, and serve hot.

In his poem, " The Morning Interview ", published in 1721, Allan Ramsay speaks of " some kettles full of Todian spring ", and appends the note:

" The Todian spring, i.e. Tod's well, which supplies Edinburgh with water. Tod's well and St. Anthony's well, on the side of Arthur's Seat, were two of the wells which very scantily supplied the wants of Edinburgh, and when it is borne in mind that whisky derives its name from water, it is highly probable that Toddy in like manner was a facetious term for the pure element."

[1] " This beverage, carried about in a bright copper kettle, is the celebrated New Year's morning Het Pint of Edinburgh and Glasgow. In Honest Aberdeen, half-boiled sowens is used on the same festive occasion. In Edinburgh, in her bright and palmy state — her days of ' spice and wine ', while she yet had a court and parliament, while France sent her wines, and Spain, Italy, and Turkey, fruits and spices—a far more refined composition than the above was made by substituting light wine for ale, and brandy for whisky."—W. Winterblossom, in the *Annals of the Cleikum Club.*

Het Pint was used also on the night preceding a marriage and at a lying-in. The writer recollects the *Bride's Cog* (Gael. *coggan*), a large wooden vessel with three iugs, or ears, often of beautiful design and workmanship, which used to circulate like a loving-cup at the Orkney rural weddings. It contained copious libations of new ale, laced with whisky, seasoned with pepper, ginger, and nutmeg, and thickened with beaten eggs and pieces of toasted biscuit.

GLASGOW PUNCH [1]
(FROM " PETER'S LETTERS ") [2]

A hundred years ago and more, the signal toast at the Glasgow clubs was " The trade of Glasgow and the outward bound ".

Rum, cold water, sugar, lemons, limes.

The sugar [3] being melted with a little cold water, the artist squeezed about a dozen lemons through a wooden strainer, and then poured in water enough almost to fill the bowl. In this state the liquor goes by the name of sherbet, and a few of the connoisseurs in his immediate neighbourhood were requested to give their opinion of it—for in the mixing of the sherbet lies, according to the Glasgow creed, at least one half of the whole battle. This being approved by an audible smack of the lips of the umpires, the rum was added to the beverage, I suppose, in something about the proportion from one to seven. Last of all, the maker cut a few limes, and running each section rapidly round the rim of his bowl, squeezed in enough of this more delicate acid to flavour the whole composition. In this consists the true tour-de-maître of the punch-maker.

Glasgow punch should be made of the coldest spring water newly taken from the spring. The acid ingredients above mentioned will suffice for a very large bowl.

(*Another way*)

Icing sugar, lemon, rum, ice.

Put into a tumbler a tablespoonful of icing sugar, the juice of a lemon, and a wineglassful of Jamaica rum. Fill the glass with chipped ice and stir well.

[1] " Rum punch was the universal beverage of the members of the Pig Club at their dinners, as it was at those of all the jovial fraternities in the city."
—Strang: *Glasgow Clubs.*

[2] *Peter's Letters to his Kinsfolk*, by J. G. Lockhart and others, 1819.

[3] Allow a tablespoonful to each lemon.—F. M. McN.

SCOTS NOYAU

(A Very Pleasant Compound)

(Meg Dods's Recipe)

Proof-spirit, water, syrup, almonds (sweet and bitter).

Two quarts of proof-spirit, a pint and a half of water, a pound and a half of syrup, six ounces of sweet and four bitter almonds blanched and chopped. Infuse for a fortnight, shaking the compound occasionally, and filter. Lemon juice or grate may be added, but the nutty or almond flavour does not harmonize well with acid or citron flavours.

BIRK WINE

(Mrs. Dalgairns' Recipe)

Juice from the birch tree,[1] sugar, raisins, almonds, crude tartar.

To every gallon of juice from the birch tree, three pounds of sugar, one pound of raisins, half an ounce of crude tartar, and one ounce of almonds are allowed; the juice, sugar, and raisins are to be boiled twenty minutes, and then put into a tub, together with the tartar; and when it has fermented some days, it is to be strained, and put into the cask, and also the almonds, which must be tied in a muslin bag. The fermentation having ceased, the almonds are to be withdrawn, and the cask bunged up, to stand about five months, when it may be fined and bottled. Keep in a cool cellar. Set the bottles upright or they will fly.

[1] About the end of March, or later if the spring is backward, bore a hole in a tree and put in a faucet, and it will run for two or three days together without hurting the tree; then put in a pin to stop it, and the next year you may draw as much from the same hole.

Pennant, writing in 1769, tells us that, in the Aberdeenshire Highlands, the birch, which grows plentifully in this district, was applicable to a great variety of purposes: for all implements of husbandry, for the roofing of houses, and fuel; whilst with its bark leather was tanned, and " quantities of excellent wine are extracted from the live tree by tapping ".

HEATHER ALE

From the bonny bells of heather,
They brewed a drink longsyne,
Was sweeter far than honey,
Was stronger far than wine.
— Robert Louis Stevenson (*Heather
Ale*: a Galloway Legend).[1]

(From an old coverless book of cottage cookery)

Heather, hops, barm, syrup, ginger, water.

Crop the heather when it is in full bloom, enough to fill a large pot. Fill the pot, cover the croppings with water, set to boil, and boil for one hour. Strain into a clean tub. Measure the liquid, and for every dozen bottles add one ounce of ground ginger, half an ounce of hops, and one pound of golden syrup. Set to boil again and boil for twenty minutes. Strain into a clean cask. Let it stand until milk-warm, then add a teacupful of good barm. Cover with a coarse cloth and let it stand till next day. Skim carefully and pour the liquor gently into a tub so that the barm may be left at the bottom of the cask. Bottle and cork tightly. The ale will be ready for use in two or three days.

This makes a very refreshing and wholesome drink, as there is a good deal of spirit in heather.

In Islay, in the eighteenth century, Pennant tells us, ale was frequently made of the young tops of heath, mixed with about a third part of malt and a few hops. "This liquor, it appears from Boethius, was first used among the Picts, but when they were extirpated by the Scots, the secret of preparing it perished with them."

SKEACHAN, OR TREACLE ALE

(Meg Dods's Recipe)

Molasses, hops or ginger or extract of gentian, yeast, water.

Boil for twenty minutes four pounds of molasses in from six to eight gallons of soft water, with a handful of hops tied in

[1] The poem tells how the Scottish king who slaughtered the Picts tried to wrest the secret of heather ale from the last survivor by offering to spare his life, and how the old man chooses death. The legend of the extirpation of the whole race of Picts, who with the Scots, Britons, and a small colony of Angles constituted sixth-century Scotland, has no historical evidence and is highly improbable.

a muslin rag or a little extract of gentian. When cooled in the tub, add a pint of good beer-yeast, or from four to six quarts of fresh worts from the brewer's vat. Cover the beer with blankets or coarse cloths.[1] Pour it from the lees and bottle it. A little ginger may be added to the boiling liquid if the flavour is liked, instead of hops. This is a cheap and very wholesome beverage.

Yule Ale was usually made in this manner.—F. M. McN.

WHITE CAUDLE

(Meg Dods's Recipe)

Oatmeal, water, sugar, nutmeg or lemon juice.

Mix two large spoonfuls of finely ground oatmeal in water, two hours previous to using it; strain it from the grits and boil it. Sweeten and add wine and seasonings to taste. Nutmeg or a little lemon juice answers best for seasoning.

BROWN CAUDLE, or THE SCOTS ALEBERRY [2]

(Meg Dods's Recipe)

Is made as White Caudle, using mild sweet small beer instead of water.

"Caudle may be made of rice flour or wheat flour, with milk and water, sweetening it to taste."—M. D.

OATMEAL POSSET

(Mrs. Cleland's Recipe)

Flour of oatmeal, nutmeg, cinnamon, sugar, milk, sack, ale.

Take a mutchkin (pint) of milk, boil it with nutmeg and cinnamon, and put in two spoonfuls of flour of oatmeal, and boil it till the rawness is off the oatmeal; then take three spoonfuls of sack and three spoonfuls of ale and two spoonfuls of sugar; set it over the fire till it is scalding hot, then put them to the

[1] Let it stand for one day.—F. M. McN. [2] Berry is a corruption of Fr. *purée*.

milk, give it one stir, and let it stand on the fire for a minute or two, and pour it in your bowl; cover it and let it stand a little, then send it up.

A HARVEST DRINK

Oatmeal, sugar, lemon, water.

Put a quarter-pound of oatmeal and six ounces of sugar into a pan. Mix with a little warm water and the juice of a lemon, and pour over it, stirring all the time, a gallon of boiling water. Boil (still stirring) for three minutes. Strain and use when cold.

This is said to be very strengthening. Half an ounce of ground ginger may be mixed with the dry ingredients.

STOORUM [1]

Oatmeal, salt, water, milk.

Put a heaped teaspoonful of oatmeal into a tumbler; pour a little cold water over it and stir well. Fill up half-way with boiling water, then to the top with boiling milk. Season with salt and serve.

This is said to be splendid for nursing mothers.

BLENSHAW [2]

(*A Cottage Recipe*)

Oatmeal, sugar, milk, water, nutmeg.

Put a teaspoonful of oatmeal into a tumbler with the same quantity or less of sugar. Pour in half a gill of good milk, stir to the thickness of cream, and then pour in boiling water, stirring till the tumbler is full. Lastly grate a very little nutmeg over it. Do not drink it too hot. It should be the temperature of milk from the cow. This is a wholesome and nutritious beverage.

The names blenshaw and stoorum seem to be used arbitrarily for any of the many varieties of oatmeal drink.—F. M. McN.

[1] In Shetland the name *stoor-a-drink* is given to a mixture of oatmeal and water or swats. In Aberdeen *Stouram* is a kind of gruel. In the Hebrides, a similar drink is made with barley-meal; if made with water, a morsel of butter is added.
[2] Fr. *Blanche eau*, whitish water; Strathmore.

APPENDICES

I. FRANCO-SCOTTISH DOMESTIC TERMS

" Mrs. Diggity-Dalgetty's forebears must have been exposed to foreign influences, for she interlards her culinary conversation with French terms, and we have discovered that this is quite common. A ' jigget ' of mutton is, of course, a ' gigot ', and we have identified an ashet as an ' assiette '. The petticoat tails she requested me to buy at the confectioner's were somewhat more puzzling, but when they were finally purchased by Susanna Crum they appeared to be ordinary little cakes; perhaps, therefore, petits gastels, since gastels is an old form of gâteau, as bel was for beau. Susanna, for her part, speaks of the wardrobe in my room as an ' awmry '. It certainly contains no weapons, and we conjecture that her word must be a corruption of armoire."

—Kate Douglas Wiggin: *Penelope's Experiences in Scotland* (1890).

SCOTS.	ENGLISH.	FRENCH (or O.F.)
Acornie.	A drinking-vessel with ears.	Acorné.
Ashet.	A dish on which meat is served.	Assiette.
	" To keep me in braws and you in ashets to break, is more than the poor creatures would face, I'm thinkin'."	
	—Neil Munro: *John Splendid*.	
Assol, aisle.	To sun; to dry, mellow, or season in the sun.	Assoler.
Aumrie.	A cupboard.	Aumoire.
	Her cozie box-bed and weel-polished aumrie	
	Wi' massy brass handles a' shinin' sae braw,	
	Her shelf fu' o' pewter a' glancin' like glamrie,	
	An' braw bawbee pictures nailed round on the wa'.	
	—*Janet's Auld Aumrie* (Gaberlunzie's Wallet).	
Backet, back, backie.	A small shallow tub for holding ashes (aiss-backet), salt (saut-backet), &c.—*Rob Roy*; Burns.	Bacquet.
Bassie.	A large wooden dish for holding meal.	Bassin.
Battry.	Kitchen utensils.	Batterie.
Beam, bein.	To beam the tea-pot: to warm the tea-pot with hot water before putting in the tea.	Baigner.
Berry.	Bread soaked in boiling milk and sweetened is called breadberry. Sim. aleberry, waterberry.	Purée.

SCOTS.	ENGLISH.	FRENCH (or O.F.)
Blenshaw.	A drink composed of meal, milk, water, &c.; Strathmore.	Blanche eau.
Bonally.	A *deoch-an-doruis*, or stirrup-cup: a drink to speed the parting guest. " I will drink it for you, that good customs be not broken. ' Here's your bonally, my lad."—Scott: *The Pirate*.	Bon aller.
Boss.	A small cask, a bottle.	Boisson.
Bouvrage.	A drink, a beverage.	Beuvrage.
Bowet.	A hand-lantern.—*Waverley*.	Boete, boîte.
Bowie, milk-bowie.	A tub or milk-pail.—*Old Mortality*.	Buie.
Brick.	A small loaf of bread sold in Edinburgh and elsewhere for a penny.	Brique de pain (patois).
Broach.	A flagon or tankard.	Broc.
Broch, brotch.	A spit.—*Bride of Lammermoor*.	Broche.
Brule, brulyie.	To broil.	Brûler.
Bufe.	Beef.	Bœuf.
Buist, meal-buist.	A box or chest.—*Acts James II; The Monastery*.	Boist.
Calander.	A mangle. " Calandering done here " was once commonly seen on sign-boards.	Calandre.
Cannel.	Cinnamon.	Cannelle.
Caraff.	A decanter for holding water.	Carafe.
Carvi.	Caraway. Carvies: confections in which caraway seeds are enclosed.	Carvi.
Chandler.	A candle-stick. " Hae ye ony pots or pans, Or ony broken chandlers?" 　　—*Clout the Cauldron*.	Chandelier.
Chauffen.	To warm.	Chauffer.
Chopin, choppin	A measure.	Chopine.
Creish.	Grease. " Even the slang of the Courts passed from France to Scotland, and to *graisser la patte* became to ' creish the hand ' of the advocate."—J. G. Mackay: K.C., LL.D.: *Relations between the Court of Session, the Supreme Civil Court of Scotland, and the Parliament of Paris*.	Graisse.
Cummerfealls.	Entertainment after an inlying.	Commère and veille.
Debosh.	Festivity, riot.—*Mansie Waugh*.	Débauche.
Deis, dess, deas.	A sort of uncushioned sofa.	Dais.
Dine.	Dinner. " We twa ha'e paidl't in the burn Frae morning sun till dine."—Burns.	Dine.
Disjeune, disjune.	Breakfast.—*Old Mortality*. " A kiss and a drink o' water are but a wersh (insipid) disjeune."—Allan Ramsay.	Desjune.

Appendices

SCOTS.	ENGLISH.	FRENCH (or O.F.)
Dortor.	A dormitory, bedroom; also a posset or night-cap taken at night-time.	Dortoir.
Dresser.	A kitchen sideboard.	Dressoir.
Dublar.	A large wooden platter.—*Wowing of Jok and Jynny*.	Doublier.
Eel-dolly.	An oil lamp (originally oil for a lamp).—Rev. W. Macgregor: *Folklore*.	Huile d'olive.
Fadge, fage.	A large flat loaf or bannock.	Fouace.
Fenester.	Window.	Fenêtre.
Flam.	A custard.	Flan.
Flamb, to.	To baste (roasted meat).	Flamber.
Fraise.	The pluck of a calf.	Fraise (id.).
Furmage.	Cheese.—*Henrysone*.	Fromage.
Gallimafray.	A hash, a hotch-potch.	Galimafrée.
Gardevyance, gardeviant.	A cabinet.	Garde-viandes.
Gardyloo.	" Before the days of sanitation, slops were thrown from the upper windows of old Edinburgh houses, with the warning cry of ' Gardyloo! ' "—Scott: *Waverley*.	Gare de l'eau.
Gardyveen.	A case for holding wine.	Garde-vin.
Gean.	Wild cherry. " Brought from Guignes in France to Scotland."—Sir John Sinclair.	Guigne, guine.
Geil, jeel.	Jelly.	Gel.
Gigot, jiggot.	A leg of mutton.	Gigot.
Girnal.	A meal-chest.	Grenier.
Gout (pr. goo).	Taste. " They do not know how to cook yonder. They have no gout."—Galt.	Goût.
Governante.	Housekeeper.—Scott: *Old Mortality*.	Gouvernante.
Grange.	Granary.	Grange.
Grosset, grosert.	Gooseberry. " A randy-like woman with a basket selling grossets."—Galt. " They will jump at them in Edinburgh like a cock at a grosset."—Scott: *Fortunes of Nigel*.	Groseille.
Haggis.	A dish with hashed liver as a principal ingredient	Hachis.
Hainberries.	Wild berries.	Haie.
Harigals.	Liver and kidneys. " He that never eats meat Thinks harigals a treat.". —Scots Proverb.	Haricot (a dish of boiled livers.)
Havil-crook.	Lowering-crook (for pots over a fire).	Avaler.
Herse.	A frame for lights, a chandelier.	Herse.
Hogue.	Tainted.	Haut goût.
Hotch-Potch.	Vegetable soup.	Hochepot.
Howtowdie.	A pullet.	Hutaudeau.
Kickshaw.	Trifle, dainty.	Quelque chose.

17a 2

SCOTS.	ENGLISH.	FRENCH (or O.F.)
Lamoo.	Wassail bowl.	Le moût (new or sweet wine).
Laundiers.	Andirons.	Landier.
Lavatour.	A vessel to wash in.	Lavatoire.
Lavendar.	A laundress.	Laver.
Lent-fire.	A slow fire.—Baillie.	Lent.
Lepron, leproun.	A young rabbit or hare.	Lapereau.
Mange.	A meal.	Manger.
Mangerie.	A feast.—Barbour.	Mangerie.
Maniory.	A feast.—Douglas.	Maniairia.
Man-miln.	Hand-mill.	Moulin-main.
Mele.	Honey.	Miel.
Menage.	Housekeeping, establishment. —Scott: *Old Mortality.*	Ménage.
Mobylls.	Furniture.	Meubles.
Mouter.	Miller's perquisite.	Mouture.
Moy.	A measure.	Moyau.
Mutton.	A sheep.	Mouton.
Napery.	House-linen.	Nappe.
Napron.	Apron.	Naperon.
Orlege, orlager.	A clock.	Horloge.
Paip.	A cherry-stone.	Pépin.
Palliase.	Straw mattress.	Paillasse.
Pands.	Valances of bed.	Pands.
Parsell.	Parsley.	Persil.
Pece.	A piece of plate. *Treas. Acts. I.* A vessel for holding liquids.—Douglas.	Pièce.
Pecher.	A pitcher.	Pichier (Languedoc).
Petté quarter.	A measure: a small quarter. Aberd. Reg.	Petit.
Petticoat tails.	Thin shortbread cakes.	Petits gastels.
Pettie-pan.	Small moulds for cakes.	Petit.
Piertryks, partrik, patrick.	A partridge.	Perdrix.
Plat.	A plate, a dish.	Plat.
Plumedame.	A prune. *Acts James VI.*	Plume-bedamas.
Pork.	A pig.	Porc.
Pottisear	A pastry-cook.—Balfour.	Patissier.
Proochey.	"Proochey, leddy, proochey-moo (moi)!" Milkmaids' call to the cows in many parts of Scotland.	Approcher.
Pultie.	A short-bladed knife.	Poêlette.
Purry.	A kind of porridge, Aberd. Sim. tart-an-purry.	Purée.

Appendices

SCOTS.	ENGLISH.	FRENCH (or O.F.)
Ravelled (bread).	A species of wheaten bread.	Ravailler.
Reefort, ryfart.	Radish.	Raifort.
Regale.	Entertainment.—Scott: *Old Mortality*.	Régale.
Repater.	To feed, to take refreshments.—Douglas.	Repaître.
Revay.	Festivity.—*Gawan and Gol.*	Reviaus.
Rizards, riz-zer-berries.	Currants.	Ressoré.
Rizzared.	Dried in the sun.	Ressoré.
Rooser.	A watering-can.	Arrouser.
Saim.	Lard.	Sain.
Sauty or sooty bannock.	A pancake.	Sauter.
Sawcer, sawster.	A maker or vendor of sauces.	Saucier.
Say.	A bucket.	Seau.
Scaud.	Scald.	Eschauder.
Schoufer.	A chaffern.—*Inventories.*	Eschauffer.
Scrutoire.	A desk, generally forming the upper part of a chest of drawers.	Escritoire.
Serge.	A taper, a torch.—Wyntoun.	Cierge.
Servite, Servet.	A napkin.	Serviette.
Soss.	A savoury chop-steak stew.	Sausse.
Spairge.	Sprinkle.	Asperger.

    " Auld Hornie, Satan, Nick, or Clootie,
    Spairges aboot the brimstane cootie
           To scaud poor wretches."
        —Burns: *Address to the Deil.*

Spence, spens.	The place where provisions are kept; the room where the family sit at meat.	Despence.

    " Our Bardie lanely keeps the spence
        Sin' Mailie's deid."
        —Burns.

Squiss.	To beat up (an egg).—Z. Boyd.	Escousser.
Stoved.	A method of cooking potatoes, howtowdie, &c.	Étuvé.
Sucker.	Sugar. " Neeps like sucker!" An old Edinburgh street cry.	Sucre.
Sybo.	A young onion, with its green tail.	Cibo.

    " A lee dykeside, a sybo tail
        An barley-scone shall cheer me."
        —Burns.

Syes.	Chives.	Cives.
Tantonie bell.	A small bell.	Tintoner.
Tartan purry.	A dish of chopped kail and oatmeal.	Tarte-en-purée.
Tash.	To soil.	Tacher.

    " An' cauld and blae her genty hands,
    Her feet a' tashed and torn."
        —W. B. Crawford: *The Wandered Bairn.*

SCOTS.	ENGLISH.	FRENCH (or O.F.).
Tasse, tassie.	A cup.	Tasse.

> " Gae bring to me a pint o' wine
> And fetch it in a silver tassie,
> That I may drink, before I go,
> A service to my bonnie lassie."
> —Burns.

Trayt.	A superior kind of wheaten bread.	Panis de Treyt.
Trest.	The frame of a table. *Acts James V.*	Tresteau.
Tron, trone.	A public beam for weighing merchandise.	Troneau.

> " The beam known as the salt-trone, to distin-
> guish it from the butter-trone in Lawn-
> market . . . gave its name to the Tron
> Church."
> —Reid: *New Lights on Old Edinburgh.*

Vantose.	A cupping-glass.	Ventose.
Veal, veil.	A calf.—*Acts James VI.*	Veau.
Verry.	Glass or tumbler.	Verre.
Vittall.	To supply with provisions.	Vitaille.
Vivers.	Victuals.	Vivres.

> " The dainty vivers that were set before them."
> —Scott: *The Fortunes of Nigel.*

Vodure.	A tray for removing fragments after a meal. (Lit. a voider or emptier.)	Vodeur.
Wyandour.	" A gud wyandour ", one who lives or feeds well.—Wyntoun.	Viander.

II. OLD SCOTTISH MEASURES

4 gills	=	1 mutchkin
2 mutchkins	=	1 choppin
2 choppins	=	1 pint
2 pints	=	1 quart
4 quarts	=	1 gallon
8 gallons	=	1 barrel

SCOTTISH		IMPERIAL
1 mutchkin	=	1 pint
1 choppin	=	1 quart
1 pint	=	2 quarts [1]
1 quart	=	1 gallon
—		—
1 lippie	=	1 peck

[1] " The Scottish pint of liquid measure comprehends four English measures of the same denomination. The jest is well known of my poor countryman who, driven to extremity by the raillery of the Southern on the small denomination of the Scottish coin, at length answered, ' Ay, ay! but the deil tak them that has the least pint-stoup!' "—Scott: *Redgauntlet*, Note.

III. OLD SCOTTISH CUTS

The names of the various pieces, according to the Scottish method of dividing the carcass, says Mrs. Dalgairns (1829), are as follows:

BEEF

The Middle Sirloin—Top of the Rump and Hook-Bone—Middle Hook-Bone and Round—the Hough—the Spare Rib—the Flank and part of the Hough—the Fore Saye—the Breast and Nine-Holes—the Lair—Neck and Sticking-piece—the Knap—Cheek and Head.

Besides these are the Tongue and Palate. The Entrails consist of the Heart—Sweet-breads—Kidneys—Skirts—and three kinds of Tripe, the Double, the Roll, and the Red Tripe.

MUTTON

The Leg—the Loin—the Fore Quarter. The two loins joined together are called a Chine. A Saddle of Mutton is the two Necks joined together.

The finest mutton is that of the mountain or black-faced sheep of Scotland, and that of the South Downs and Welsh Sheep.

PORK

Spare Rib—Breast and Shoulder—Sirloin—the Ham or Gigot. The Entrails are named the liver, crow, kidney, skirts, sometimes called the harslet, also the chitter-lings and guts.

IV. OLD SCOTTISH FESTIVAL CAKES AND DISHES

" Some of the cakes which have a prominent place in folk usage at certain periods of the year, e.g. Christian festivals and holy days, as well as on other occasions, are probably lineally descended from cakes used sacrificially or sacramentally in pagan times. This is suggested by the customs observed in the making of these cakes, or the eating of them; by their division among the members of the family, or by their being marked with sacred symbols."—J. A. MacCulloch: *Encyclopædia of Religion and Ethics*, article on " Cakes and Loaves ".

Jan. 1.	New Year's Day.	See Hogmanay (Dec. 31).
Jan. 5.	Twelfth Night.	Twelfth Cake.[1]
Jan. —	Auld Handsel Monday. (First Monday of New Year, O.S.)	Gudebread (various).[2]

[1] A rich plum- or pound-cake, ornamented, and containing a lucky bean, the recipient of which became King or Queen of Bane. In one of his Latin epigrams, Buchanan commemorates the choice of Mary Beaton as Queen of the Twelfth Tide Revels at Holyrood. Possibly Black Bun was the original Twelfth Cake. See p. 188, note to recipe for Black Bun.—F. M. McN.

[2] *Gudebread* is the Scots term for all bread and cakes specially prepared for festive occasions.—F. M. McN.

Jan. 25.	Burns Night.	Haggis.
Feb. 1.	St. Bride's Day (Candlemas Eve).	St. Bride's Bannock (Highland Quarter Cake: Spring)
Mar. —	Fastern's E'en (Shrove Tuesday.)	Fastyn, Festy, or Fitless Cock; Skairskons, Car-cakes, or Sauty Bannocks; Crowdie or Matrimonial Brose or Matrimonial Bannock (with ring).
Mar. —	Car Sunday (a week before Palm Sunday).	Carlings (peas, birsled or broiled).
Mar. —	Pasch or Easter.	Pays or Pasch Eggs; Hot Cross Buns.
May 1.	Beltane.	Beltane Bannock (Highland Quarter Cake: Summer); Beltane Caudle.
June 9.	St. Columba's Day.	St. Columba's Cake (with coin) (Hebrides).
Aug. 1.	Lammas.	Lammas Bannock (Highland Quarter Cake: Autumn).
Sept. 29.	Michaelmas.	St. Michael's Cake (Hebrides).
Oct. 18.	St. Luke's Day.	Sour Cakes (Rutherglen).
Oct.	Harvest Home.	Cream Crowdie; Meal-and-Ale (with ring).
Oct. 31.	Hallowe'en.	Buttered Sowans; Crowdie or Champit Tatties (mashed potatoes) or (modern) cake, with charms; *Bonnach Salainn* (Highlands); Apples and Nuts.
Nov. 1.	Hallowmas.	Hallowmas Bannock (Highland Quarter Cake: Winter); Hallowfair Gingerbread.
Nov. 11.	Martinmas.	(Killing of Mart.) Haggis, Black and White Puddings.
Nov. 30.	Andermas (St. Andrew's Day).	Sheep's Head, Haggis, and other national dishes.
Dec. 24 to Auld Handsel Monday (q.v.)	The Daft Days.[1]	Gude-bread (various).
Dec. 25.	Yule or Christenmas.	Yule Brose; Yule Bread; Sowans; Goose, Goose-pie, or (modern) Turkey; Plum Porridge or (modern) Plum Pudding.
Dec. 31.	Hogmanay	Cheese and Oat-farles; Sugared Bread and Sweet Cakes (Shortbread, Black Bun, Currant Loaf, Ankerstock Gingerbread, &c.); Oranges; Het Pint (Edinburgh and Glasgow); Sowans (Aberdeen); Athole Brose.

> * When merry Yule-day comes, I trow,
> You 'll scantlins * fin' a hungry mou †;
> Sma' are our cares, our stamacks fou
>   O' gusty gear ‡,
> An' kickshaws §, strangers to our view,
>   Sin' fairn year ‖.
>
> — R. Fergusson: *The Daft Days.*

* Scarcely.   † Mouth.   ‡ Savoury fare.   § Dainties.   ‖ Since yester-year.

Births.	*Inlying*: Blythe Meat, Merry Meat or Wanton Meat; Cheesing Meat [1] (Orkney); Crying Bannock; Crying Kebbuck.
	Christening: Bonnach Baiste or Christening Bannock, or (modern) Christening Cake (ornamented).
	Teething: Teething Bannock.
Marriages.	Infar Cake or Wedding-cake (originally a rich oat-cake; later shortbread, ornamented with favours; now more commonly a rich fruit-cake, elaborately iced)[2]; Spice Brose; The Bride's Pie; The Bride's Cog.
Funerals.	Gude-bread, various (seed-cake perhaps a specialty).

V. MEG DODS'S SUGGESTED BILL OF FARE FOR ST. ANDREW'S DAY, BURNS CLUBS, OR OTHER SCOTTISH NATIONAL DINNERS.

First Course

Friar's Chicken, or Scots Brown Soup.

(*Remove*—Braised Turkey.)

Brown Fricassee of Duck.   Potted Game.   Minced Collops.

Haggis.

Salt Cod, with Egg Sauce.   (*Remove*—Chicken Pie.)   Crimped Skate.

Smoked Tongue.   Tripe in White Fricassee.

Salt Caithness Goose, or Solan Goose.

Sheep's Head Broth.

(1. *Remove*—Two Tups' [3] Heads and Trotters.)

(2. *Remove*—Haunch of Venison or Mutton, with Wine Sauce and Currant Jelly.)

Second Course

Roast Fowls, with Drappit Egg, or Lamb's Head Dressed.

Buttered Partans.[4]   Small Pastry.   Stewed Onions.

Calves-foot Jelly.   Rich Eating Posset   Blancmange.
in a China Punch Bowl.

Apple-puddings in skins.   Small Pastry.   Plum-damas [5] Pie.

A Black Cock, or three Ptarmigan.

---

[1] This consists of a stoupful of eggalourie (a caudle of eggs and milk) and a cubbie (a special kind of basket) full of bannocks.

[2] The wedding-cakes of the Royal Family are supplied by a well-known Edinburgh firm.

[3] Sheeps'.   [4] Crabs.   [5] Prune.

VI. SOURCES OF RECIPES

M. Martin, Gent.	*Description of the Western Islands.*		1703
Mrs. Glasse.	*The Art of Cookery Made Plain and Easy, by a Lady.*	Edinburgh,	1747.
Mrs. Cleland.	*A New and Easy Method of Cookery.* By Elizabeth Cleland. Chiefly Intended for the Benefit of the Young Ladies who attend her School.	„	1759.
Mrs. McIver.[1]	*Cookery and Pastry, as Taught and Practised by Mrs. McIver.*	„	1773
Mrs. Frazer.	*Practice of Cookery.*	„	1791.
Mrs. Dods.	*The Cook and Housewife's Manual.* By Mistress Margaret Dods, of the Cleikum Inn, St. Ronans.	„	1826.
Mrs. Dalgairns.	*Practice of Cookery.*	„	1829.
Mrs. McEwen.	*Elements of Cookery.*	„	1835.
—	*New Statistical Account of Scotland.*	„	1845.
Sir Walter Scott.	Waverley Novels.	„	
Mrs. Williamson.	*The Practice of Cookery and Pastry.*	„	1862.
Lady Harriet St. Clair.	*Dainty Dishes.*	„	1866.
—	*The Highland Feill Cookery Book.*[2]	Glasgow,	1907
Lady Clark of Tillypronie.	*The Cookery Book of Lady Clark of Tillypronie.*	London,	1909
Old Family MSS.			
Oral Tradition.			

[1] "A celebrated Caledonian professor of the culinary art."—Dr. Kitchener, in *The Cook's Oracle.*

[2] Published by *An Comunn Gaidhealach* (The Highland Association).

INDEX TO RECIPES

(Dishes, &c., mentioned in the notes are printed in italics)